The Baldrige

The Baldrige

What It Is, How It's Won, How to Use It to Improve Quality in Your Company

Christopher W. L. Hart

Christopher E. Bogan

McGraw-Hill, Inc.

New York St. Louis San Francisco Auckland Bogotá
Caracas Lisbon London Madrid Mexico Milan
Montreal New Delhi Paris San Juan São Paulo
Singapore Sydney Tokyo Toronto

Library of Congress Cataloging-in-Publication Data

Hart, Christopher W. L.
    The Baldrige : what it is, how it's won, how to use it to improve
quality in your company / Christopher W. L. Hart, Christopher E.
Bogan.
        p.   cm.
    Includes bibliographic references (p.   ) and index.
    ISBN 0-07-026912-2 :
    1. Malcolm Baldrige National Quality Award.   2. Total quality
management—United States.   I. Bogan, Christopher E.   II. Title.
    HD62.15.H37   1992
    658.5'62—dc20   92-12344
                                                                    CIP

1 2 3 4 5 6 7 8 9 0   DOC/DOC   9 8 7 6 5 4 3 2

ISBN   0-07-026912-2

The sponsoring editor for this book was James H. Bessent, Jr., and the production supervisor was Pamela A. Pelton. It was set in Baskerville by Publication Services.

Printed and bound by R. R. Donnelley & Sons Company.

Contents

Part 2. The Seven Pillars

6. The Baldrige Structure   69

7. The First Pillar: Leadership   85

8. The Second Pillar: Information and Analysis   103

9. The Third Pillar: Strategic Quality Planning   119

10. The Fourth Pillar: Human Resource Development and Management   133

Foreword

The pre-Socratic philosopher Heraclitus observed that "There is nothing permanent except change." Based on my experiences as a member of the United States Congress, I must concur; no truer words were ever spoken. The world is changing at what seems to be an ever-quickening pace. The world economy is changing; centers of economic power and high value-added jobs are shifting. The U.S. economy is being challenged not only by Japan and other countries in the Far East but also by Europe. After 1992, the European Economic Community will constitute a single integrated market larger than the U.S. and Canada. Our ability to compete as a nation in the rapidly emerging global economy of the 1990s will ultimately depend on the quality of our products and services. The handwriting is on the wall: If we do not produce well, we will not live well. Our jobs, our standard of living, and our personal and national futures are at stake.

On Capitol Hill, and throughout the country, "competitiveness" has become one of the dominant issues. At the same time, increasing America's competitiveness by improving the quality of everything has been proven to be a winning strategy.

The movement to improve quality in America gained momentum in the 1980s, particularly after the creation of the Malcolm Baldrige National Quality Award in 1987. Having been instrumental in framing the legislation that created the award and formulated its guidelines for assessing an organization's quality or performance capabilities, I feel tremendous pride in our nation as I watch the Baldrige galvanize the quality-improvement efforts of thousands of corporations, communities, governmental agencies, and other nonprofit organizations throughout the country. Millions of workers in these organizations have come alive with commitment and enthusiasm for their work.

The opportunities for continuing to improve individual and national quality levels are limitless, but already we can proudly point to a growing number of achievements. Many private and public corporations have used total quality management principles to help assert their leadership positions and to turn away challenges from foreign competitors. Just where would Xerox, Ford Motor Company, Motorola, and so many others be without their commitment to quality? They would probably be out of business. Likewise, a growing number of quality-conscious educators and administrators have committed to change and enhanced performance through total quality in education. State and federal governments have also awakened to the opportunity to do business in new ways and have committed to quality principles. The revolution is underway.

In my opinion, the Malcolm Baldrige National Quality Award—the result of collaboration between the public and private sectors—has been the single most important force spurring greater American competitiveness in the 1980s and 1990s. Authorized by Congress in 1987, the Baldrige Award has emerged as this country's symbol of quality achievement. The award and its comprehensive criteria have helped companies large and small, in both the manufacturing and service sectors, recognize the power of total quality management.

The award criteria are a stunning achievement, reflecting a consolidated wisdom of scores of management experts. They have established a national standard for ways to achieve high performance. Global quality concepts such as "Leadership" and "Customer Focus and Satisfaction" are distilled into operational issues such as worker empowerment and design processes. The Baldrige guidelines, oriented toward systems, probe relationships that reach across departments and disciplines. Consequently, they have helped many organizations develop insights about their operating strengths and opportunities to improve. Insight and diagnosis are the first steps in continuous improvement. In this fashion, the Baldrige Award is serving as a catalyst for greater national competitiveness. We simply cannot afford to do without it or its facsimiles. The new global economy won't permit us to.

And yet, even though the Baldrige criteria describe many quality principles that are requisites of high performance, the criteria themselves are not prescriptive. In other words, there is no single right way to pursue total quality management. As a framework for continuous improvement, the Baldrige framework truly embodies our American spirit of ingenuity and individuality. Each company is encouraged to develop and use the tools and techniques that best fit its own culture and quality objectives.

Even though only six companies can actually win the Baldrige Award in any given year, many companies are using the award criteria for training, self-assessment, quality-system development, and strategic planning. These organizations—the "silent majority" of the Baldrige participants—are laying a solid foundation of quality practices and contributing to the snowballing effect the Baldrige framework is having on industries throughout the country. For example, a growing number of Baldrige practitioners have stipulated to their suppliers that they must make the commitment to quality or risk losing business. Although the Baldrige criteria, as a management and work evaluation system, focus most specifically on operating processes and results, there is a growing body of powerful evidence correlating total quality management practices and bottom-line financial results.

As a member of the House Committee for Science and Technology that oversees the Baldrige program, I initiated a study by the Government Accounting Office (GAO) to measure the impact of TQM programs on the performance of a representative sampling of American companies. This study, which became the GAO's all-time best-seller, replaced anecdotal evidence about quality and single-company testimonials with hard data. The study, entitled "Management Practices—U.S. Companies Improve Performance Through Quality Efforts," surveyed 22 companies, all high scorers in either the 1988 or the 1989 Baldrige Award competition. The results strongly suggest that a strategy built around the principles of total quality as embodied in the Baldrige framework can contribute substantially to a company's long-term competitiveness and bottom line.

As the representative from Pennsylvania's Lehigh Valley, one of the most manufacturing-intensive districts in America, I am deeply committed to improving the quality and, by extension, the health of manufacturing industries throughout America. Service industries must not be excluded from this commitment because total quality services are inseparable from manufacturing success. That is why I believe this book is so important. Christopher Hart and Christopher Bogan give readers a detailed look at what the Baldrige Award is all about. Although it concentrates on the award's positive aspects, the book doesn't ignore criticisms and deals with them effectively. Drawing on their years of general experience working with clients to design and implement total quality management systems, and drawing on their specific experience in helping organizations apply the Baldrige criteria to their own quality improvement efforts, they provide an excellent overview of the Baldrige framework and its core principles.

The value of the Baldrige, as they correctly point out, is not in "bagging a trophy," but rather in using the criteria to improve quality continuously. In my estimation, the Baldrige Award will eventually rival the Nobel Prize in capturing the imagination of the American people. At this stage of our national life, I frankly believe it's more important. The benefits of quality, after all, are clear, and the potential reward for the American people is enormous. In today's competitive world, the Baldrige framework will be a focal point for ensuring a bright future for America in terms of jobs, standard of living, and global leadership.

My message to America? Go do it!

HONORABLE DON RITTER
U.S. House of Representatives

Preface

Thanks in part to the Malcolm Baldrige National Quality Award, managers of U.S. companies today are concerned as never before with the mega-issue of quality. Everyone wants to "do quality," to work quality into every aspect of the business. Countless different approaches to quality have blossomed and proliferated. We are truly living in the "Age of Quality."

But the result has not been uniformly positive. Many managers find that quality is not happening as they would like, or that it is not delivering the benefits they expected. Consequently, they may feel confused, or even betrayed. They may find themselves in one of five basic quality predicaments, or "boxes":

- Although their intentions are good, they've not yet taken the quality plunge. They see a dozen different approaches they might use—statistical process control, benchmarking, six sigma, Juran, Deming, guarantees—and wonder which is best for their company. A pack of different consultants are pounding on the door, each one saying, "Me! No—me! *My* approach is best."

- They think their company is already working hard to improve quality, but they're perplexed because other companies are pushing quality in very different ways. These managers want to know if they are on the right track or if their quality processes are wrong for them.

- Maybe their company has been improving quality for a while, but it's not paying off in higher profits or sales. "Where is the Great Transformation everyone promised?" they ask. "Why isn't our company achieving the kinds of results obtained by Motorola, Milliken, and Xerox?"

■ Maybe the company has been improving quality, but lately the quality-improvement effort has been running out of gas. "We've been improving quality for several years now, but the excitement is gone, and we're starting to flag. How do we regain our momentum? What are other companies doing that we are not?"

■ The gospel of quality may not be widely accepted in the organization. "No matter how much effort we put into quality, the organization remains skeptical. No matter how excited top management is, the rank and file don't believe it. How do we overcome this wall of resistance?"

These confusions will not go away with the mere passage of time. They keep getting worse because our notions of quality, and the quality discipline, keep changing. Quality is not standing still. Every year it becomes more sophisticated and more diverse, splintering into different subspecialties. At present, quality is not only a moving target, but a rapidly moving one.

The question everyone is asking about these boxes is, "How do we get out of them?" This book is designed to be a stepladder that will help managers climb out of these boxes—to install quality, or restore it in its proper place. The keys are the Malcolm Baldrige National Quality Award assessment, and the philosophy of total quality management.

Four years after the first Malcolm Baldrige National Quality Awards were given out, many Americans have been exposed to the award in some way, if only through a television commercial. Year after year, the Baldrige Award is altering how business is done in our country, in ways both subtle and sensational.

American industry has been the wonder of the world, but in recent years the giant has been stumbling. The Baldrige Award is evidence of America's practical ingenuity; it helps a business diagnose its problems—indifference to the quality of its processes, and to the eventual satisfaction of its customers—and develops ways to solve them. What makes Baldrige work is that its approach to quality improvement is *total*; it asks that quality be pursued on all fronts, by everyone associated with an organization. This fits well with our definition of total quality management:

> Total quality management is a business management methodology that aligns the activities of all employees with the common focus of customer satisfaction, through continuous improvement in the quality of all processes, goods, and services.

The Baldrige assessment methodology is an ideal means to the total quality management end. This book marries the two concepts of total quality management and the Baldrige methodology to produce a single, state-of-the-art approach to quality management.

The development of the Baldrige criteria has reversed much of the splintering of the quality movement, pulling the increasingly different elements together again. Managers no longer have to rely on the last article or book they read, or on the heart-stopping presentations of the guru of the moment, in order to drive their companies toward world-class excellence. Now companies have a single, cogent, understandable, and workable methodology to apprise them of their greatest opportunities and to drive them single-mindedly toward success.

The approach prescribed by this book is based on the premise that Baldrige is best used not to "bag a trophy," but as a process that helps a company learn more about its strengths and weaknesses, and then helps the company take steps to improve itself.

This book is therefore for a variety of readers. It is for

- *CEOs* and other *senior executives, division* and *functional heads* of manufacturing and service companies who want to know how to make their businesses more productive, more communicative, and more profitable. Senior executives are having a hard time right now, trying to pick their way through a large number of ideas and possible directions, all included under the umbrella of quality. They want someone to stop and explain, in simple terms, which quality initiatives are on target and which are not. This book intends to do just that.

- *Quality managers* at every level, whose job it is to train, test, and communicate for quality. These managers are having a hard time, too. Managing the multiple dimensions of quality in a rapidly changing business environment is like juggling in a wind tunnel.

- *Executives* and *managers* at all companies selling to companies who are committed to the Baldrige process, and who may be asked to put their companies through Baldrige as well.

- *Economists, policy makers, researchers, business teachers, business students,* people in the *business media,* and *general business readers* who want to better understand an important trend in modern management and global competition.

Quality guru Philip Crosby is famous for his observation that "quality is free"—that any costs associated with quality improvement are inconsequential compared to the gains quality improvement will inevitably produce. We take a different tack, acknowledging that quality costs—and sometimes costs plenty. We agree with Crosby from the standpoint that, when quality is done right, it becomes a kind of obsession, one that begins in the hearts and minds of top management and is transmitted from there down through every nook and cranny of even the largest multinational corporation.

Take that emotional commitment, combine it with a map that will guide a company's quality-improvement investments toward concrete payoffs—increased sales and profitability, improved market share, greater customer satisfaction and employee retention—and you have a formula for unsurpassable success.

You supply the obsession, and the Baldrige criteria will supply the map.

Christopher W. L. Hart
Christopher E. Bogan

Acknowledgments

One thing we know about quality, and the Baldrige Award in particular, is that it is a team endeavor. The same is true for this book. Although only two names appear on the cover, dozens more could have appeared alongside them.

In quality, the present builds on the past. There have been many leaders in the quality discipline who have contributed to this book, from the well-known gurus to the quality professionals in the trenches, inside and outside corporate walls. Others include colleagues at Harvard Business School and elsewhere in academia, who placed a brick here, some mortar there, and together built the Baldrige house of quality.

We are grateful to the sponsors and to the participants in the annual "Quest for Excellence" conference, whom we have quoted extensively here. Participants include some of the most respected names in industry: John Wallace, Robert Galvin, David Kearns, Donald Berwick, Larry Osterwise, Roy Bauer, Kent Sterett, John Grettenberg, and Paul Vita. We thank the National Institute of Standards and Technology for supplying us with a wealth of materials, including the list of Baldrige resources.

Special thanks to our colleagues at the TQM Group, Ltd., Boston, for their brainstorming, critiquing, and proofreading—especially Steven Kett, Chris Lemley, Joan Livingston, and Norman Klein, all of whom acted as an informal "critic's corner" in the final stages of writing. Christina Mullin, Jim Garrett, and Jane Gallagher, all of whom helped develop exercises and other materials for use with clients, and now for use in this book, also deserve special thanks.

Gary Spizizen was of inestimable value at every stage of this project: researching, planning, and helping with the actual writing. Likewise, Michael Finley helped polish the final product. To them, and to everyone else who helped with a phrase, an idea, or an improvement, our deepest thanks.

Christopher W. L. Hart
Christopher E. Bogan

PART 1

The Meaning of Baldrige

1

The Background
to Baldrige

The Evolution of
the Quality Spirit

What is the Malcolm Baldrige National Quality Award? Where did it
come from? What is its purpose? How does it work? How does it relate
to you and your company?

The first and most obvious thing that must be said about the Baldrige
Award is that you cannot win it with a single achievement. You cannot
bring home the gold by scoring high in only one of the seven categories
of Leadership, Information & Analysis, Strategic Quality Planning, Human Resource Development and Management, Management of Process
Quality, Quality and Operational Results, and Customer Focus and Satisfaction.* Achievement under Baldrige must be total.

The Greek runner Pheidippides ran the original marathon, 150 miles
in two days, to alert Sparta to the arrival of Persian ships in 490 B.C.,
and dropped dead after running back to Athens to deliver news of the
Greek victory. Pheidippides is a hero forever in the annals of one-shot
deeds. But if there were a Baldrige Olympics, Pheidippides might not
even make it to the semifinals.

---

*It is recommended that you have a copy of the guidelines on hand as you read this
book. If you don't have a copy of the Baldrige guidelines, individual copies are free, and
may be ordered from the National Institute of Standards and Technology in several ways:

By mail:
National Institute of Technology
Route 270 and Quince Orchard Road
Administration Building, Room A537
Gaithersburg, MD 20899

By telephone:
301-975-2036

By FAX:
301-948-3716

The Baldrige Award is conferred not for suicidal eleventh-hour individual heroics, but for *total quality management*. That immediately makes Baldrige less exciting than the Olympic Games, at least as a spectator sport. But, for companies, Baldrige represents an approach that more and more companies are turning to in order to create new jobs, new markets, new customers, and new profits.

Total quality management requires that everyone in an organization work together toward these common objectives. Managers who try to do it all by themselves may, like Pheidippedes, exert themselves remarkably—but their final moments may not be so glorious.

Winning the Malcolm Baldrige National Quality Award is, indeed, a remarkable victory. But the real winners of the Baldrige process are all who put it, and its philosophy of total quality, to work for them.

The Problem of Defining "Quality"

Much of the wrangling in the field of quality has been about terminology. QC (quality control), QA (quality assurance), TQC (total quality control), CWQC (company-wide quality control)—the list of quality acronyms, and the separate ideologies governing each, constitute a confusing stew of *-isms* for the innocent onlooker.

Quality is something we all think we understand; it is almost too simple for words. A *quality* car. A *quality* individual. An inexplicable *quality*. But it means different things to different people. Different quality movements have focused on different aspects or dimensions of quality. People in training, marketing, engineering, and service all have their own specific notions of what quality is, where it begins and ends, and how it may be measured. As the quality movement has grown, defining quality has only become more difficult. The Baldrige framework itself makes no effort to define quality. Curt Reimann, director of the award process, says that meaningful definition is simply not possible.[1]

But it may be said that Baldrige does define total quality management by identifying a full landscape of areas where organizations will want to be proficient in order to ensure their success and continuous improvement. What path an organization takes to develop those proficiencies is left to the individual organization.

Quality before Baldrige

In the eighteenth century, defining quality as "conformance to specifications" would have been unthinkable. Manufacturing then was what the word suggested: "making by hand." Handmade goods were not expected to fit together as interchangeable sets of parts, as later mass-assembled goods would be. Until the nineteenth century, industry lacked the means for even rudimentary quality control—technology, management, training, everything.

One of the first figures in the history of quality control—manufacturer, inventor, and entrepreneur Eli Whitney—was only intermittently successful. Whitney's career was a string of startling claims and unreproducible results. Contrary to popular belief, he was not the first inventor to patent a machine for deseeding cotton. And he was never able to manufacture rifles with reliably interchangeable parts—the achievement on which his reputation in the quality field rests. He did mount demonstrations using hand-tooled parts that somehow did interchange.[2] Not until the Civil War, however, would munitions makers even begin to get right the task of interchangeable weapons parts—and then not often enough to inspire confidence among the men on the front lines.

Frederick Taylor and Frank Gilbreth

With the dawn of the age of mass assembly in the twentieth century, modern manufacturing began to assume its current shape. Part of this system was a new philosophy of quality. Scientific management method, as preached by Frederick Taylor,[3] and time-motion productivity study, as advocated by Frank Gilbreth,[4] took as their touchstone the idea that every business behavior was intrinsically perfectible through the application of testable work methods.

The quest for quality followed almost as naturally upon the advent of mass assembly as exhalation follows inhalation. Too many mismade parts were showing up at the end of the assembly line; too many assemblies and components were breaking down during testing; too many finished products came back to the factory under warranty; and too many sales were lost because of the growing suspicion in the customer's mind that Company X was simply not capable of turning out reliable products.

G. S. Radford and Inspection

In its early days, quality control was a dimension of cost control, with emphasis on eliminating waste. The first important book on quality, was *The Control of Quality in Manufacturing,* by G. S. Radford, published in 1922. It established inspection as the bulwark of a company's quality control efforts.[5] In Radford's view, it was the inspector's job to examine, weigh, and measure every item prior to its being loaded on a truck for shipment. Inspection thus became a kind of industrial safety net.

Walter Shewhart and Statistical Process Control

In 1931, Walter Shewhart's pioneering book, *Economic Control of Quality of Manufactured Product,* gave the fledgling quality profession a foothold in scientific method.[6] Shewhart was one of a team of individuals, working together at Bell Telephone Laboratories, whose mission was to devise techniques to improve standardization and uniformity throughout the national Bell System. The six of them—Shewhart, W. Edwards Deming, Harold Dodge, Harry Romig, G. D. Edwards, and late arrival Joseph Juran—fashioned the modern-day discipline of statistical quality control (SQC).[7]

Shewhart and his team saw that, in reality, there was no such thing as 100 percent conformance to exact manufacturing specifications; in any phenomenon, there is some degree of naturally occurring variability due to such factors as aging machines, differences among parts, or differences in worker skills. Hence the challenge of quality is to *control* variability between like things so that they fall into acceptable limits. Statistical process control does this by *mathematically determining acceptable levels of variation.* Workers select samples of what they are making during the course of production and plot critical specification variables (e.g., size, weight, tensile strength) on a graph. They use the graph to determine whether the variation in the process under way is "in control" (i.e., producing a predictable quality of output), or whether variation in the process is "out of control," which would be due to some "special cause"—a problem with a particular worker or machine, or a one-time environmental condition, such as a hurricane or missed delivery.

SPC was a leap forward for quality because it allowed workers on the factory floor to monitor the quality of their own work by visually plotting variations of output. If variations became too wide or too frequent, then workers intervened and did whatever was necessary to control the variation. In addition, managers could tell, by looking at the data in the charts that were created, when the system was stable and when structural changes—new technology or new methods—were called for.

Harold Dodge and Harry Romig—Sampling

Sampling, techniques of which were advanced by Dodge and Romig, is an approach to inspection. Instead of measuring every manufactured item, sampling showed how to measure representative samples of manufactured items, thus eliminating the need to spend too many resources on inspection.

The Deming Synthesis

Yoked together, statistical process control and sampling lifted quality control to a new level, beginning in the Bell system. W. Edwards Deming, after whom Japan's coveted Deming Prize for Quality was named in 1951, has become the most famous guru of statistical process controls. Deming is also well known for the Fourteen Points, a broad set of simple, but profound quality principles; the Seven Deadly Diseases, common obstacles to quality improvement; and the PDCA (Plan, Do, Check, Act) cycle, a systematic approach to problem solving. Deming's influence has been so pervasive that whatever form a quality program takes, it is bound to include some elements of his philosophy.

The Birth of the American Society for Quality Control

With the industrial fury that World War II engendered, and the life-or-death necessity of decent product quality, the profession took another major step forward. The sudden increase of inspectors and quality engineers resulted in the formation of an academic and professional society to further the spread of quality techniques and technologies. This group, formally established in 1945, was originally called the Society for Quality Engineers. We know it today as the American Society for Quality Control (ASQC). Its creation went a long way toward legitimizing quality control as an integral part of the industrial scene.

During the statistical quality control revolution, industrial quality made enormous strides. It was nevertheless only a partial approach, one lacking corporate-wide authority. Quality control professionals were engineers, standing at the end of the line, sorting product into pass and fail buckets. It was never quite certain for whom these engineers worked. Production people were suspicious of them. Their status was nebulous, and their loyalty to the company's bottom line could be perceived by upper-level management as "compromised by quality." Quality professionals were typically excluded from high-level corporate deliberations.

The Juran Breakthrough

The next development, the evolution of quality control into quality assurance, was a pivotal one, one that intensified the notion of quality as a pathway to cost control. Joseph Juran published *The Quality Control Handbook* in 1951. In it he articulated the principle that quality ought not to be seen solely as an expense but as an investment in profitability. Avoidable quality losses were, in fact, a "business" unto themselves;

care in reducing them had the potential, by his calculations, of saving as much as $1000 per worker per year.[8]

Armand Feigenbaum and Total Quality Control

Following on the heels of Juran's breakthrough was Armand Feigenbaum, the first proponent of *total quality control*. His insight was central to what Baldrige would become 40 years later: quality was too central to a company's identity to be entrusted to an isolated corps of inspectors. Factory-door inspections were a *partial response* to failure. For a *total response*, every single employee and vendor had to be brought into the process.[9]

Philip Crosby and the Popularization of Quality

Consultant and author Philip Crosby, who coined the phrase *Quality Is Free*, popularized quality assurance as no one before him had. His approach is driven by the principle that quality is conformance to requirements and by his battle-cry, "zero defects." The elegant crux of *Quality Is Free* is that the costs of good quality, though real, evaporate over time, as they are enveloped by the very real and very measurable benefits of quality improvement.[10]

By the onset of the 1970s, thanks in large part to Juran, Feigenbaum, and Crosby, the perception of quality as a detective function had given way to the quality-assurance movement, in which quality was treated as a preventive function. Quality was something to be done before and during the making of a product or the delivery of a service, not afterward.

The topic of quality was now becoming layered and deep, drawing on the contributions of process control, reliability engineering, and the "zero defects" movement. Consultants were called in to help companies design quality systems that would minimize errors. This created a major advancement in the raw sense of improved efficiencies—fewer mistakes meant lower costs and fewer unhappy customers.

But those heady days were nothing compared to what was to come. American industry sometimes assumes it is the source of all great business ideas. From World War II to the 1970s, the United States did lead in many areas. But until the Arab oil embargo of 1972, and the sudden emergence of Japan as a fierce competitor in the 1980s, U.S. quality ideas had existed in a kind of noncompetitive vacuum. Indeed, the topic was generally given lip service and little more.

The intensified competition of the 1970s and 1980s took American business by surprise. And the surprising news was that quality-as-cost-containment was not a strong enough concept to guarantee American competitiveness in the years to come. By internal measures, American companies had indeed improved over their own quality benchmarks since the complacent 1950s and 1960s. But compared to the intense culture of continuous improvement *(kaizen)* of many major Japanese companies, the United States had fallen far behind.

The Call for an Industrial Policy

Think back to the deep recession the United States slipped into around 1980. America had spent the previous fifteen years hobbling along with inflation getting 0.5 percent or so worse with each passing year. In the final months of the Carter administration, prime interest rates hit a mind-numbing 18 percent. Factory after factory padlocked its gates and sent workers packing.

With two consecutive billion-dollar annual losses at Chrysler,[11] the auto industry groaned, awakening to the realization that foreign competitors, whom United States business had scoffed at since the end of World War II, were suddenly overtaking the United States. When the oil shocks of the 1970s hit, the Japanese share of United States auto sales grew to 25 percent in less than two years.[12] In 1980, the Big Three U.S. carmakers held 77 percent of U.S. market share. By decade's end, market share had dropped to 67 percent. Japanese share over the same period rose from 20 percent to 26 percent.[13] Unable to compete on quality, American industry pushed through a plan requiring Japan to limit auto exports.

Japan bashing became the order of the day. Americans took great and solemn umbrage at the idea that MITI, Japan's Ministry of International Trade and Industry, was working with such a sense of purposefulness to coordinate and consolidate that country's efforts in the automotive, steel, and electronics industries. Commentators, politicians, and certain business people all clamored for something to add to the American arsenal to match the help Japanese companies were getting from their government. Talk was of a "level playing field," on which American companies could engage Japanese companies in combat with no unfair advantage to either side.

Economists and policy specialists called for an American industrial policy; Japan's MITI had the power to establish national business priorities, and Americans wanted a government policy that would do something similar. Japan clearly appeared to be doing things better than the

United States was, though exactly what their superiority was based upon was something of a mystery. (One team of multinational managers visiting Japan reported that the main distinction between American and Japanese workers was that Japanese workers wore white uniforms and hats.) Whatever the Japanese were doing, Americans reasoned, Americans should be doing, too. The call for an industrial policy was a call for an "American MITI."

Things were so bad in the grip of the 1981–82 recession that some people seized on the idea of government control of American business as The Answer. If only that paragon of competence, flexibility, and delivery of fine quality goods—the government—would step in and tell American corporations what to do! Such was the depth of the American malaise.

Japan's success owed less to centralization and government assistance, however, than it did to what was happening in design and engineering departments, among its market researchers, and on the factory floors. While American industry was paying out its regular dividends, and growing fatter and weaker, Japanese industry was beefing itself up at the workteam level. Stripped of a military, Japan brought a warrior's attitude to the conduct of business, essentially free of the perks and vanities that characterized—or caricaturized—stickpin American capitalism.

The clamoring in the early 1980s for an American industrial policy was a first step toward the development of a national strategy of greater competitiveness. But it was only a first step. American industry lacked the language and the discipline in 1980 to understand just how radically different the Japanese approach was. But an American MITI? It should have been obvious from the moment it was suggested that American businesses would not (1) sit down at a table to discuss new products, export ideas, competitive strategies, and industrywide labor arrangements, or (2) meekly submit to the superior management wisdom of Congress and the Executive branch. Given the American appetite for independence, self-reliance, and go-to-it leave-me-alone-ism, such actions would have been completely out of character.

What could the government and business do together that *would* be "in character," and that would push U.S. business in the direction of greater competitiveness with foreign nations? That was a question on which there was no agreement. Regulation, deregulation, new taxes, no taxes—there existed no consensus either in the corridors of government or in the boardrooms of big business about what the proper, constructive role of government in the rebuilding of American industry might be.

Until talk began circulating around Washington, D.C., about a national quality award.

2
The Baldrige Era

Where the Award Came from, and Why

In October 1982 President Reagan signed a bill recommending a study looking at different ways the government might reward productivity and competitiveness. "Productivity improvement can be restored in the U.S.," that bill said, "through the application of policies and management techniques which have brought substantial productivity gains on a broad scale in other countries and in some businesses within the United States."[1]

But it was on the private side that action began in earnest. In Milwaukee, the American Society for Quality Control (ASQC) was spearheading an effort to advise labor, management, and government on ways to develop greater quality awareness.[2] The idea of a national quality award was at the center of the quality revolution ASQC wished to see. The ASQC's efforts led to the formation of the National Advisory Council for Quality (NACQ), a group of top managers from both the public and private sectors concerned about improving competitiveness through quality. The idea was that NACQ would become a kind of academy of quality, an ongoing information center for the exchange of ideas and research.

In December 1983, a presidentially appointed group called the National Productivity Advisory Committee recommended the creation of a national medal for achievement in productivity. Unfortunately, the motion was tabled by the Cabinet Council on Economic Affairs, on the grounds that the Council needed more detail about where the money would come from, who would be eligible, how achievement would be defined, and who would actually run the program.

Much the same thing was happening over at ASQC's rival, the American Productivity Center (APC), a nonprofit professional group pushing

11

industrial excellence from the productivity angle. APC, since renamed the American Productivity and Quality Center (APQC), sponsored a series of symposia on what the United States needed to do to regain industrial primacy. The idea of some sort of quality award came up repeatedly. APC Chairman C. Jackson Grayson, Jr., contacted Roger Porter, Deputy Assistant to the President, to plant APC's vision of a quality award. They finally drafted a statement calling for the establishment of an American prize roughly parallel to the Japanese national industrial award for quality, the Deming Prize.[3]

Almost immediately after APC's report came out in September 1983, the ground-breaking White House Conference on Productivity was held. On hand to dedicate the event and its aims were Reagan himself, Vice President George Bush, Treasury Secretary Donald Regan, White House Chief of Staff Ed Meese, and Commerce Secretary Malcolm Baldrige. A transcript of the conference opened thus:

> America is the most productive nation in the world, but its growth in productivity has faltered. Some of the factors contributing to slower productivity growth are within our control and some are not, but it is important that we respond to this challenge.[4]

The report concluded that a public/private sector effort *could* succeed, if all parties in the process—business, government, labor, and higher education—rolled up their sleeves and went to work to find a solution together.

Everyone seemed to think that an award was a good idea—but what kind of award? Names were bandied about by a group of officials appointed from government and industry calling themselves the Committee to Establish a National Quality Award. The idea of a national quality award was widely hailed, though some people wanted to ensure that the award would not be simply a copy of Japan's Deming Prize.

Companies participating in the selection process included Ford Motor, McDonnell Douglas, and Florida Power & Light (which would later go on to be the first company outside Japan to be awarded the Deming Prize). The names they suggested indicated the factionalism within the group: the National Quality-Productivity Award, or the National Productivity-Quality Award, or simply, as was finally adopted, The National Quality Award.[5]

Congress Acts

Private industry input may have given the National Quality Award its initial impetus, but Congress had to decide on its final character—a concept that, by itself, did not much console corporate proponents. But Florida

Power & Light's two leaders, Chairman-CEO Marshall McDonald and FP&L Group Chairman John Hudiburg, met with Florida Democratic Rep. Don Fuqua, at that time the chair of the House Committee on Science & Technology, to talk up the idea of a quality award. Fuqua was agreeable, and after a fact-finding trip with Hudiburg to Japan, worked with the House Science, Research & Technology Subcommittee to draft legislation. In August 1986, Fuqua introduced House Bill 5321, titled The National Quality Improvement Act. The bill acknowledged the competitive problems American industry faced and called for an award that would spotlight quality performance by American corporations.

Congress ignored Fuqua's bill, however, and Fuqua himself did not return to office in 1987. But Doug Walgren, a Pennsylvania Democrat, picked up the quality award flag and reintroduced Fuqua's bill. On June 8, the House passed Walgren's bill. At the same time, support had been building in the Senate, largely as a result of the energy and salesmanship of John Hudiburg of FP&L.[6]

It was at this point that Malcolm Baldrige, Secretary of Commerce and an amateur rodeo rider, was killed in a riding accident. In the wake of that development the Senate moved rapidly to rename the award after Baldrige. Passage was swift. On August 20, 1987, President Reagan signed the Malcolm Baldrige Quality Improvement Act into law, and a new era in American industry was under way.

The Goals of the Baldrige Award

The Malcolm Baldrige National Quality Award was created to promote the following four goals:

- Helping to stimulate American companies to improve quality and productivity for the pride of recognition while obtaining a competitive edge through increased profits;
- Recognizing the achievements of those companies that improve the quality of their goods and services and providing an example to others;
- Establishing guidelines and criteria that can be used by businesses, industrial, governmental and other organizations in evaluating their own quality improvement efforts; and
- Providing specific guidance for other American organizations that wish to learn how to manage for high quality by making available detailed information on how winning organizations were able to change their cultures and achieve eminence.

After the award had been thus designated, a trophy was designed. Created by Steuben Glass, it is an attractive sculpture—a 14-inch solid crystal with a medal embedded in it, emblazoned on one side with the Presidential seal and on the other with the name of the award and the phrase "The Quest for Excellence." Its exposure in TV and print media commercials would soon make it recognizable to millions of Americans.

Giving Meaning and Legitimacy to the Award

But in point of fact, neither the House, nor the Senate, nor the Executive branch, had ever stipulated how exactly the new award would work. Would candidates apply or would they have to be nominated? If candidates were to be examined, what questions would be asked? Who would ask them? Who would decide which answers were "right"? The world is full of phony awards—would Baldrige turn out to be another platinum-plated honorarium, the property of whichever company mounted the biggest publicity campaign? Would the largest corporate contributors to the Foundation for the Malcolm Baldrige National Quality Award walk off with the trophies every year? That was the nightmare the Baldrige could conceivably have become. Certainly, nothing Congress required guaranteed that the Baldrige be a legitimate award. The Baldrige could easily have turned out to be merely a public-relations gimmick, adding glamour to corporate profile ads but doing little to alter the industrial skyline. Indeed, some skeptics in the early offing insisted that was exactly what the Baldrige would become—window dressing.

Fortunately, the Baldrige process was entrusted to the administrative oversight of the National Institute of Standards and Technology (NIST), formerly the National Bureau of Standards. NIST, located in Gaithersburg, Maryland, has a long tradition of impartiality. NIST and the Baldrige Foundation adopted a strict policy of withholding information from the public about contributions for a given year until that year's awards have been announced. Such information is likewise withheld from Baldrige examiners. The result is that gifts, although necessary to the continuance of the program, are kept apart from the judging process, so that they cannot influence it.

Perhaps even more important to the strong start of the award, however, was the selection of Curt Reimann as its first director. He had begun his career in 1962 as a research chemist, with a B.A. from Drew University and a Ph.D. from the University of Michigan. At the time of his selection to head the Baldrige Award, Reimann was Deputy Director of the National Measurement Laboratory, the NIST organization responsible for developing and maintaining the nation's basic physical, chemical and radiation measurements and standards.

Suddenly, Reimann the scientist found himself in the unfamiliar realm of business, charged with the task of defining quality in a way that American companies could accept and feel motivated to attain, each in its own way. In their research, Reimann and his colleagues at NIST talked to over 200 quality professionals, picking and choosing which criteria to incorporate into the—at that point, empty—Baldrige framework. "We conceived of the framework in a number of ways," Reimann said. "First, as a communications tool in a field that has historically resisted adopting a common framework for communication. Second as a diagnostic tool that allows companies to self-assess. And finally, as an evaluative scoring system."[7]

Reimann and his colleagues fashioned their list of criteria into the structural underpinnings of the Baldrige Award. These assessment criteria were assigned values, totaling 1000 points, to be used in scoring, with some criteria weighted more heavily than others. Taken together, these criteria constitute the "Seven Pillars" of the Baldrige quality framework:

- Leadership
- Information and Analysis
- Strategic Quality Planning
- Human Resource Development and Management
- Management of Process Quality
- Quality and Operational Results
- Customer Focus and Satisfaction

Each pillar symbolizes a wide variety of issues; together they require that interested companies master an arsenal of different quality techniques. Taken as a whole, they do not favor any "guru" or system or dogma. They tread a fine line: Reimann intended the framework to be nonprescriptive, in the sense of not identifying specific quality tools and techniques that *must* be used. Yet it still had to present a useful road map to guide companies aspiring to world-class quality (see Fig. 2-1).

After a period of fitful development, the Baldridge criteria have stabilized around some broad, core quality principles, supported by specific items and "areas to address" that accommodate virtually every type of business. Clearly, the criteria can be changed if necessary. The guidelines state, "The items and areas to address have been selected because of their importance to virtually all businesses. Nevertheless, the importance of the items and areas to address may not be

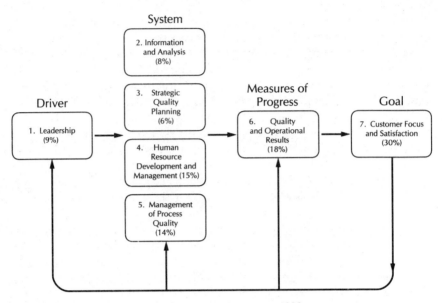

Figure 2-1. The Baldrige Award Examination Categories, 1992

equally *applicable* to all businesses, even to businesses of comparable size in the same industry." (Emphasis is ours.) The award is still young and malleable. A major strength of the Baldrige process is the continual cycle of evaluation and improvement of its guidelines.

Flexibility is the byword. The criteria are written in such a way as to give examiners the latitude to judge each company's quality efforts independently. "Specific business factors that may bear upon the evaluation," say the guidelines, "are considered at every stage of preparation for evaluations, as well as in the evaluations themselves. It may be judicious to include a section of the criteria which addresses how business factors—such as size and resources of the applicant, etc.—are considered in the award criteria." Thus, the quality systems and techniques found in two businesses—say, a rapidly growing retail chain and a mature manufacturing operation—may both be rated very highly in the Baldrige criteria, even though they are very different.

There are three award categories: manufacturing, small business, and service. Only two awards can be conferred in any category per year; and judges are free to withhold awards in any category. In the award's first two years, for example, they gave no awards to service companies. This flexibility on the part of the judges can lead to controversy. Service companies fumed that the service sector was getting short shrift from NIST. Numerous letters from service companies criticizing the omission appeared in periodicals such as *Quality Progress*. But when service businesses Federal Express and Wallace finally did win the award in 1990, the event carried great weight.

The Baldrige Review Process

The main review body for the Malcolm Baldrige National Quality Award is its Board of Examiners, comprising more than 250 quality experts selected from business, professional and trade organizations, accrediting bodies, universities, and government agencies. Membership on the Board has increased as the number of award applications has increased.

Selected each winter through an application process, Board members are evaluated according to expertise, experience, and peer recognition. Consideration is also given to creating a range of expertise on the entire Board, covering both manufacturing and service businesses. In addition to their examination responsibilities, Board members participate in informational exchanges within their professional, trade, community, and state organizations and collectively represent a large and growing corps of experts promoting the national quality effort.

Board appointments are of three types: examiners, senior examiners, and judges. All Board members take part in a preparation course designed to ensure understanding, consistency, and fairness throughout the examination process. The course addresses the intent of the examination items, the application of the scoring system, the preparation of feedback reports, and other details of the examination process. In addition, examiners are taught how key business factors, such as the applicant's regulatory environment and size and resources, should be taken into account in the examination process.

When assigning Board members to review applications, business and quality expertise are matched to the business of the applicant. Accordingly, applications from manufacturing companies are assigned primarily to board members with manufacturing expertise, and applications from service companies are assigned primarily to those with service expertise. Each award category—manufacturing, service, and small business—is considered separately. Judges monitor the review process to ensure thoroughness and integrity.

The Four Stages of Review

Stage One

In the first stage, each application in each of the three award categories is reviewed by at least four members of the Board of Examiners. They individually score all the items, record their comments on worksheets, and begin preparation of a list of site-visit issues (i.e., questions to be answered if the applicant is selected for a site visit).

Stage Two

On the basis of the scores and comments from the first stage of review, the Panel of Judges selects which applicants will receive a *consensus review*. The Judges's selection process is anonymous; applicants are identified by code number only. All the scores of the stage 1 review, to the item level, are given for each applicant. Various charts and graphs displaying the data are provided to each member of the Panel of Judges.

In the consensus review, a uniform set of scores is developed. A scoring difference of 20 percent or less on a particular examination item is considered acceptable; above that level, the original examiners must confer and resolve their differences. For example, the examiner who gave the lowest score may point out several serious inconsistencies in the applicant's survey data that were overlooked by the other examiners. The consensus process also leads to revisions in the list of site-visit issues.

The concensus scores and all of the individual Examiner scores for each applicant are returned to the judges, who discuss each application, beginning with the one that received the lowest score. Eventually, some company gets a majority of judges's votes, qualifying for a site visit. Every company scoring higher than this "threshold" company is then automatically accorded a site visit. Applications during this stage are still identified only by number.

Stage Three

The third stage of the process is the site-visit review, in which an on-site "verification" of the application is conducted by at least five members of the Board of Examiners, including a Senior Examiner who leads the team. At the end of a week-long site visit, the team prepares a report for the panel of judges.

The primary objectives of the site visit is to verify the information provided in the application and to clarify the issues and questions raised during the review of the application. The site-visit plan is cooperatively developed by the applicant and the site-visit team, and an agenda is provided to the company at least two weeks in advance of the visit.

The site-visit agenda includes, but is not limited to, a schedule of planned visits to the applicant's facilities and operating units, a list of corporate officials to be interviewed, an estimate of time requirements for the visits, and the names of the examiners who will participate. To minimize the potential for "dressing up" errors, a site-visit team typically makes several unannounced visits to parts of the organization not included in the planned agenda. The actual site visit consists primarily of interviews and reviews of pertinent records and data, although applicants are given the opportunity to make introductory and concluding presentations.

Stage Four

In the fourth and final stage of review, all the evaluation reports submitted by the site-visit teams are reviewed by the panel of judges. Judges with any conflicts of interest or appearance of conflicts of interest are not allowed to participate. The judges's discussions focus on overall strengths and weaknesses of each company. Questions are referred to the senior examiner who oversaw the company's site visit. Applications in each of the award categories are discussed one at a time and eliminated by unanimous vote. When the number of applicants in each category has been reduced to two, the process of elimination is terminated. All Judges with no conflict of interest with the two remaining applicants can then vote on the final recommendation. There is a separate ballot for each candidate so that either, both, or neither may be recommeded for a Baldrige Award. Decisions are made by a simple majority of the voting judges (for example, 5/9, 5/8, 3/4, and so on.)

Award recommendations, if any, are sent to the Secretary of Commerce who makes the final decision based on the ability of the prospective award recipient(s) to serve as appropriate models of total quality achievement for other U.S. companies. A wide margin of safety is built into the review process. Judging procedures ensure that applicants are not eliminated based upon small differences in scoring. Kent Sterett, formerly Chief Quality Officer at Florida Power & Light and currently Assistant Vice President for Quality at Southern Pacific Transportation Co., compared the Baldrige process to that of the judicial system in that both are based on "reasonable doubt." If, for example, there is "reasonable doubt" in the judges' minds whether or not a company deserves a site visit, then that company receives one.

Strong conflict-of-interest rules apply and are carefully monitored at all four stages of review. Members of the Board of Examiners receive no information regarding the content or status of applications to which they are not assigned. Board members sign agreements to abide by a code of ethics, which includes nondisclosure of information from applications. Information is available only to those individuals directly involved in the evaluation and application distribution process. Applications are confidential and not available to the public.

The Baldrige Award versus the
Deming Prize: A Comparison

First, the Baldrige is not a spinoff of Japan's Deming Prize. The Baldrige Award may have been inspired by the Deming Prize, but it is far from a carbon copy of it. There are important differences between the two awards. The Deming Prize, named after W. Edwards Deming and instituted in 1951, has a much longer history than the Baldrige. It is often given credit for guiding Japanese manufacturing beyond its second-class reputation for poor quality, to its current position of excellence.

The Deming Prize is awarded in six categories:

- The Deming Application Prize for Companies (or public institutions)
- The Deming Application Prize for Small Enterprises
- The Deming Application Prize for Divisions
- The Deming Application Prize for Work Sites
- The Deming Application Prize for Overseas Companies
- The Deming Prize for Individuals

The first step of the Deming Prize process requires a company to submit an application, including a history of the company and a précis of its company-wide quality control (CWQC) efforts. If the application advances to the next level, the company must then prepare—in Japanese—a much more exhaustive report on its quality systems. This report is called the *Description of Quality Control Practices.*

If this document passes muster with Deming judges—who, unlike Baldrige judges, are also consultants who *must* be engaged by companies interested in the Deming Prize—an on-site examination is scheduled. The examination involves a presentation by the company, a series of reviews and question-and-answer sessions by the examining body, and a series of interviews with top management.

The primary similarity between the Deming and the Baldrige is the value system upon which each is based: Both awards are steeped in the principles of continuous improvement and customer satisfaction. Both require initiative by individual companies, which must apply to be considered. Likewise, both involve site inspection by examiners.

But there are many differences as well. The Baldrige Award is far more *result-oriented* than is Deming. In addition to information about processes, applicants for the Baldrige must demonstrate measurable, performance results. The Baldrige guidelines set aside an entire pillar to consider the real-life, measurable results of what process improvements achieve. Deming, by contrast, is much more single-minded in its focus on processes. The logic behind the Deming Prize is that if a company's processes are improving, its results (productivity, profitability, etc.) will improve as well.

The evaluation of applicants for the Baldrige is conceived as a *true competition*, with a limited number of awards for which applicants openly compete. Any number of companies can win the Deming Prize, depending on how many firms the examiners deem worthy of the award. U.S. companies compete aggressively for the Baldrige Award, and they spend money both on the application and on subsequent advertising, using the award in their marketing efforts. (NIST prefers that winners not use winning the Baldrige Award too nakedly in advertisements, but most winners have not been shy about including the Baldrige logo in their marketing pieces.)

The Baldrige Award takes a much closer look at *customer satisfaction* and *service quality* as criteria for excellence than the Deming Prize does. This difference is intentional, and it is hoped that these factors will be distinguishing factors for American business in the decades to come.

The Baldrige and the Deming awards are given to different types of entities. As a recognition of the burgeoning growth of America's service sector, the Baldrige has made a special point of including service companies. On the other hand, the Deming offers awards to individual employees and work sites.

The Deming Prize process is a bit mysterious. Deming examiners use a brief 2-page checklist of criteria as guidelines when examining a company. They are free to improvise from the checklist, interpreting items on a case-by-case basis. The Baldrige guidelines, by contrast, are compiled in a 35-page booklet. As such, they constitute a methodology that companies can use without outside assistance—and without ever applying. The same can not be said for the Deming. Indeed, Deming Prize judges routinely serve as consultants to the companies seeking the Deming Prize, helping the companies improve and control their processes to the point where they become Deming Prize contenders.

Finally, the Baldrige is different from the Deming, and from most industrial awards, in that it is diagnostic, not prescriptive. Thus, its overall message to American business is not "Here is the tune, now dance to it." Clearly, the Baldrige was not created to provide all the answers. It encourages applicants to develop their own approaches to achieving competency. The Deming, on the other hand, rightly or wrongly, stipulates its own quality criteria against which companies must measure themselves.

It is true that the Baldrige is prescriptive in the sense that applicants must exhibit that they have developed quality systems directed toward accomplishment in the areas of leadership, customer satisfaction, continuous improvement, response time, employee empowerment, and quantifiable results. That said, there is no official Baldrige "recipe" that an applying or self-assessing company must follow down to the quarter-teaspoon. In the final analysis, the Baldrige methodology does not tell an organization how to be excellent. Rather, it serves as a roadmap that shows an organization the many routes that can be taken to attain world-class quality, daring the organization to find its own way.

Winning in the True Sense of the Word

The original title for this book was *Winning through Baldrige,* but this was changed to avoid any misconception that winning refers primarily to a prize or award. This decision reflects the belief that the Baldrige process is its own reward. Companies that commit to its core beliefs of customer focus and continuous improvement and develop the discipline to build these beliefs into everything they do will have already entered the winner's circle.

The most frequent misrepresentation of the Baldrige is that the object is to win it outright and cart the trophy back to the corporate headquarters lobby. Some companies covet the Baldrige as a kind of hood ornament for their profile marketing. And some consultants hawk their services with the strong implication that retaining them assures prompt installation of the hood ornament.

Actually *winning* the prize is probably the single worst reason for applying. This misunderstanding is probably, in a way, a sign that the Baldrige is on the right track. From the beginning, it sought to bestow prestige on those companies awarded the prize. The problem here is that a few companies are performing mental shortcuts. They confuse the symbol of excellence with the reality of creating total organizational excellence. They concentrate so hard on winning the prize that they lose sight of the process that guides this achievement.

Positive Results of the Baldrige Award

Baldrige creates a common language and a common standard for quality. It takes the former confusion of slogans, concepts, and dogmas that peppered the quality landscape and unifies them under a single rubric. As a consequence of this unification, many different things have started to happen on the quality scene, all of them good.

- The most immediately noticeable result is that the Baldrige has altered the landscape of *quality education* in America, dramatically accelerating learning. Baldrige gives companies, educational institutions, pub-

lic agencies, and consultants a common curriculum, a shared understanding of the many concepts, disciplines, and practices that, taken
together, constitute total quality management.

- A second major consequence of the Baldrige is a new level of communications within companies. Whereas in the past companies may
have encouraged departmental and divisional goal setting, participation in the Baldrige process ups the ante by including *cross-functional
communications*—communications that vault across old barriers and accepted boundaries, connecting team to team, and level to level. The
common language of the Baldrige process accelerates this development.

- The Baldrige process comprises a *body of quality knowledge* that serves
as a resource for companies. It establishes common values and common standards. It identifies and celebrates national models that other
companies are inspired to study, imitate, or follow. It creates a basis
for flexible self-assessment that any company or any part of any company can use for its own internal purposes. And it serves as a lightning
rod for governmental and private sector commingling of talents and
resources.

The single best reason for a company to commit to the Baldrige process is probably to learn about itself. The process is first and foremost
internal, as indicated by the disparity between the number of Baldrige
applications requested for information purposes and those actually submitted to formally compete for the Baldrige Award. Thousands of companies are taking the Baldrige criteria and adapting them internally for
their own purposes, without formally applying.

	Requested	Submitted	Site visits
1988	12,000	66	13
1989	65,000	40	10
1990	180,000	97	12
1991	205,000	106	19

The Power of an Idea Whose
Time Has Come

One of the clearest signs of the power of the Baldrige idea has been
the proliferation of similar quality programs and awards developed
within companies, communities, and states. From IBM to AT&T, from
Connecticut to North Carolina, the Baldrige Award and its approach
to assessing organizational quality are serving as a model for fostering

greater competitiveness among organizations and communities of all sizes (see Chapter 17). The core concepts of quality embodied by this model represent crucial knowledge for modern managers.

At Westinghouse, IBM, AT&T, Baxter Healthcare and other organizations, business units all undertake Baldrige-style quality assessments each year. In 1990 AT&T trained over 1000 senior and mid-level managers to be its own internal Baldrige examiners. At Xerox, promotions are based in part on a manager's ability to serve as a quality role model to his or her team; the basis for role model behavior at Xerox draws heavily upon the concepts of customer focus and quality leadership identified in the Baldrige criteria. GTE Management Education and Training Program has a special course in which it exposes its business unit teams to the Baldrige framework.

Ford Motor Company, for instance, has tied its fortunes to the quality concept since the 1970s. But with the emergence of the Baldrige standards, Ford successfully implemented its own Ford Total Quality Excellence Award, made to recognize major quality improvements by suppliers. Motorola wants to have the Baldrige both ways—having won the award in 1988, it requires thousands of its vendors to commit to the criteria as well, as tangible evidence of their shared commitment to Motorola's quality standards and objectives. IBM, Xerox, and other companies have followed Motorola's example, urging external partners to commit to quality as it is understood through the Baldrige criteria.

In community after community, the Baldrige process is being enlisted as a platform on which to base excellence councils, user groups, and homegrown quality awards. Cities stepping forward with their Baldrige-inspired programs include Erie, Pennsylvania; Madison, Wisconsin; Philadelphia, Pennsylvania; Austin, Texas; and Seattle, Washington. And numerous states have leaped into the fray with their statewide offerings: Connecticut, Maine, Maryland, Massachusetts, Minnesota, New York, Texas, Virginia and Wyoming. More states are expected to follow.

The Baldrige is having an enormous impact on business today, and its influence can be expected to grow in the years ahead of us. The entire world is in need of a quality standard, and the new world-class quality standards—the Baldrige Award, Japan's Deming Prize, and the ISO 9000 standards in Europe—are emerging as the cornerstones for a new era of excellence.[8]

Winners of the Malcolm Baldrige National Quality Award

A list of the winners from Baldrige's first four years is given in Fig. 2-2.

Year	Manufacturing	Small Business	Service
1988	Motorola, Inc. Commercial Nuclear Fuel Division of Westinghouse Electric Corporation	Globe Metallurgical, Inc.	[None]
1989	Milliken & Company Xerox Business Products and Systems	[None]	[None]
1990	Cadillac Motor Car Company IBM Rochester	Wallace Co., Inc.	Federal Express Corporation
1991	Solectron Corp. Zytec Corp.	Marlowe Industries	[None]

Figure 2-2. Winners of the Baldrige

1988

Motorola, Inc. Motorola, which leads the nation in the manufacture and sale of semiconductors, has been described as "fanatical about quality." This fanaticism was inculcated by founder Paul Galvin, who headed the company until 1959, and his son Robert, who stepped down as chairman in 1988. It was Robert Galvin whose ambitious commitment to perfection led to winning the Baldrige Award. In 1981 he called for a tenfold reduction in defect rates. Having achieved that, Motorola set long-term goals in both defect *and* cycle-time reduction. The company's guiding vision has spawned the business phrase "Six Sigma Quality"— to reduce failures to a minuscule 3.4 per million. Its defect reduction and other quality strategies are credited for saving over $500 million in manufacturing costs in 1990. Motorola's has set itself a "stretch goal" of achieving $1 billion in savings in 1992.[9]

Westinghouse Commercial Nuclear Fuel Division.   Before this Westinghouse division seized the quality initiative, quality in the fuel-rod assembly industry meant meeting regulatory standards, period. Quality throughout Westinghouse was likewise a laid-back affair—John Marous, then CEO and chairman and now retired, admits the company was satisfied with 95 percent defect-free level of quality.[10] But the demands of competitiveness forced the division to improve its quality performance by a factor of 10 while sharply reducing product cycle times. The approach followed at Westinghouse is a total quality management concept, parallel to the Baldrige guidelines, pushing continuous improvement on all fronts at once, through a central quality council comprised of "champion" managers and employees, tracking progress at 60 critical "Pulse Points." The company achieved its goal of being the best in the industry, as defined by customer satisfaction, four years ahead of schedule. In so doing they reduced defects per thousand from 50 to 0.5.

Globe Metallurgical.   The first small business awarded the Baldrige. Globe's story is one of great resourcefulness, in which "just another" maker of commodity ferroalloys (iron-based metals) decided to differentiate itself, to distinguish its products from the competition by making them better and cheaper. In effect, the Cleveland-based company reconfigured itself as a specialty provider of high-grade supplies to foundries, chemical companies, and the automotive and aluminum industries. The company hitched its quality-progress cart to a statistical, control-driven quality improvement process and to a down-to-earth philosophy of human observation and attention. Ken Leach, then Vice President for Administration, led the way, establishing a participative style of communication within the company and a relentless round of daily quality sessions. Among the company's achievements were the reduction of customer complaints by 91 percent and the reduction of returned products in 1987 to zero.

1989

Milliken.   As the top U.S. textiles company in annual sales, this privately owned Spartanburg, South Carolina-based company is deeply committed to competitiveness. Under the stewardship of its flinty chairman, Roger Milliken, to whom author Tom Peters dedicated *Thriving on Chaos*,[11] Milliken initiated its total quality siege in 1981 with its

"Pursuit of Excellence" campaign. Anti-union by disposition, the company of 14,300 associates encouraged instead the formation by 1990 of 1600 *corrective action teams* to spot and fix internal problems, 200 *supplier action teams* to build cooperative alliances with vendors; and another 500 *customer satisfaction teams* to focus on meeting customer needs. Milliken has fashioned an open information system, centrally located but accessible to all 47 work sites. In the 10 years since the inception of "Pursuit of Excellence," Milliken has seen productivity increase by 42 percent.

Xerox Business Products and Systems. The history of Xerox is an interesting one. It began life as a unique superstar, slipped to the status of an also-ran in the 1970s, and then was reborn like a phoenix in the 1980s as a fiery, quality-minded competitor. Xerox Business Products and Systems, makers of more than 250 different copier and other office-machine products, devised a comprehensive quality process focusing on customer-defined quality, drawing on a monthly survey from over 55,000 Xerox equipment owners. The company's "Leadership through Quality" program, begun in the mid-1980s and headed by then-CEO David T. Kearns, balances the principles of strong central management and an empowered "Team Xerox" workforce. Xerox greatly advanced the practice of corporate benchmarking—continuous self-measurement against other companies and industries—a concept so useful, so strong and so portable that it was subsequently incorporated as a fixture in the Baldrige criteria.

1990

Cadillac Motor Car Company. Throughout most of this century, Cadillac has been synonymous with quality in automobile manufacture. But in the 1970s and 1980s, its reputation was hit hard by competition at home and abroad. Sales plummeted even further when the division shortened its cars by two feet in 1984.[12] In 1987, company management, along with the United Auto Workers, recognized that a consistent, joint quality-improvement process was needed to increase competitiveness. In its revamping, Cadillac redefined its relationship with the autoworkers' union, as well as its relationships with customers, vendors, and dealers.[13] One of the first efforts was Cadillac's simultaneous engineering approach, an information and implementation process designed to anticipate and exceed the needs of potential customers. Today the division's customer-based program of continuous improvement is addressing a changing menu of "targets of excellence."

IBM Rochester. IBM Rochester (Minnesota) has worldwide development and U.S. manufacturing responsibility for the AS/400 line of minicomputers and for a wide array of large system hard-disk devices. Its character as a recipient of the Baldrige Award grew naturally out of the PRIDE (People Responsibly Involved in Developing Excellence) program instituted in 1981. Every year that vision deepened. In 1984 its "quality journey" was expanded to include process efficiency and effectiveness, and cycle-time improvements. In 1986 the focus broadened to include planning, the product development cycle, and inviting customers and vendors to become partners in quality. And in 1989 the company once again altered the focus of its quality process under a concept it called "market-driven quality," in which customer satisfaction replaced advanced technology as the engine driving the division to continuous improvement. Between 1986 and 1989 the company saw a 30 percent improvement in productivity. Product development time was sliced in half, and the manufacturing cycle was cut by 60 percent.

Wallace Company, Inc. Working from 10 offices in Texas, Alabama and Louisiana, the Wallace Company is a distribution company serving regional chemical and oil companies. Products include pipe, valves, fittings, and a variety of specialty products. Wallace took the quality plunge in 1985, when it formally instituted its quality-improvement program, and soon established itself as the quality provider of products in its industry. The company has forged quality alliances with both customers and suppliers and has inculcated its 280 associates with a strong focus on total customer satisfaction. One facet of its quality process is a guarantee that customer complaints will receive a response within 60 minutes. As its quality has improved, so has Wallace grown. Sales increased by 69 percent between 1987 and 1990, and profits increased by 740 percent.*

Federal Express. Federal Express invented the overnight air delivery industry in 1973. Since then, its 29,000 white, orange, and purple vans have become familiar sights to every businessperson. Its approach to quality is implicit in its slogan: "Absolutely, positively the best in the business." In an industry where mistakes can have life-threatening consequences, FedEx's "People-Service-Profit" values have been cornerstones of its world-class quality, guaranteeing fair treatment and stability to employees while galvanizing them to deliver innovative and efficient customer service.

---

*Wallace has encountered business difficulties since winning the Baldrige Award. See Chapter 14.

1991

Zytec Corp. Zytec Corp., of Eden Prairie, Minnesota, a supplier of electronic power-supply units to original-equipment manufacturers, won a Baldrige award in the manufacturing category. But with $56 million in annual sales, its lessons are also instructive for small businesses. The company's efforts to improve quality date back to 1984, when it first began implementing the "Fourteen Principles" of quality expert W. Edwards Deming, as well as heeding his insistence that good management be rooted in hard data. All activities at Zytec are charted, including how long a phone rings before it is answered. Employees are empowered to spend up to $1000 at their own discretion to ensure customer satisfaction. Product quality continues to rise: In 1991 Zytec units worked correctly when customers first tried them 99.8 percent of the time, up 0.1 percent from the year before.[14]

Marlowe Industries. Started in 1973 as a five-person operation, Marlowe Industries employed 160 people in 1991. It is the market leader in the production of customized thermoelectric coolers. In 1987 Marlowe decided to implement a structured program for continuous quality improvement. Since that time employee productivity has increased at a 10 percent annual rate, cycle time from design to manufactured product has been reduced substantially, and the cost of rework, scrap, and other non-conformance errors has been cut in half. Over 90 percent of Marlowe's products are customer-designed to meet individual requirements. The company has an advanced system for providing customer feedback, from surveys to individual quarterly meetings. An information system listing 500 separate data categories helps the company track every important aspect of quality performance. Two statistics are especially remarkable: over the past 10 years, Marlowe has not lost a single major customer; and the company's top 10 customers rated the quality of Marlowe TE coolers at 100 percent.

Solectron Corp. Founded in 1977 in Milpitas, California, as an electronic assembly job shop, Solectron specializes in the custom manufacture of printed circuit boards and subsystems for makers of computers, work stations, tape drives, and telecommunications equipment. At the heart of the company culture is a commitment to continuous improvement and customer satisfaction, driven by a weekly survey of all 60 of its customers. Solectron uses statistical process control in all its departments and feeds this information into a customized relational database. The company was quick to adopt "surface mount technology," allowing it to place integrated circuits on both sides of a circuit board and giving customers increased performance in a more compact package. Solectron's quality improvement efforts have won it 37 superior performance awards over the past decade, 10 of these in 1990. After a recent audit, a major customer named Solectron as the "best contract manufacturer of electronic assemblies in the U.S."

3
Navigating Baldrige

The pre-Socratic philosopher Heraclitus said that one can never step in the same river twice. He meant that the world is a place of constant change; so, too, is the Baldrige assessment process. The Baldrige criteria are not perfect. Consistent with principles of continuous improvement, the award's criteria have been revised and improved every year. Like the companies evaluated by it, the Baldrige Award itself is continuously improved; every year, the Baldrige program administrators solicit from Baldrige examiners and other knowledgeable parties ideas about how to improve the award process.

Despite this internal cycle of continuous updating, simplification, and improvement, the Baldrige criteria are still not exactly "gripping" reading. Many people find the criteria to be downright "user-unfriendly." The language can be dense, and the concepts can seem obscure to managers unfamiliar with quality. In an effort to boil down the Baldrige criteria's hundreds of points and subpoints to a handful of understandable principles for the uninitiated, Curt Reimann himself compiled an informal list of "Eight Essentials"—eight things that really ought to be in place for a company to qualify as truly quality-minded:

- A plan to keep improving all operations continuously.
- A system for measuring these improvements accurately.
- A strategic plan based on benchmarks that compare the company's performance with the world's best.
- A close partnership with suppliers and customers that feeds improvement back into the operation.
- A deep understanding of the customers so that their wants can be translated into products.

- A long-lasting relationship with customers, going beyond the delivery of the product to include sales, service, and ease of maintenance.

- A focus on preventing mistakes rather than merely correcting them.

- A commitment to improving quality that runs from the top of the organization to the bottom.[1]

But even this list of "musts" may seem tantalizingly short, abstract, or less than perfectly clear. This chapter looks at, expands, and clarifies these essentials. It also is intended to help you make sense of the complexity and navigate the pitfalls of the Baldrige guidelines.

Continuous Improvement

The main theme in the Baldrige Award, of course, is the notion of *continuous improvement*. At the Quest for Excellence II Conference in 1990, Donald Berwick, a Baldrige judge, associate professor of pediatrics at Harvard Medical School, and member of the faculty at the Harvard School of Public Health, called continuous improvement the "meta-issue in Baldrige." If you intuitively understand continuous improvement, negotiating the Baldrige process is not difficult. Improvement is easy to define—it simply means taking steps toward a goal. But most improvement is not continuous. Once we reach our goal, improvement slows to a halt. We solve the problem, and we walk away. To continuously improve, however, means to repeat the improvement process over and over and over again. Once you refine the process, you then refine the refined process, and so forth and so on, forever. Simple improvement addresses and solves discreet *problems;* continuous improvement addresses and manages ongoing *processes.*

Continuous improvement, as embodied in the Baldrige criteria, boils down to two basic questions: *How do you do it?* and *How do you evaluate what you've done?* The first question, "How do you do it?," is about approach. It asks you to describe your company's processes in each of the seven basic topical categories. What methods did you use? What tools? What techniques? (We will talk more about the idea of approach in the next chapter, dealing with the three dimensions of quality assessment—approach, deployment, and results.) The second question, "How do you evaluate what you do?," comprises the feedback loop of the Baldrige process. The question, "How do you know how well you're doing?," lays down the conditions for learning and exposing additional opportunities for improvement.

The evaluation question is asked again and again in the Baldrige criteria. It will ask you to explain:

- how the company evaluates and improves the scope, sources, and uses of competitive and benchmark data; or
- how the goal-setting and strategic planning processes are evaluated and improved; or
- key indicators the company uses to evaluate and improve its recognition, reward, and performance measurement processes.

Get used to thinking in terms of these two questions, for they are essential to grasping the full meaning and consequences of continuous improvement as it is contemplated in the Baldrige framework. Indeed, by the time the 1990 guidelines were issued, nearly every single point was discussed in explicit terms of "How do you do it?" and "How do you evaluate and improve it?"

W. Edwards Deming laid down the law on continuous improvement. "Constantly improve design of product and service," he tells us. "This obligation never ceases."[2] "Everyone everyday," Deming says, "must ask himself what he has done to advance his learning and skill on the job."[3] The reason continuous improvement has become important is simple. Quality goals are moving targets. There is no single thing you can do to change your company from zero quality to all quality. Quality is incremental and competitive. Other companies are continually "upping the ante": refusing to stand still once their quality levels have been surpassed. Rather than reinventing the "improvement wheel" every time a problem or opportunity presents itself, companies are finding that it is more efficient to keep the wheel constantly turning, to build continuous improvement into processes themselves by putting in place planning-and-feedback mechanisms. Improvement *must* be continuous, or it quickly becomes obsolete and irrelevant.

Donald Berwick has a story about a quality management expert who was asked to visit Singapore Airlines and give them advice about their processes. When he asked why he was hired to evaluate and review their already outstanding operations, their reply was, "That's easy—because we want to *stay* the best."

Planning and Processes

It's no surprise that astute planning is key to winning the Baldrige Award. In the Baldrige category called *Strategic Quality Planning* the guidelines specifically request that companies summarize their quality plans. But the Baldrige Award goes beyond calling for *planning;* it also demands *prognosis*—that companies predict or project how their most important measures of quality will change over time. It is at this point that companies grappling with the Baldrige guidelines first wrestle with the concept of *process*. Process is a major stumbling block for many people, who think of business in terms of things—products, services—and not the processes underlying the creation of things.

What is a process exactly? It is simply a repeatable activity or sequence of activities (sub- or microprocesses) that somehow changes something. Processes take an input and convert it into an output. Businesses are made of many, many processes, complex and interwoven—"wheels within wheels." Coming to grips with the health or quality of each of these processes is central to the Baldrige framework. Indeed, managing and improving processes are arguably the most critical challenges for organizations pursuing total quality initiatives.

What are some examples of processes? The production of nails and the production of automobiles are obviously both manufacturing processes. But resolving customer complaints is a process, too, as are the recruiting, orientation, training, and development of employees. Virtually every repeatable activity in an organization can be viewed as a process of events. To a total quality manager, processes are more important than things, because they are part of the system—indeed, processes *are* the system. A common mistake companies make in assessing their quality position is to think that recurring problems are attributable to an individual or to some special event. The fact is that most problems with service and production are usually not isolated incidents—they are built into the system. They are flaws in the process that impair the desired end result. Deming says that fully 94 percent of the "troubles" in a company can be attributed to systems—the plans upon which the company is founded. Only 6 percent, Deming asserts, are due to so-called special causes.[4] The bottom line? Fix the processes, and the products and services will take care of themselves.

Questions about process in the Baldrige criteria are always phrased in terms of *how*. An appropriate answer to a *how* question includes a description of sequential activities, along with a discussion of the tools, techniques, and methods employed during these activities. One of the great benefits of using the Baldrige criteria is that they compel companies to define, study, and understand their many processes. Indeed, some companies have gone to great lengths to identify *all* their processes and subprocesses and to compile books of process flowcharts. Lori Kirkland, IBM Quality Consultant and a member of IBM Rochester's Malcolm Baldrige Process Team, told us that working through the Baldrige assessment was the greatest lesson she ever had in terms of teaching her about business at IBM.

Think of the Baldrige assessment as a "census of processes" at your company: processes for motivating workers, processes for designing products and services, processes for strategic quality planning, and so on. Because there are so many avenues for improvement, systemwide quality improvement is possible only if everyone in every phase of the business contributes. The identification and study of processes lead inevitably to the concept of continuous improvement. Why? Because processes, by definition, can never be solved—they can only be improved. Total quality managers are not inspectors, whose sole function is to cull out flawed products and services. Rather, total quality managers are architects and designers who seek to improve the systems that create the things that customers purchase.

Processes and Prevention

This focus on processes is the heart and soul of a *prevention-based approach to quality*. Under this approach, the target is not defects in the products or services themselves, but rather in the processes that created them. A process approach such as the Baldrige Award forces a company to take a close look at every link in the production chain and to identify and eliminate problems *before* they lead to defective products in customers' laps.

Internal and Low-frequency Processes

Many companies question whether they need to invest the time or money to evaluate and improve their internal and low-frequency processes. In the Baldrige view, a chain is only as strong as its weakest link; your processes to deliver products and services are only as strong as the many subprocesses that compose them. Problems with supplier processes and internal support processes have a way of negatively affecting the products and services you offer your end customers.

The Baldrige Award seeks to encourage companies to apply continuous-improvement techniques to all processes. A quick look at winners of the award, in fact, reveals that they view *every* process—no matter how large or small—as a candidate for improvement. Consider Xerox, a 1989 Baldrige Award winner. When it completed its first Baldrige assessment, it had identified more than 500 improvement opportunities—it referred to them as "warts"—throughout the organization.

The Concept of Satisfaction

Process improvement is ultimately defined, not by cycle time or standard deviations, but by the requirements of customers, both external and internal. Customer satisfaction lies at the heart of the Baldrige framework. The concept of customer satisfaction is interwoven through virtually every section of Baldrige, coming most clearly into view in the last category, which examines a company's knowledge of its external customers and its skills in satisfying them, relative to competitors. Think broadly about customer satisfaction, for total quality managers understand that it is the objective of every provider-receiver relationship.

Meeting customer requirements and expectations is an aspect that requires an exceedingly close fit between product or service features and customer needs. The Baldrige Award is also very demanding about using data to make informed decisions about what product or service features to provide. Once you know what features your customers want, you can work backwards—reverse engineering—to design processes that provide those customer-satisfying features. Customer-focused organizations also pay close attention to customer satisfaction trends, knowing that what won customer applause and loyalty last year will probably seem inadequate this year or next year. Customer satisfaction, in the era of the Baldrige Award, is a dynamic concept.

Quality as an Ongoing Relationship

From the Baldrige perspective, satisfaction is not a one-time event. It is a dynamic state implying an ongoing relationship with the customer. Customers must be satisfied with the company and its products and services, and satisfaction must be established and nurtured throughout their entire relationship with the company—before, during, and after the actual sale.

It was with this realization that Cadillac stopped focusing on just "selling" cars in the 1980s and began focusing instead on the customer experience—on what it meant to *own a Cadillac*. This led the company to add services and build an ongoing relationship between the customer and itself. For example, Cadillac maintains 21 toll-free telephone numbers so that customers are able to get assistance, make complaints, or just plain offer comments.

Determining the changing requirements of customers, setting customer service standards, and managing the customer relationship through well-trained and empowered customer contact employees are all requisites of building a strong ongoing customer relation. The Baldrige framework requires that systems be in place to support such relationships. Moreover, the Baldrige framework is structured to motivate managers to ask themselves how their company's customer-satisfaction results compare with those of competitors who provide similar products and services. This helps managers to ensure that the company's systems are truly functioning at levels that will keep customers happy in an increasingly competitive marketplace.

Benchmarking

Benchmarking is the process of studying the practices of well-run, world-class companies in order to establish operating targets for your company. Benchmarking managers, like those at Milliken and Company, do not apologize for adopting or adapting whole processes and practices from other companies. Their credo is cheerfully plagiaristic: "Steal shamelessly." By doing this, they are able to accelerate the rate of improvement in their organizations and provide the rationale for both continuous improvement and strategic quality planning.

Benchmarking has grown rapidly in importance, both inside the Baldrige framework and inside American companies. When the Baldrige Award first appeared in 1988, there were no specific references to benchmarking. By 1991, there were over twenty references to the benchmarking concept. An entire examination item was dedicated to "Competitive Comparisons and Benchmarking," and almost half of the criteria's total points were influenced by this subject. Benchmarking is now so central to the Baldrige Award and its commitment to fact-based management that the award criteria quiz companies that are applying for the award about their benchmarking processes for both products and services.

Before benchmarking, the typical approach to goal setting was to extrapolate future performance gains from internal, historical results. Benchmarking also relies on internal measures, but focuses more on performance standards achieved by *other* companies. In fact, the search for benchmarks covers not only a company's direct competitors, but also companies in other industries throughout the world. Once these benchmarks have been discovered, the objective is not simply to "copy" them, but rather to be innovative and smart, to go beyond simple solution-borrowing, and to improve them.

Benchmarking may result in discouraging data at first, but it is absolutely essential for companies seeking accelerated improvements and meaningful targets that have been validated against the competition and other best-in-class companies. On the basis of comparisons with its competitors, Xerox, a pioneer in benchmarking, found that it had been using the wrong customer-satisfaction indicators! The company also learned that the gap between its quality performance and that of its competitors was so large that it had to make fundamental changes in the way its products were made.[5]

A Roadmap to Continuous Improvement

If the Baldrige Award took the view that quality was static, the only question in the guidelines would be, "How do you do it?" Baldrige would be no more challenging than a connect-the-dots puzzle.

Instead, because companies compete against continuously changing standards, the writers of the guidelines couple, "How do you do it?" with a question about feedback loops, "How do you evaluate and improve?" The result is a cycle for renewal and continuous improvement, a navigational tool helping companies move from the *here* of current quality to the *there* of a company's true potential.

Be creative. Companies can add or subtract steps as necessary and appropriate. Florida Power & Light, for example, recently dismantled its highly regarded but also highly structured quality-improvement program in favor of a less regimented, less formal approach. A fast-moving, creative enterprise such as an advertising agency, no doubt, would and should develop a quality process tailored to its culture and operating environs. That process would and should look different from the quality improvement process of a utility. Developing a quality approach appropriate to your organization is the challenge of the '90s and of the the Malcolm Baldrige National Quality Award.

4

The Baldrige
Assessment Process

Winning the Baldrige Award is a dream come true. Yet, in a sense, "winning" is counter to the ethic of continuous improvement that motivates any quest for the Baldrige Award; it implies that a finish line must be crossed in order to succeed. In the Baldrige view, however, the pursuit of total quality is a race without a finish line, in which the reward lies in the participation.

No one can guarantee that any given course of action will allow you to capture the Baldrige trophy for your company showcase. It *is* possible to guarantee that, should your company pursue a total quality initiative in the light of the Baldrige, your processes can be significantly improved—some may match, or even surpass, those of world-class companies. And improved processes are, in large part, what the quest is all about.

The Baldrige criteria are remarkable for their many applications, ranging from training to quality-system development ("blueprinting") to strategic planning. Some companies have even developed or re-cast their own internal quality awards based on the Baldrige criteria. For example, AT&T's Network Systems Group, which designs and manufactures telecommunications hardware and software systems, reformatted its own internal award to follow the Baldrige criteria precisely.

This chapter considers two preliminary tasks that must be completed before using the Baldrige criteria. First, you must decide what type of assessment to undertake—whether to do it all alone, solely for your own internal purposes, or whether to utilize outside resources and to compete for the prize itself. Second, you must decide how to set up the assessment process that will work best for the type that you choose—how to create an assessment team, who should lead it, and which company division to spotlight.

It is important to remember that Baldrige assessments are not simply reports of the kind that companies create and file away routinely. Baldrige assessment not only uncovers new information, but it shows you what to *do* with it. Every flaw in every process is magnified under the scrutiny of the Baldrige criteria, and each one is referred back for change under the Strategic Quality Planning category. There is no rug to sweep the crumbs under. Which approach your company takes to identifying and disposing of its crumbs depends on what your company wants.

Five Types of Assessment

An initial, fundamental use of the Baldrige criteria is self-assessment—to identify areas for improvement. Assessments or audits of one kind or another are familiar activities in most organizations. Indeed, Baldrige considers them important enough to devote an entire item to assessments (an *item* is a component of the Baldrige guidelines less important than a *category* but more important than an *area to address*) under the Managing Process Quality category. However, the difference in scope between routine audits (e.g., accounting, product, regulatory, or safety audits) and Baldrige-style total system assessments is immense. The latter are more comprehensive and, because they look at the relationships between functions, they provide a great deal more insight into the nature of complex problems affecting the company.

For example, a routine customer satisfaction audit will not uncover the reasons why quality is poor. A Baldrige assessment, on the other hand, may indicate potential root causes in the related areas of information and analysis, identification of customer requirements, or human-resource training.

The basic purpose of a self-assessment or audit is to identify defects or inefficient practices. The assessment concept originated and is most often used in the financial field to verify to management and regulatory agencies that accepted accounting procedures are being followed. Quality control managers seized on this accounting concept as a way to measure quality control systems. Today, the idea of mounting a serious quality-improvement effort without any assessment process is difficult to imagine. The challenge is to determine the Baldrige assessment approach that best suits your company.[1] The trade-off you will make is between resource requirements (time, people and money) and information quality (see Fig. 4-1).

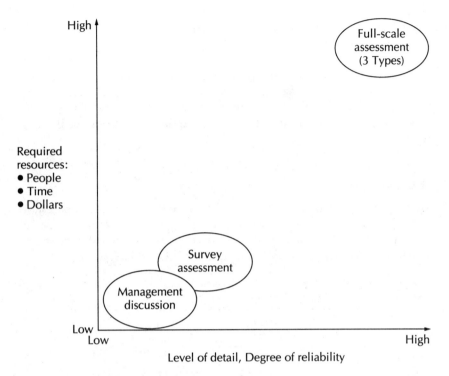

Figure 4-1. Baldrige-based Quality Assessment Options

The Baldrige Short Course

The simplest Baldrige assessment is discussion-based. Managers use the criteria to guide their discussions of organizational performance. This approach can be fast, inexpensive and engaging. It is, however, limited to the knowledge and insight of the participants. For some organizations this can be an effective and easy first step forward.

Many companies pursuing the Baldrige short course use total quality management questionairres that collapse Baldrige criteria into summary statements requiring survey respondents to assess current performance of their organizations on a relatively simple scale. Surveys are the second type of assessment.

The beauty of Baldrige-based surveys is their reach. Scores of employees can be polled very quickly and at a low cost. The result is a snapshot of the level of quality perceived within the organization. Survey responses are based on individuals' perception, not hard data, so there is no fact-based justification for creating recommendations and action plans using the findings. And unless the survey is given to a

large number of employees, it is difficult to define statistically significant segments—departments or hourly workers, for example—and draw
meaningful conclusions about them.

Despite these shortcomings, however, the discussion-and-survey forms
of Baldrige assessment can still be useful. Important performance gaps
may surface into public light only when employees and managers are
asked to review their organizations through the new lens of the Baldrige
criteria.

The Long Course

More thorough, data-driven approaches to Baldrige assessments require
gathering information and formally profiling an organization's practices
and processes. There are three approaches to this kind of assessment:
(1) Do-It-Yourself, (2) Collaborative, and (3) Outside Expert.

Division of Repsonsibilities for the Assessment Effort

	Data collection and report writing	Scoring and evaluation
Do-it-yourself	Self	Self
Collaborative	Self	Others
Outside expert	Others	Others

Do-It-Yourself Assessment

When a company follows the Do-It-Yourself model, assessments are conducted, scored, and evaluated almost entirely by its own staff, possibly
with some help from outside experts such as Baldrige-based consultants
or experts from another division, or even from another company. The
Do-It-Yourself approach is closer to pure self-assessment than is any
other approach. Data is collected, and a report is written, scored, and
evaluated. The brunt of this assessment labor falls to internal staff; external experts, if consulted, step in only to help evaluate the total quality
profile assembled by the internal team.

The learning experience for the internal team serves as an overrid-
ing reason for trying the Do-It-Yourself approach. Preparing a concise
description of your organization's complete quality practices, scoring it
yourself, and developing your own set of strengths and improvement
opportunities can be a rewarding—albeit humbling—experience. You
learn more about your business during this process than if you hired an

outside expert to review your operations. By going through the assessment process, companies often gain major insights and discover literally hundreds of opportunities to improve.

If your organization has no experience performing broad operational reviews or assessments, then consultants can help in the first assessment and provide your internal team with a "hands-on" learning experience. Training programs for internal assessors are offered by both the American Society for Quality Control ("Baldrige Award Self-Assessment Training") and the American Productivity and Quality Center ("Internal Assessment Training"). The ASQC programs have been offered since 1989; the APQC program since 1990. A rapidly growing number of other management organizations and private groups also offer Baldrige assessment training.

Even if a company has its own cadre of internal examiners, an outside expert is a valuable addition to any internal team. The outside expert is not biased by corporate experience and culture that can blind an organization to other, different ways of operating. This "second opinion" can provide unexpected insights. Consultants can also act as expert facilitators and help in the creation of recommendations, the follow-up to assessment findings.

As outsiders, external experts working on the evaluation phase of an internally generated total quality profile can also provide extra credibility and objectivity to the overall assessment process. This is more true of independent consultants and examiners on loan from other companies, and less true of examiners from another of the company's own divisions. If this is your first Baldrige assessment, an experienced external examiner who knows the ropes can save you valuable time by helping you avoid common pitfalls in the assessment process.

When selecting assessment team members, you should choose people the rest of the company knows and respects—frontline employees as well as managers from a broad cross-section of functions. A team comprised of widely credible, high achievers will help ensure participation and buy-in to the process and its findings from others in the organization.

An alternative to hiring an independent consultant is hiring an examiner from another company, one that is versed in the Baldrige criteria and in TQM assessment generally. Managers from about 100 companies have established an informal Baldrige Award Users Network coordinated by Baxter Healthcare. Network participants have discussed creating a shared pool of managers trained in Baldrige-based quality assessment. This group would be available to serve network members as consultants and examiners for site visits and quality assessments. It is an admirable system for broadening a company's quality experience base at low cost.

Who should manage the assessment team? It must be someone who has good rapport with top management; who is comfortable working across all functional areas—a generalist capable of viewing the corporation in "holistic" terms; and who has the ability to motivate—not merely to keep other team members on track and enthusiastic, but to communicate the idea that assessment is a pathway to improvement and success, not a headache. The assessment team manager need not be a quality manager, though a solid knowledge of quality practices is a definite plus.[2]

Collaborative Assessment

In a Collaborative approach data is collected by company staff, but the report is scored and evaluated entirely by outside experts. The advantage of using outsiders, of course, is that they are more objective and, at least for the first assessment, more experienced than company staff. Certainly, if you are applying for the Baldrige award itself, as opposed to using the Baldrige framework for the purpose of learning more about your company, you should prepare a strong written profile of your organization's best practices. Consultants, who have their own insights and skills to add to yours, can help accomplish this task. Consultants can critique applications and help organizations identify and clearly articulate how their processes work. This clarification can be extremely useful when preparing for a Baldrige site visit.

The model for the Collaborative assessment is the Baldrige competition itself, in which your company is judged by some of the nation's top quality experts. The official Baldrige assessment is an extraordinary opportunity for companies seeking an external view of their quality progress. For a nominal fee of $4000 ($1200 for the small business category), applying companies get a grade (a point score of up to 1000 points) plus a thorough report highlighting their strengths and "areas to improve" in each of the seven categories of Baldrige criteria. For those companies fortunate enough to reach the final examination stage, on-site examination by a team of Baldrige examiners is an extremely valuable experience. It provides both feedback and the sheer stimulation of having your processes reviewed first-hand by world-class quality experts.

The written feedback contained in the report is useful but short, usually focusing on a handful of the most important points in each Baldrige area. The questions asked by on-site examiners, on the other hand, are often very detailed and can cover all of the nearly 100 areas to address in the criteria. So detailed and valuable is this kind of question-based feedback that Federal Express, upon learning it had been selected as a 1990 finalist, hired a consulting firm to conduct mock site visits and interviews in advance.[3] Another consultant scored the application in a test run.

Outside Expert Assessment

In this third type of assessment, data collection, scoring, and evaluation are all performed entirely by outside experts. A good alternative when time and resources are limited, the Outside Expert approach can be either exhaustive or "quick and easy," to uncover the most serious quality gaps and galvanize top management's attention.

Because it taps the talents of outside experts, Outside Expert assessment achieves a high degree of objectivity and credibility. In the data collection part of the assessment process in particular, outsiders have a much greater ability to ask politically tough questions and get answers. Outsiders are also more inclined to present data in a frank and unbiased manner, rather than telling managers "what they want to hear."[4]

The Benefits of Self-assessment

Assessments are an important part of the continuous quality improvement process. With all of the preceding approaches, the Baldrige assessment process can be used as a precision diagnostic tool to identify weaknesses in the organization, providing focus for improvement and goal-setting activities. By measuring the levels of quality in a company's products, services, and processes, systematic assessments both confirm the results of past quality efforts and form the basis for planning future improvements.

Assessments are required, in particular, for companies that have "stabilized" after a period of rapid, unstructured growth. During the accelerated growth period, solutions get cobbled together and approaches are improvised to meet immediate concerns. As the company matures and as competitive and market conditions change, however, these approaches may no longer be appropriate or effective. When this happens, a systems engineering approach, as embodied in the Baldrige process, can be used to assess and revamp the organization.

The Outcome of Self-assessment

Any assessment approach, whether Do-It-Yourself, Collaborative, or Outside Expert, should yield a score and a set of strengths and weaknesses. The resources required to perform each approach differ, as do the depth, detail and breadth of the findings and feedback. The improvement opportunities, or weaknesses (both IBM and Xerox call them "warts"), feed directly into Strategic Quality Planning, a process which is examined in Category 3 of the application. Here, they are converted into quality-improvement objectives and the systems, methods, tools, and techniques needed to achieve those objectives are defined.

For example, Baldridge examiners told IBM Rochester in their feedback in 1989, the first year the IBM division applied (though it did not win the award), that it had done a spectacular job of competitive comparisons (comparisons within the industry) but lacked effectiveness when comparing itself to the "best of the best" (comparisons outside their industry). So, in early 1990, Larry Osterwise, Rochester Site Manager at the time of the winning Baldrige application, now VP-U.S. Market-Driven Quality Assessment, asked his Market-Driven Quality team to develop a benchmarking plan, complete a critical benchmarking project by June in order to learn the process, and make benchmarking a part of ongoing operations by August.

IBM Rochester worked hard to address other improvement opportunities as well. The examiners said that the division didn't have a consistent, focused education program. "A college catalogue, take-what-you-need" approach was the way Larry Osterwise, described it. This criticism resulted in a basic, mandatory education for all employees in areas such as quality principles. The company also suffered from a lack of consistent, focused leadership. "Ricochet Rabbit" and "action without vision" were the expressions used to describe the situation. Other weaknesses included a gap between customer feedback and planning and insufficient assistance to suppliers performing assessments. With determination and a structured process, IBM Rochester fought to correct these problems and align the organization's activities in a common focus. The rest, as they say, is history.

A Comparison of the Five Assessment Types

Each assessment type has advantages as well as disadvantages. Management discussion can yield some startling insights, but is not empirically based. The Short Course survey based on the Baldrige criteria is excellent for measuring employee perceptions of quality in a company. Until these perceptions are verified through research, however, they remain opinion, not fact.

Do-It-Yourself assessments represent pure self-assessment, in which the company itself gathers information, scores it, and generates a list of strengths and improvement opportunities. Although it is a terrific learning experience, the Do-It-Yourself approach can suffer from a lack of objectivity. Including an external expert on the assessment team, though, can help eliminate bias in the scoring and evaluation process.

In a Collaborative assessment, the company still gathers the information, but outside experts perform the scoring and evaluation. The Baldrige competition is an example. Its drawback is the short period of time—only about four months from the day applications are available until the day they are due—in which a large or diverse company must create a concise, 75-page document. It is, therefore, helpful to have conducted at least one self-assessment before entering the actual Baldrige Award competition. Yet, because the assessment is so rigorous, some companies, on their first attempt, have submitted an application, received feedback from the examiners, and decided to spend one or more years implementing improvements before applying again.

Outside Expert assessments are useful for an initial introduction to the quality-assessment process. Such assessments indicate the most serious quality gaps in a relatively short amount of time and provide a reliable baseline against which to measure future progress. The involvement of outside experts gives such assessments the advantage of credibility with top management.

The Baldrige framework, given by these five approaches, represents the instrument of choice in conducting a quality assessment. It is broad-reaching in its requirements, comprehensive as a methodology and effective as a diagnostic tool. No wonder it has emerged as an international standard for talking and thinking about total organizational performance excellence. With it, companies can shine a light into every nook and cranny of the organization, illuminating the path to continuous quality improvement.

How to Do a Baldrige Self-assessment

Because they may require a major commitment of time and resources, Baldrige assessments warrant considerable planning. The first issue facing large companies comprising two or more divisions is where to begin. Performing an assessment on an entire company, especially for a first-time effort, can seem overwhelming. Concentrating on one division or operating unit is more manageable, and as the company becomes increasingly familiar with the methodology of Baldrige assessments, they can be applied to other divisions in a kind of a "rolling assessment."

McDonnell Douglas

As part of McDonnell Douglas's quality plan, the corporation
established an annual competition among its seven subsidiaries. Each
subsidiary must complete a full Baldrige assessment, just as if it
were getting ready to apply, but minimizing graphic presentation
and supplements. The corporate quality office has trained managers
from each of the seven major subsidiaries in Baldrige assessment
techniques. This cadre of examiners evaluates each subsidiary's
assessment/application, offering extensive written feedback on
strengths and areas for improvement for each question. The
examiners also conduct a site visit at each subsidiary to confirm their
quality assessment findings and to give each company the benefit of
a site-visit experience.

Following the evaluation process, the McDonnell Douglas
examiners assign a score for each criteria category. The subsidiary
with the highest score wins the McDonnell Douglas President's
Quality Award, and may then, if its score is high enough, be
selected to represent the corporation as an applicant for the
Baldrige Award.

In addition to providing detailed evaluation of each subsidiary's
quality performance and creating healthy competition, the award
process identifies internal quality benchmarks for each of the
Baldrige categories. Along with their own score, the subsidiaries also
learn which of them achieved the highest score in each category.
The corporation plans to develop seven internal benchmarking
conferences, one for each criteria category. Each conference, to be
attended by managers from all subsidiaries, will be hosted by the
highest-scoring subsidiary and will highlight that subsidiary's quality
practices.

Baxter Healthcare Corporation

Baxter Healthcare Corporation launched an internal quality award
program in 1989 to recognize and promote quality excellence
throughout the company and to identify potential candidates for the
Baldrige and other international quality awards. Interestingly, the
Baxter award differs from the Baldrige in several key ways: It
reorders the Baldrige criteria, placing Customer Focus and
Satisfaction first rather than seventh; defines its award categories in
terms reflecting company organization; and recognizes an
unspecified number of winning applicants in each category.

Debra Owens, Baxter's Director of Corporate Quality, Strategy
and Planning, believes that an award program is easier to market
internally than an assessment tool alone. "Maybe it's a sugar-coating
for the assessment pill," she says, "but most managers react
favorably to the perceived benefits of a quality award program;
there's an actual, tangible prize, plus there are all the goodies of
internal recognition. Psychologically, it's just more attractive."[5]

Building the Assessment Team

Companies opting for the Do-It-Yourself or Collaborative assessments, in which data is collected internally, will want to consider the optimal size and composition of the assessment team. In a small company, where the senior executives are aware of everything that happens, two or even one individual(s) can collect the data and write the report. In what now amounts to Baldrige legend, Ken Leach completed tiny Globe Metallurgical's winning Baldrige application in one long weekend on a Macintosh home computer with the help of a single co-worker. What this wonderful and true story overlooks is the fact that Globe's quality processes were well developed and well documented, making the Baldrige application process much easier than in organizations where hundreds of pieces of data and information are unconsolidated.

For most companies, the assessment task is simply too large and broad-reaching to be left to one individual, so a team approach is necessary. IBM Rochester assigned teams of employees to write each section of the assessment report. The core team was supplemented by representatives from functional areas. Teams of reviewers read and scored each draft of the application.

Cadillac used a similar structure of a core team comprising thirty members and representing all functions and employee grades (hourly and salaried). Team members worked part-time on the Baldrige assessment while holding down their regular jobs. They drew on the knowledge of 100 different "content" experts who were responsible for providing written descriptions of how the system actually works as it related to each area to address. Each draft was reviewed by Cadillac general manager John Grettenberger, the entire executive staff, the plant managers, UAW leadership, and key "quality-process" champions.[6]

In general, assessment team members should be attentive to detail, have a knowledge of quality concepts, and be committed to the audit process. In addition, an assessment manager or leader is needed to keep the process on track. The assessment manager should be someone who has good rapport with top management, understands the organization's overall operations, and has a good grasp of the Baldrige criteria and basic quality concepts.

IBM Rochester used a single individual to drive and guide the assessment process. "The biggest problem in keeping things going and in focus," said Roy Bauer, Director of Market-Driven Quality, Rochester, and architect of the Baldrige-winning effort, "was to keep our enthusiasm during the review process. The teams that wrote the sections were invariably disappointed when they received only half of what they expected or a lower score than what they got on the first draft. I had to keep reminding them how much they were learning by going through the process."[7]

A related issue is involving senior managers in the assessment process. At IBM Rochester, each executive asked himself or herself the following questions on the assessment process: Am I answering the questions or not? Am I thinking globally or not? Through this effort executives came to understand what is involved in self-assessment. "Once they understand what it means to understand their business and see how it operates," Bauer said, "executives are completely committed to Baldrige."

When You Need Help?

Basic learning theory tells us that people learn best when they do the work themselves rather than being given the answers. Companies can derive enormous benefit from struggling with the criteria, working to articulate their core processes, comparing their processes to those of other companies, and learning first-hand about quality in their businesses.

Although undertaking a full-scale Baldrige assessment in a large organization is a complex project, help is available in many forms. First of all, companies can turn to other companies. Cadillac, for example, asked Globe and Motorola to give presentations introducing the Baldrige assessment process. Federal Express had a representative from Westinghouse Nuclear Fuels, a 1988 winner, visit and tell them what Baldrige was all about.

Baldrige-based user groups are another useful source of guidance. The Malcolm Baldrige National Quality Award Users's Network, cited earlier in this chapter, is a "non-profit facilitating network" created to promote use of the criteria for non-award-based internal assessments. Over 100 companies, with varying levels of knowledge and experience with quality improvement, use the network to share their expertise (e.g., Owens recently sent Baldrige-related information *gratis* to a company that requested it).

Is such collaboration fruitful? Does this openness enable participating companies to make noticeably more progress in improving their own quality process? "Absolutely," says Tom McElwee, Vice President for Quality at Mortgage Guaranty Insurance Company. "Those (companies) that give probably do the best because they learn the most."[8]

Who Should Lead?

Putting a company's functional leaders in charge of collecting data in an area in which they currently work is acceptable because these people obviously know better than anyone else how their systems work and where to go for information.

At IBM, a senior manager was responsible for, or "owned," each category. Larry Osterwise, then Rochester Site Manager, owned Category 1, Leadership; the site financial controller owned Category 2, Information and Analysis; Roy Bauer, head of Market Driven Quality, owned Category 3, Strategic Quality Planning; the personnel director owned Category 4, Human Resource Development and Management; Category 5, Management of Process Quality, was handled by a senior engineer; Category 6, Quality and Operational Results, belonged to the plant manager; and Category 7, Customer Focus and Satisfaction, to the manager of the customer-satisfaction management team. With ownership, there can be no passing of the buck, no "tossing responsibility over the wall."

Although the assignment of the responsibility for data collection is relatively straightforward, scoring, evaluation and preparing feedback are as much art as science and many employees have difficulty shedding their biases and anxieties. They may be more concerned with protecting their jobs and reputations than with the assessment, the purpose of which is to uncover problems and improvement opportunities in the organization.

Which Division to Spotlight?

Among conglomerates and very large corporations with different businesses, it may be difficult to choose which division to assess first. The division in most dire need of quality improvement is a logical candidate for your first assessment. The Collaborative assessment, in which outside counsel provides feedback on quality efforts, would provide an excellent approach to solicit feedback on how to improve the division. The Collaborative assessment approach would also be appropriate if you are vying for the Baldrige Award and want to put your best division in the spotlight. The best division might even be determined by internal quality awards, competitions in which the award guidelines are modeled on the Baldrige criteria.

IBM Rochester, for example, was selected to apply from among various IBM sites based on the fact that it won the IBM U.S. Annual Market-Driven Quality Award for Best Site two years in a row. Westinghouse Nuclear Fuels, a 1988 Baldrige Award winner, was selected because it won the George Westinghouse Total Quality Award, a company award whose criteria blends the company's own quality ideas with concepts from the Baldrige criteria. Local and regional quality awards (e.g., the Minnesota State Quality Award, Erie (PA) Quality Award, etc.) can also serve as screening mechanisms for the Baldrige competition.

5

The Baldrige Scoring and Evaluation Process

Assessment is about measuring—the effectiveness and efficiency of one's processes. But it is not enough to set one's processes against a yardstick. One must also understand what the yardstick is and what it means. Whether a company undertakes to apply the Baldrige criteria for internal assessment purposes or to compare its operating processes in direct competition with other companies vying for our nation's highest level of recognition for business excellence, it is important to understand how the Baldrige quality assessment process scores and evaluates organizational quality.

The system for scoring examination items is based upon three evaluative dimensions: *approach, deployment,* and *results* (see Fig. 5-1). All the Baldrige items require applicants to furnish information relating to one or more of these dimensions.

Approach

Approach refers to the methods, tools, and techniques the company uses to achieve the purpose stated in the examination item. The Approach concept itself is a composite of seven different criteria, one or more of which will apply to most items. The seven criteria hold that an excellent approach should:

SCORING GUIDELINES

SCORE	APPROACH	DEPLOYMENT	RESULTS
0%	■ anecdotal, no system evident	■ anecdotal	■ anecdotal
10-40%	■ beginnings of systematic prevention basis	■ some to many major areas of business	■ some positive trends in the areas deployed
50%	■ sound, systematic prevention basis that includes evaluation/ improvement cycles ■ some evidence of integration	■ most major areas of business ■ some support areas	■ positive trends in most major areas ■ some evidence that results are caused by approach
60-90%	■ sound, systematic prevention basis with evidence of refinement through evaluation/improvement cycles ■ good integration	■ major areas of business ■ from some to many support areas	■ good to excellent in major areas ■ positive trends — from some to many support areas ■ evidence that results are caused by approach
100%	■ sound, systematic prevention basis refined through evaluation/ improvement cycles ■ excellent integration	■ major areas and support areas ■ all operations	■ excellent (world-class) results in major areas ■ good to excellent in support areas ■ sustained results ■ results clearly caused by approach

Figure 5-1. A Page from a Baldrige Application Showing Scoring Guidelines for Approach, Deployment, and Results

1. Be prevention-based.
2. Demonstrate evaluation/improvement cycles.
3. Be appropriate, in terms of tools, techniques, and methods.
4. Be effective, in terms of use of tools, techniques, and methods.
5. Be systematic, integrated, and consistently applied.
6. Be quantitative-based.
7. Be innovative.

Let us look at these seven criteria in greater detail.

Prevention-based

Prevention is one of *the* basic quality concepts. The idea of a prevention-based approach is to prevent errors or defects in the final product or service by ensuring the quality of all the inputs into the process. Why is prevention so important? Because scrap and rework are unnecessary and costly and because customers, internal and external, are invariably more satisfied when things are done right the first time.

At first glance, it may be hard to tell how prevention applies to concepts like public responsibility and employee well-being and morale. Remember, though, that for the purposes of the Baldrige evaluation everything is regarded as process or the result of a process. *Public Responsibility*, for example, is a process because it involves promoting quality awareness and sharing with external groups. Some of the inputs into this process might be paying employee dues and giving them time off from work to participate in the quality activities of various external organizations. Similarly, employee well-being and morale in the Human Resources Development and Management category are the results of a process of maintaining a supportive, nurturing work environment. Inputs into this process are health, safety, job satisfaction, and ergonomics. When you think about an item in terms of prevention, try to get a sense of how well the company ensures the quality of all the inputs *upstream* in the process and how the process itself prevents errors *downstream*. Whether suppliers, customers, and employees are being brought into the Strategic Quality Planning process early, for example, is a good way of determining whether the approach is prevention oriented. Statistical sampling at receiving inspection might be another indication that a preventative approach is being taken toward supplier quality, itself a critical input into a company's production or service-delivery process. Supplier training and assessment programs, however, would indicate a much stronger orientation toward prevention.

In another more limited but still important sense, prevention consists of testing or validation techniques to reduce failure rates while products and services are still in the design stage. Determination of customer requirements, for example, is a prevention-based approach to ensuring a new product or service does not fail in the marketplace. Exhaustive prototype testing under a variety of conditions illustrates prevention in the item, "Design and Introduction of Quality Products and Services." In services, which are often produced and consumed simultaneously, prevention is often complemented by a focus on *recovery*. Recovery refers to the fast, coordinated response of a company to unexpected, sometimes unavoidable, service failures—delay of an airline flight due to weather, for example.[1] Service companies will score points for prevention-based approaches. However, the disciplined handling of recovery situations can and should be documented in the "Process Control" item in the category, Management of Process Quality, and in "Customer Relationship Management" under Customer Focus and Satisfaction.

Evaluation/Improvement Cycles

The flip side of error prevention, the evaluation/improvement cycle refers to continuous quality improvement. This dimension was discussed in Chapter 3, and it will come up again in this book. In nearly all process-related items, there is explicit reference, usually in a separate "area to address," to feedback loops and continuous-improvement methods:

- "How the goal-setting and strategic processes are evaluated and improved."
- "Key indicators the company uses to evaluate the extent and effectiveness of (employee) involvement...and how the indicators are used (for improvement)," and so on.

Quality improvement is relentlessly self-critical; consequently, virtually every process can and should be followed by an evaluation-and-improvement cycle seeking to make the process even better.

Appropriateness of Tools, Techniques, and Methods

This is a very simple concept. Are the proper tools, techniques, and methods being used to accomplish the stated objective? If so, then you are on target. Employee surveys, focus groups, and interviews are appropriate ways of measuring the adoption of quality values throughout your company. An appropriate technique for problem solving is the cross-functional team. An error-classification scheme that classifies errors into only two broad categories, "Type A" and "Type B," on the other hand, is not a good method if it does not reflect the complexity of problems and does not generate adequate data for identifying root causes.

Effectiveness of Use of Tools, Techniques, and Methods

Everyone understands what it's like to use the wrong end of a hammer to pound a nail. That is the message in this criterion. In the example above, surveys are not effective if they take place infrequently and are poorly designed. (If they are not given to all appropriate employee groups, that is a problem with deployment, which will be discussed shortly.) Conditions on a guarantee that make it difficult for customers to invoke ("Must be invoked within 24 hours of purchase") illustrate ineffective use of an otherwise perfectly appropriate tool. Where inspection is required (in connection with regulations, government contracts, etc.), it needs to be rigorously performed. Improper sampling techniques, insufficient number of inspectors, and too little time spent actually examining goods are examples of the ineffective use of inspection methods. A suggestion system that does not acknowledge receipt of a suggestion or provide constructive feedback is simply not effective.

In scoring this criterion and the previous one, companies need to consider the appropriateness and effectiveness of "unconventional" tools, techniques, and methods such as meetings, committees, and policies. Senior management meetings that do not follow agendas, reach decisions, or address important issues can be considered as ineffective and wasteful of time, which for managers and professionals should be counted every bit as significant as excessive scrap from a manufacturing process.

Systematic, Integrated, and Consistently Applied

A "system" is fairly easy to define from a manufacturing point of view: a sequence of activities that produces a predictable output. Some providers of complex services like management consulting, education, and nonroutine health care, however, have resisted this definition, arguing that what they do does not always involve an orderly sequence of steps and that the results are not always predictable. The consequence of this attitude? Resistance to the Baldrige methodology itself.

Upon reflection, this seems unreasonable. The process labeled "unsystematic" may in reality only be one process or subprocess in the core service-delivery process. Other processes, like leadership, complaint resolution, billing, recruitment, planning, and so on should all have the characteristics of conventional systems. Discounting the entire Baldrige methodology on the basis of one "unconventional" process is like throwing the baby out with the bathwater.

Even though a delivery process in complex services is modified as new information becomes available, the process is, in a meaningful way, still "systematic." Break delivery of a professional service into two phases and what do you have? Diagnosis and response. Diagnosis consists of analytical procedures performed in a sequence of steps until, by the process of induction, the problem is identified. Solutions are proposed based on standardized responses or trial and error.

While not quality engineers, the Webster-dictionary wordsmiths have turned out a definition of *systematic* that should please most everyone: "methodical, according to plan, not casual, sporadic or unintentional." This definition seems useful because it is loose enough to accommodate processes that are nonsequential, nonrepetitive, open-ended, and creative—and because it gives providers of complex services the well-deserved opportunity to score points in a Baldrige assessment.

Examples of "systematic" and "nonsystematic" approaches:

- *Nonsystematic:* An educational program consisting of a grab-bag of elective courses that do not build on each other and which employees may choose not to take.

- *Systematic:* An educational program consisting of quality orientation and a basic quality-tools training class required by all employees, specialized training for key functions, and training in advanced quality tools, also for key functions.

- *Nonsystematic:* A management consulting firm that does a cursory job of identifying client requirements and fails to monitor customer satisfaction during the engagement.

- *Systematic:* A consulting firm that spends a great deal of time managing client expectations, setting objectives, and surveying clients regularly during the engagement to ensure that objectives are being met.

Besides being systematic, approaches need to be "integrated." Integration is an extremely important concept in the Baldrige framework. Its footprints are seen throughout the criteria:

- "...relationship of benchmarks and competitive comparisons to company goals and priorities....,"

- "...how human resource plans are derived from strategic quality goals, strategies, and plans....,"

- "...how designs are coordinated and integrated to include all phases of production and delivery....,"
- "how the company analyzes key customer-related data and information to assess costs and market consequences for policy development, planning, and resource allocation...."

In scoring items on this dimension, you should look for connections, linkages, and alignments. Integration refers to the degree of alignment or harmony within an organization. Integration involves real-time, continuous cooperation and coordination among functions; find out where information goes. Look for open communication and unimpeded information flows between processes.

The keys to achieving company-wide integration are collaboration in the goal-setting process, and excellent communication of goals and objectives. Broad quality objectives ("increased customer satisfaction with our service") are set at the corporate level, then progressively narrowed and quantified at lower levels of the organization. The result of interrelated goals, consistently communicated to all employees, is an organization in which everyone knows what he or she is doing and why.

Once the approach is systematic and integrated, it must be "consistently applied." Approaches that are consistently applied are sustained over time, as opposed to episodic, on-again, off-again approaches. A company that stresses a team culture yet rewards only individual achievement is guilty of this kind of inconsistent application.

Quantitative-based

"In God we trust; all others must bring facts" is a favored saying at Milliken. In judging the quality of an approach, do not overlook the value of qualitative data (e.g., focus-group interviews) but be especially alert for quantitative measures that take the guesswork out of decision making and provide accurate performance data that can help set clear standards and goals. Check to see that processes and techniques are in place to ensure the objectivity and reliability of data by referring to the category, Information and Analysis.

Innovative Approaches

Are the Baldrige criteria prescriptive? Yes. And no. *Yes* if you believe, as some critics do, that Baldrige is ideologically biased toward participative management. *Yes* if you accept the fact that to score points in the Leadership category, senior executives have to be totally immersed in their company's quality activities. The writers of the Baldrige criteria assume there are certain broad requirements that high-performing—and high-scoring—companies must have. On the other hand, the answer may be *No*, since the Baldrige criteria do not specify how to implement any particular requirement. Companies are "encouraged to develop unique, creative, or adaptive approaches to achieving the goals of the [Baldrige] criteria." The evaluative criterion "innovation" is a critical point demonstrating that the Baldrige criteria are nonprescriptive; indeed, they reward flexible new approaches.

Why innovation? Because the Baldrige, as its creators and supporters will readily admit, only represents the best thinking of the current year. In the spirit of continuous improvement, the criteria are adjusted annually to stay abreast of the evolving nature of the quality discipline. Interestingly, companies do not have to wait years for their new approaches to be validated by the quality community. The Baldrige is an immediate reward for innovation—provided that the new approach meets the criteria discussed in this section: prevention-based, systematic, integrated, consistently applied, based on reliable information, and so on. There is indeed more than one way to achieve the Baldrige goal of excellence. In the words of Curt Reimann, "If a company has something they're doing that is superior, consistent with the spirit of Baldrige, then we want to capture that. That kind of information is extremely valuable. Not discovering these practices would be unforgivable."[2]

Innovation may be seen as a kind of tie-breaking criterion in the Baldrige framework. The scores of world-class companies tend to cluster at the high end. If two companies each score 800, the award may go to the company that broke new ground in its improvement processes. Innovation can be the distinguishing edge that separates companies that achieve excellence using conventional methods and measurements, and those that "go the extra mile" by pioneering new methods and measurements.

The emphasis on innovation—through adoption or invention—is consistent with Public Law 100-107, otherwise known as the Malcolm Baldrige Quality Improvement Act, which endorses information sharing and improving our collective quality and productivity. To paraphrase: the Baldrige Award will provide specific guidance for American companies by making available detailed information on how winning organizations were able to change their cultures and achieve excellence. To be sure, applications are confidential and companies are under no legal obligation to reveal their precise approaches. Call it rather noblesse oblige. In fact, Baldrige winners have been remarkably forthcoming about their strengths as well as weaknesses.

It is up to companies to define their systems, to be able to say, "This is what quality means throughout our organization." Therefore, companies and examiners should give as much credit as they can for any quality practice that fits the so-called "spirit of Baldrige," including significant and effective new adaptations of tools and techniques used in other applications or types of businesses. Wallace Company's adaptation of failure mode and effect analysis (FMEA), a technique traditionally used in manufacturing settings for systematically reviewing the way a product can fail and on that basis proposing alternative designs, is an example of an innovative approach taken by that service business. Federal Express's use of customer-satisfaction measures—its SQI (for service quality indicator), for example—in determining manager and employee pay also qualifies as "innovative." A technical point about scoring a company on innovation: These are really "brownie points," extras. If an approach is *not* prevention-based, systematic, and so on, then it does not matter how innovative it may be. Note also that an approach does *not* have to be innovative to score 100 percent of point value.

This completes the description of the seven criteria of Approach. The key criteria, as displayed in the scoring-guidelines grid, are systematic, prevention-based, evaluation/change cycles, and integration. To score any points at all, approaches have to be systematic and prevention-based. In improving from 0 percent to 100 percent, however, approaches need to exhibit more and more evidence of "refinement of existing methods through evaluation/change cycles" and integration. Adjustments to the mid-range scores (i.e., 50 percent of point value) would be made based on the presence or absence of the other criteria (e.g., quantitative based, consistency, innovation, or the appropriateness and effective use of tools, techniques, and methods). In other words, if the approach has a "sound, systematic prevention basis" that includes "evaluation/improvement cycles" and "some evidence of integration," but there is a lack of a quantitative approach and some of the tools are not being used very effectively, then some downward adjustment, based upon examiner judgment, would be made to the point-value score.

Deployment

Deployment, the second evaluative dimension, refers to the extent to which approaches are applied to all relevant areas and activities, those explicitly addressed and those implied, in the examination items. The scoring criteria used to evaluate deployment include one or more of the following:

Application by All Work Units to All Appropriate Processes and Activities

The company must implement processes and programs in all appropriate work units. A new performance review process that is used in only one factory, department, or work group, for instance, is not fully deployed.

Product/Service Characteristics

An organization must effectively apply its approaches to all product and service features. The company must benchmark and measure customer satisfaction with all critical product/service characteristics, for example, safety, reliability, durability, features, and so on. Processes must be in place to continuously evaluate and improve performance across all dimensions. Cadillac Vehicle Systems Management Teams, part of their overall Simultaneous Engineering approach, are responsible for developing plans to achieve world-class attributes in the six major vehicle systems for each of Cadillac's products: Exterior Component and Body Mechanical; Chassis/Power Train; Seats and Interior Trim; Electrical/Electronics; Body in White; and Instrument Panel, Heating, Ventilation, and Air-Conditioning.

Transactions and Interactions

Quality processes need to be in place to address all types of transactions and interactions with customers. In addition, supplier quality programs need to be extended not only to suppliers of raw materials but also to suppliers of ancillary goods and services (e.g., office supplies, internal suppliers, consulting services, advertising, etc.). The Baldrige judges even consider transactions with the public when they assess "full deployment."

Internal Processes, Activities, Facilities, and Employees

The message here is the same as in the previous two criteria: make sure every process is fully deployed to all appropriate points in the business. Benchmarking activities, for example, should be deployed to all support functions as well as major production functions. Every plant and field office needs to be covered. A typical deployment "error" is not extending quality training to all categories of employees, for example, hourly employees.

As in Approach, potential point values increase as certain Deployment criteria increase in importance. For example, in order to score the minimum number of points, companies need to have processes deployed to "many" major business areas. The more processes are deployed to support areas, the higher the number of points.

Results

The bulk of results are reported in the category, Quality and Operational Results, including the quality of products and services, business processes and support services (e.g., finance and accounting, software services, etc.), and suppliers. Other items and "areas-to-address" scattered throughout the criteria also ask for results, in particular, "customer-satisfaction results" located in the last category, operating results, and financial and market share results. In scoring on this dimension, there are eight characteristics to keep in mind:

- The absolute quality levels
- Comparison with industry and world leaders
- The rate of quality improvement
- The breadth of quality improvement
- The duration of improvement, demonstrating sustained gains
- The significance of improvements to the company's business
- The company's ability to show that the improvements derive from their quality practices and actions
- The contributions of the outcomes and effects to quality improvement

The four major characteristics of Quality and Operational Results, as presented in the Baldrige Award scoring-guidelines grid, are positive trends in major business areas, evidence that results are caused by approach, positive trends in support areas, and sustained (i.e., continuously improving) results. Companies that exhibit the four characteristics *plus* world-class performance score the highest percentage of possible point value. Companies that provide nothing more than anecdotal evidence, on the other hand, will score the minimum number of points. "Anecdotal" means isolated information, unsupported by quantitative data, and lacking context—random descriptions that may have little relevance to the larger events in an organization. Whereas anecdotes are useless, examples are not. Examples are representative of overall trends and patterns. They are the rule, rather than the exception to the rule.

Note that the guidelines make a subtle distinction between two similar phrases: "evidence that results are caused by approach" and "results clearly caused by approach." In the first instance, what is being asked for is evidence that your company's approaches "contribute" or "have had an effect on" quality improvement. In the second instance, Baldrige is asking for *proof* that the approaches—rather than, say, a favorable economy—have resulted in your company's performance.

Proof is normally established by varying one factor and holding all the others constant. If output changes as a result of this controlled experiment, then the cause can be attributed to the independent variable. Linear processes, like those described in standard statistical control charts, are amenable to this kind of procedure. To the extent that a company can conclusively establish a causal relationship between approach and results, it boosts the diagnostic and predictive value of the criteria immensely (which is the real purpose of the question). In a complex system like an organization, on the other hand, with lots of interactive subsystems and variables, establishing proof is much more difficult. This is why trend data is so important. If a company can demonstrate that approaches and results are coterminous for at least three years, then an examiner can reasonably infer a causal relationship. In legal parlance, a company does not need a smoking gun, but should have strong circumstantial evidence.

A few final comments about Results: Note that the term "world-class" refers to the results at the item, not company, level. Although we expect Baldrige winners to be top performers, we do not expect them to be world-class in all phases of the business. An analogy would be a championship baseball team that does not field world-class, that is, all-star, players at all nine positions.

The administrators of the Baldrige program recognize that examiners may not be knowledgeable about an applicant's industry. Therefore, it is the responsibility of the applicant to demonstrate superior results by comparing its results with the results of other companies in the industry. If you cannot obtain specific numeric comparisons, make sure the internal standard you do use is high enough. Twenty years ago, AQL (acceptable quality levels)—the poorest quality that a company could maintain over time and still be considered satisfactory—might have been an acceptable standard in the business community. Today, though, a PPM (parts per million) requirement that identifies errors or defects per million pieces or opportunities expresses a much more rigorous standard.

Unraveling the Mysteries of Scoring

Approach, Deployment, Results—how are the three evaluative dimensions scored? To begin with, each examination item is scored on one or more of the three dimensions. Baldrige uses a "build-up" or incremental scoring methodology, in which an approach first has to qualify as systematic and prevention-based, then evaluation/change, and so on, through the list of TQM characteristics. Fifty percent of point value is the threshold for an effective system, good deployment, and respectable results. As much as the Baldrige administrators would like scoring for the award to be utterly scientific, it is, of course, prone to variability. One of the largest swings in scores (and evaluations) derives from examiners's acceptance of evidence given in applications. Official examiners's guidelines state that data, information, and facts should be accepted at face value. Likewise, assertions that cannot be supported by plausible data, information, or facts should be barred from your assessment.

A related problem is whether there may be additional indicators, not required in the criteria, that would demonstrate the effectiveness of the company's quality activities. Reporting requirements are set forth in each of the "areas to address." Applicants have limited space to devote to addressing these topics, and hence may not be able to prove or adequately document every statement. For example, in a manufacturing organization, measures such as yield, reject rate, and scrap rate may be pertinent, although they are not explicitly requested. On a site visit examination, team members can request additional data demonstrating results. However, designating something as a "site issue" should not always be used as a basis for deferring judgment. The Baldrige judges use the concept of "reasonably supported" to weigh the value of evidence. Accordingly, emphasis is given to facts and information that, taken together, convey a complete picture of the applicant's achievements in relation to the item.

Any quality story can be told in terms of the Baldrige criteria. A different concern, though, is reflected in the assignment of point values to categories and items. Some professional-service firms, for example, have argued that, because of the relative importance of client-management skills and professional judgment, human-resource management is more important in their businesses than in typical manufacturing firms or logistically-based services like telecommunications, airlines, and banking. Thus, professional service firms may argue that Category 4, Human Resource Development and Management, is worth more than its current point value (150 points) and that something like Management of Process Quality, Category 5, is worth less. As the quality discipline evolves to encompass complex, highly discretionary services like management consulting, nonroutine health care accounting, and law, one might expect that the Baldrige criteria and scoring weights would also evolve to reflect the special aspects of these businesses.

The Baldrige framework assigns points to items, but for internal assessment it is best to weight and score every area to address. The additional precision will be particularly helpful in developing recommendations to address specific weaknesses.

Evaluation

Evaluation is the final phase of the assessment process, and one deserving equal emphasis with the others. Sometimes scoring and evaluation are confused. Whereas scores provide a baseline against which to measure future progress, evaluations—lists of strengths and improvement opportunities—go beyond scoring to offer objective inputs into the strategic planning process (Category 3 in the criteria). Weaknesses, or "areas to improve," are turned into formal quality-improvement objectives. Organizational strengths are cited to encourage refinement and complete deployment of existing systems in the spirit of continuous improvement.

Evaluation occurs simultaneously with scoring. On their worksheets, examiners develop both positive and negative observations concerning each Baldrige item. Typically, there are three to four short (three- or four-line) comments as required to record the most significant points. Comments are nonprescriptive, as illustrated by the following examples:

- Approach
  + The company has six process-based and highly structured approaches to ensure that managers are involved in quality.
  − The company provides no evidence that it systematically collects and examines complaints to assess whether it is meeting customer requirements.

- Deployment
  + The company has deployed a wide range of teams, user groups, and quality councils to promote cooperation among managers and supervisors.
  − In five of its six strategic business units, the company does not track key performance indicators reflecting employee morale and well-being among hourly workers—indicators such as absenteeism, turnover, satisfaction ratings, grievances, and so on.

- Results
  + Ratings for the firm's training courses have improved steadily over the last four years.
  − The company provides no evidence that it attempts to compare its current quality levels for internal and administrative functions with those of competitors and world-class companies in either related or unrelated industries.

PART 2
The Seven Pillars

6
The Baldrige Structure

This section will take a look at each of the seven major topics, the "pillars," of the Baldrige evaluation:

- Leadership
- Information and Analysis
- Strategic Quality Planning
- Human Resource Development and Management
- Management of Process Quality
- Quality and Operational Results
- Customer Focus and Satisfaction

This is the heart of the book. This section will show you what the categories mean, what the logic is behind them, what constitutes a successful performance, and what constitutes a poor showing in each category.

The Baldrige scoring system is based upon 1000 total possible points that are distributed among the various categories and items according to their importance in a total quality management system. In the feedback report they receive, applicants are not given an exact score. Rather, they are told in which of seven "point ranges" their score fell (see Fig. 6-1), Range Seven (876 to 1000 total points) is the highest. No company has yet scored in this range. In fact, all the winners have come from Range Six (751 to 875 points). The purpose in providing ranges rather than exact scores is twofold. First, scoring is not an exact science. To provide an "exact score" would be misleading and could result in

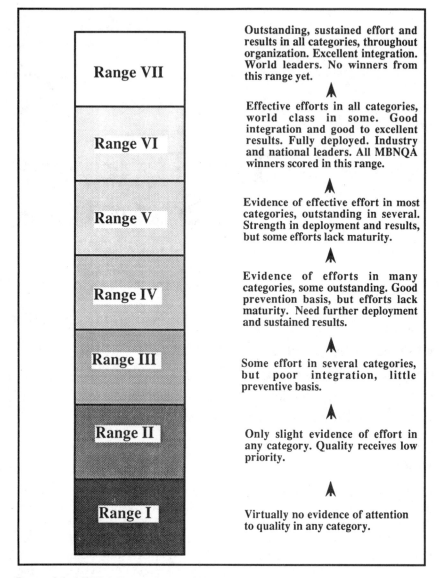

Figure 6-1. MBNQA Scoring Ranges: What Do They Mean? (1000 Points)

arguments between applicants and examiners over a few insignificant points. Second, scoring by ranges forces applicants to focus on the continuous-improvement aspect of the Baldrige process rather than on adding to the number of points they received.

Baldrige examiners do not provide applicants with ranges in each category. However, we have extended the concept of ranges to the category level. We have also provided a general descriptor for each range so that readers can quickly grasp how quality improves as a company "moves up" or ascends a pillar. Included are many examples, showing how world-class companies made their way from pillar to pillar. The purpose of these examples is not to tell you how your company must satisfy Baldrige requirements. Examples are just that—examples of ways some companies satisfied the Baldrige requirements. You are not only free to find your own way but encouraged to do so. A fundamental part of quality improvement is fresh, creative thinking. Think of these examples as door-openers, not door-closers.

The Baldrige Design

Before you move on to the seven sections, it would be well to take note of patterns throughout the guidelines and concepts that keep popping up. The first thing you will notice as you walk among the pillars is that information and questions are stated hierarchically—big concepts at the top; clarifications at the bottom.

Big concepts in the criteria fall under the heading "categories" (see Fig. 6-2). Examples of categories are Leadership, Human Resource Development and Management, Customer Focus and Satisfaction, and so on. Next, in descending order, are "items." Each item focuses on a particular idea within its category. Public responsibility is an aspect of leadership; benchmarking and competitive comparisons are elements of Information and Analysis; and so on. "Areas to address" represent an even greater level of specificity. They illustrate and clarify the intent of the items.

But if you squint you will see that there are barely perceptible levels above and below as well—call these levels "mega-concepts" and "descriptors." Mega-concepts are the supreme, overarching concepts (bigger than the "big" concepts) in the Baldrige framework. Descriptors are factors that help you to interpret each area. Mega-concepts are large-scale and strategic; descriptors are small-scale and tactical. The mega-concepts transcend categories and keep you focused on the big picture. Let's start with them, go to descriptors, and then discuss each of the seven categories, or pillars.

1992 EXAMINATION

1.0 Leadership *(90 pts.)*

The **Leadership** Category examines senior executives' *personal* leadership and involvement in creating and sustaining a customer focus and clear and visible quality values. Also examined is how the quality values are integrated into the company's management system and reflected in the manner in which the company addresses its public responsibilities.

1.1 Senior Executive Leadership *(45 pts.)*
Describe the senior executives' leadership, personal involvement, and visibility in developing and maintaining a customer focus and an environment for quality excellence.

AREAS TO ADDRESS

a. senior executives' leadership, personal involvement, and visibility in quality-related activities of the company. Include: (1) reinforcing a customer focus; (2) creating quality values and setting expectations; (3) planning and reviewing progress toward quality and performance objectives; (4) recognizing employee contributions; and (5) communicating quality values outside the company

b. brief summary of the company's quality values and how the values serve as a basis for consistent communication within and outside the company

c. personal actions of senior executives to regularly demonstrate, communicate, and reinforce the company's customer orientation and quality values through all levels of management and supervision

d. how senior executives evaluate and improve the effectiveness of their personal leadership and involvement

Notes:

(1) The term "senior executives" refers to the highest-ranking official of the organization applying for the Award and those reporting directly to that official.

(2) Activities of senior executives might also include leading and/or receiving training, benchmarking, customer visits, and mentoring other executives, managers, and supervisors.

(3) Communication outside the company might involve: national, state, and community groups; trade, business, and professional organizations; and education, health care, government, and standards groups. It might also involve the company's stockholders and board of directors.

1.2 Management for Quality *(25 pts.)*
Describe how the company's customer focus and quality values are integrated into day-to-day leadership, management, and supervision of all company units.

AREAS TO ADDRESS

a. how the company's customer focus and quality values are translated into requirements for all levels of management and supervision. Include principal roles and responsibilities of each level: (1) within their units; and (2) cooperation with other units.

b. how the company's organizational structure is analyzed to ensure that it most effectively and efficiently serves the accomplishment of the company's customer, quality, innovation, and cycle time objectives. Describe indicators, benchmarks, or other bases for evaluating and improving organizational structure.

c. types, frequency, and content of reviews of company and work unit quality plans and performance. Describe types of actions taken to assist units which are not performing according to plans.

d. key methods and key indicators the company uses to evaluate and improve awareness and integration of quality values at all levels of management and supervision

Figure 6-2. A Page from a Baldrige Application Showing Categories, Items, and Areas to Address

Baldrige Mega-concepts

Speaking in reference to quality improvement at the 1990 Quest for Excellence II Conference, Motorola CEO Robert Galvin, proclaimed, "There are only about 15 or 20 things you need to do with the right emphasis and right enthusiasm." Call these 15 to 20 things what you will—mega-concepts, critical success factors, or whatever. These are the essential, high-leverage activities, the wisdom and sense of the Baldrige criteria distilled to their pure essence. Together, they comprise the touchstone—the conceptual core of quality.

In his conference speech, Galvin did not specify what the "15 or 20 things" are. However, we've drawn up our own list based on what's in Baldrige and what we've observed in the winners. These "things" are not presented in any particular order; there will be some overlap. However, taken as an aggregate, they comprise a "bouquet" of desirable TQM attributes. You might say they are requirements for excellence. This is not necessarily the definitive list. You are encouraged, in fact, to step back occasionally from the almost 100 areas of the criteria and jot down your own 15 or 20 things. Do it just to remind yourself that what matters is the big picture! The activities that make up this list are things you absolutely, positively have to do. The Baldrige criteria do not tell you what specific tactics to use or what metrics to adopt. But the Baldrige criteria do clearly advocate specific strategies—principles and systems that have been shown consistently to move companies in the direction of superior quality.

The need for quality planning and systematic goal deployment, for example, is not controversial. It works, it is essential, and total quality management cannot occur without it. However, it is up to individual companies to flesh out the finer details—the tactics, the *how*—of those systems. Refinement of the system through evaluation/improvement cycles, leaving the door slightly ajar for innovative approaches, is what drives an organization to the highest levels of achievement. Consider the 15 or 20 things (19, to be exact) as action verbs.

Involve everyone in the organization	Involve suppliers
Continuously improve	Shorten cycle time
Measure	Develop a vision
Benchmark	Make quality strategic
Integrate	"Think systems"
Build teams	Tie approach to results
Define quality from customers' point-of-view	Empower
Educate	Deploy systems
Plan	Take charge
	Simplify

Involve Everyone in the Organization in Quality

Achieving a company's quality objectives requires everyone to contribute. Tap into your organization's brainpower and creativity. Get people to work solving problems. Cadillac does just this, calling people its "most significant competitive advantage." Federal Express gives people first-mention in its "People-Service-Profit" philosophy. Among Baldrige winners, all levels and all functions of the company get into the act—hourly and salaried workers; support services and major functional areas; senior executives, managers and supervisors, and frontline personnel. Frontline personnel are especially important. They have the greatest knowledge of the system details that are undermining quality. They are *there*. They see it happening. Not to take advantage of their knowledge, not to give these workers the tools to improve quality by team building and problem solving, for example, would be like trying to improve quality with one hand behind your back.

There are many references in the Baldrige criteria, both explicit and implicit, to the concept of involvement. The category Human Resource Development and Management has, in fact, an item entitled, "employee involvement." The item "senior executive leadership" in the Leadership category contains a list of quality-related activities in which senior executives need to participate. Also within this category is an item related to the involvement of middle-level managers and supervisors, along with an item addressing public responsibility and employees's involvement in quality activities in the external community. Implicit in the Strategic Quality Planning category is the participation of all levels of employees in validating, refining, and elaborating the goals set by senior managers. The Management of Process Quality category refers explicitly to the involvement of support services—finance and accounting, software services, sales, marketing, and the like—in the company-wide quality process. Customer-service personnel are given special treatment in the item "Customer Relationship Management" under Customer Focus and Satisfaction.

Building involvement, however, is an enormous challenge. Employees oftentimes do not feel that management has their best interests at heart, and, as former Xerox chairman David Kearns points out, the pace of change is increasing exponentially, causing great insecurity in people. "Companies that get (involvement) figured out," says Kearns, "are going to win. No question." One approach is to give employees the skills they need to participate. The topic of quality education is addressed in the human-resource category. Suggestion systems, teams, empowerment policies, and reward-and-recognition systems are other methods that, the Baldrige criteria strongly suggest, aid in promoting participation. Employee morale and well-being are also factors to consider. Involvement can only take place in an atmosphere of trust and "blameless error" in which processes and systems, not individual employees, are the focus of attention. Trust and open communication should be prominently featured in the company's pantheon of quality values, a topic addressed in the Leadership category.

Continuously Improve

The spirit of the Malcolm Baldrige National Quality Award is not just the spirit of quality improvement; it is the spirit of *continuous* quality improvement. A constant refrain in the criteria, continuous improvement is applied to all work units, all activities, and all processes— even the huge-and-hairy ones like strategic planning. Two of the components of the continuous improvement process—measurement and benchmarking—are significant enough to merit their own places in the list of "15 or 20 things."

Measure

Measurement can be boiled down to a simple rhetorical question, "How do you know how well you're doing, unless you measure it?" Measures must be objective, reliable, and preferably quantitative. Even subjective evaluations of quality, including satisfaction, can be assigned numeric values by asking customers to indicate, for example, on a scale of 1 to 7, their degree of satisfaction with products or services—"1" being dissatisfied, and "7" being greatly satisfied. With this subjective data in hand, companies have a clearer idea which areas to focus company resources on. An important decision in measuring is the selection of performance indicators. Indicators are characteristics of products, services, and processes that the company uses to evaluate performance and track progress. Indicators should be selected to best represent attributes linked to customer requirements, customer satisfaction, competitive performance, and critical operational factors. A well-conceived system of indicators thus represents a way of aligning all activities of the company toward common goals and objectives.

Measurement permeates the Baldrige. One entire category, Information and Analysis, addresses data collection, analysis, and benchmarking and competitive comparisons. An item on "quality assessment" can be found in the Management of Process Quality category. One entire category, Quality and Operational Results—including product and service quality; business process, operational, and support service quality; and supplier quality—turns on the principle of measurement. Measures and indicators are requested in the Human Resource category in items related to employee involvement, quality education and training, recognition and performance measurement, and employee well-being and morale. Customer satisfaction measurement methodology comes under close scrutiny in the criteria. In particular, Baldrige wants to know about gains and losses in numbers of customers, satisfaction—not just of the company's customers but also of *competitors's* customers—and trends in adverse indicators such as complaints, recalls, claims, refunds, and so on.

Benchmark

Benchmarks are basically internal and external reference points derived from best practices, both within and outside a company's industry, and used to validate and guide a company's goals and performance. Internal comparisons alone ("better than last year") are not sufficient to satisfy the Baldrige criteria. External comparisons ("world-class") are also needed.

Integrate

The operational environment in most companies consists of "walls" and "chimneys." Walls are barriers between departments or functions, while chimneys connote isolation and the vertical (top down), rather than horizontal (cross-functional), flow of information. Where walls and chimneys exist, operations occur in sequential fashion. Marketing will come up with a pie-in-the-sky idea, which engineering translates into precise tolerances and dimensions. The design is then "thrown over the wall" to manufacturing, which often is unable to match the design with existing equipment, production, and material methods and specifications; consequently the design goes back to the drawing board.

Contrast that clunky process with its rigorous opposite, as described in "Design and Introduction of Quality Products and Services" in the Management of Process Quality category:

> "All quality requirements are addressed early in the overall design process by appropriate company units."
> "Designs are coordinated and integrated to include all phases of production and delivery."

Integration is not confined to production processes. Two models for integration are Cadillac's and IBM's strategic planning processes, in which there is a coordinated effort at all levels of the company to meet broad quality objectives. Earlier, the importance of involvement and getting everyone to work on problems was discussed. They do not have to be horrific Gordian knots—small problems will do just fine, as long as they relate to the bigger priorities. This is what is meant by "an integrated approach to strategic planning."

How important is integration? Baldrige gives its highest scores for approach to companies that have strategically linked systems. Process mapping will indicate precisely which systems need to be integrated by showing the flows, both actual and potential, of information, products, and services among functions. For example, you do not necessarily have to integrate your systems for reward and recognition with systems for process control. However, you do need to integrate reward and recognition systems with performance-measurement systems, and you do need to integrate process control with the design and introduction of products and services. Sometimes the linkages are not very obvious. That's why "potential flows of information" is the operative phrase. Breaking with tradition, Cadillac recognized that its dealers could be a valuable source of information and brought them into the design loop.

Build Teams

Team building is an essential tool for achieving functional integration; consequently, it merits careful consideration. The Baldrige criteria also regard teams as an ideal tool for involving managers and workers in the quality process, for instilling quality values, and for problem solving. For most companies, an emphasis on teamwork entails enormous cultural change. Employee and managerial performance, for example, need to be evaluated not only in traditional terms of individual effort and results, but also in terms of cooperation and involvement in team projects. Group recognition and team awards reinforce the cross-functional nature of complex problem-solving and create a framework for building integration into the organization.

Define Quality from the Customer's
Point of View

In our list of "15 or 20 things," this one is a superstar—not difficult to understand, but enormous in its implications.

Most businesses already accept that customer satisfaction at the point of sale is a good idea. To satisfy a customer at the point of sale, however, is not enough for a company trying to win the Baldrige or improve itself by using the Baldrige criteria. Value, satisfaction, and preference also include "distant" life-cycle costs such as installation, instruction, repair, maintenance, and replacement. Systems have to be designed that address all these aspects of the relationship. Extending the customer-focus-and-satisfaction concept internally to relationships inside the organization results in a strange hybrid known as the "internal customer." The internal customer concept is useful in brainstorming the requirements of company units downstream in the production or service-delivery process *(What if that man or woman standing next to you on the assembly line were your customer . . . ?)*

Educate

Employee involvement, teamwork, and integration—these conditions of excellent companies do not occur because of executive mandate. Employees must be enabled to create such conditions of excellence. Education and training of all employees is the most powerful enabler of people in the Baldrige view. Consequently, education—the continuous improvement of employee skills and knowledge—is an important area in Category 4, Human Resources Development and Management. The Baldrige criteria seek to learn how an organization plans and set goals for its education requirements, segments employee groups with different education needs, and makes quality education an ongoing process for all employees. Investment in education is the capital expenditure in the human side of quality. As such, it is of primary interest and importance to Baldrige examiners.

Involve Suppliers

Just as a fullback and blockers work together to score a touchdown, so should a company and its suppliers work together in a joint total quality effort or partnership. Supplier quality is key to the Baldrige process. Companies must involve suppliers and vendors to raise the quality of the inputs (raw materials and services) and thereby raise the quality of the outputs (the finished product or service). In essence, companies need to communicate quality requirements to suppliers and work to elevate supplier quality performance through such methods as partnering relationships. Assuring supplier quality is a fundamental prevention-based activity for every company.

Shorten Cycle Time

The concept of cycle, or response, time has an odd way of popping up again and again in the criteria. You will find it in the "business process and support service quality" item in the Management of Process Quality category (". . . how processes are analyzed and improved to achieve better quality, performance, and cycle time."). It also shows up in "design and introduction of quality products and services" (". . . so that new product and service introductions progressively improve in quality and cycle times...."). Cycle times also come under scrutiny in data gathering and analysis, documentation, and complaint resolution. As you analyze your systems and processes, a little voice inside your head should be murmuring, "How long is it taking to perform this activity?" Shortening response time can lead to a major strategic advantage. It is also synonymous with improving quality. The logic goes something like this:

> Poor quality means lots of defects.
> Defects take time to repair.
> Repair lengthens cycle times.
> Better quality means fewer defects.
> Fewer defects means reduced cycle time.

Nowhere is this dynamic more in evidence than in design and introduction of products and services for a rapidly changing, competitive market. Here, delays caused by miscommunication and rework can seriously undermine a company's ability to survive. In short, if your organization can demonstrate that over time it has reduced the cycle time of any given process, that can be taken as at least circumstantial evidence that the organization has probably simplified the process and reduced errors. As such, reduced cycle times are a good general indicator that an organization's quality efforts are yielding results.

Develop a Vision

Vision, mission, quality values, and goals—they are all related, and they center on the idea of a sense of purpose, a guiding light. You will not find "vision" mentioned in the criteria, probably because it smacks of religious fanaticism. Still, it is clear that there is something to it, based on the achievements and testimony of Baldrige Award winners, who *definitely* are not religious fanatics. Cadillac's strategic planning process begins with a reevaluation of its vision for Cadillac Motor Car division. Roy Bauer (IBM Rochester) said at the Quest for Excellence III Conference, "I can't state with enough intensity the need for goals and vision in driving the business."

The vision process, by the way, is itself susceptible to improvement. There are bad vision processes (visions beheld over martinis at seaside retreats) and proper ones, that arise from an understanding of what customers want. Are senior executives the only ones with a vision? Not by a long shot. Their responsibility, though, is to create a shared vision through their visible personal commitment to quality and a system of durable quality values.

Plan

The most fundamental prevention-based activity of any organization is its planning process. Whether focused on organizational strategies, projects, new product development, or other initiatives, planning is the first step assuring that the sequence of events is managed in an efficient, trouble-free fashion. Developing "a long-range outlook" is one of the core values of the award. Planning, developing strategies, and allocating resources are the central activities required in developing such a future orientation. Category 3, Strategic Quality Planning, explores the organization's planning approaches, skills, and processes.

Make Quality Strategic

Quality is more than just preventing errors. Quality is an offensive strategy—the primary business operating strategy, in fact. Connect quality with basic business objectives. Quality objectives should be included explicitly in the strategic planning process. As already noted, all of Category 3 is devoted to Strategic Quality Planning, focusing on how a company's planning process helps achieve or retain quality leadership.

Simplify

An unwritten quality principle is the "KISS Rule"—short for, "Keep it simple, stupid." Experience has demonstrated that the simpler a process is, the faster, cheaper, and less error-prone it tends to be. Consequently, organizations that are aggressively pursuing total quality are on a relentless quest to improve their products and services by simplifying the processes and reducing the number of components it takes to create them. Work simplification is an important means to improved quality.

Think "Systems"

As the criteria guidelines state, "Quality excellence derives from well-designed and well-executed systems and processes." However you define "system"—as a sequential series of activities or merely a methodical approach—you have to look at your organization in terms of systems. Employee development, for instance, is not the result of just education, or orientation, or performance reviews. It occurs through the interconnected effect of various processes and programs that function interactively as a system.

Tie Approach to Results

Demonstrating a causal link between approach and results is probably not the first thing that comes to people's minds when they are asked about quality improvement, but it deserves a place on any top "15 or 20" hit parade. Planning a change and monitoring the results is part of the continuous improvement cycle, performed whenever possible on an experimental scale. If managers know which particular change has caused a certain result, they have a firm basis for planning. Empirically verifying the cause-effect relationship is probably easier said than done, but it is worth the effort. What about a company's real results—its bottom line? Evidence solidly linking customer satisfaction and quality to corporate performance (e.g., market share, profitability, and cost) such as appeared in a recent GAO report has been inconsistent to date.[1] The evidence is building, however, and the criteria linking customer satisfaction and quality improvement with financial success are being validated, report by report. Once this hard evidence linking quality with the bottom line is better established and accepted, most managers will be convinced of the strategic rationale for quality improvement. Refined research and rigorous experimentation are meanwhile needed to identify effective and ineffective quality practices and to more closely correlate quality to other measures of business performance.

Empower Employees

Empowerment—giving employees greater decision-making authority and responsibility—is closely related to the principle of involvement. In its Baldrige application a company is expected to provide specific information about what it is doing to increase employee empowerment, especially among customer-contact personnel. The purpose of empowerment is to shorten response times to customer complaints and queries and to eliminate internal bottlenecks such as the purchase of certain materials and equipment that normally require managerial approval. The effect of empowerment is to give employees a greater sense of participation and to strengthen their commitment to the organization and to quality improvement. Empowerment has become a kind of litmus test to determine whether a company's deployment of quality values and initiatives is full and effective. Examiners wishing to learn if quality within an organization is real will usually assess the degree of empowerment in front-line and first-tier employees. In those companies where quality is real in both words and actions, these front-line employees feel comfortable and have significant authority to act on the customer's behalf.

Deploy Systems Fully

One of the three evaluative dimensions, deployment refers to the extent to which approaches are applied to all relevant areas in the organization. Most companies will apply approaches only where they can be most easily utilized, where the greatest perceived need exists, or where the results are most easily monitored. The deployment issue gets at the heart of TQM—the application of quality principles and practices must be to *all* parts of the organization to be "total" quality management. Support services are an example. Most companies fail to benchmark their support services such as finance and accounting, legal services, and sales and marketing.

Take Charge

There is a reason for placing Leadership at the beginning of the Baldrige criteria. Top management commitment to the quality process is almost universally accepted as the sine qua non for successful quality improvement. Leaders must be strong role models and active contributors to the quality improvement effort. Moreover, they need to encourage leadership at all levels of the organization.

Why These "15 or 20 Things" Are Important

That's a good starting list of the major themes running throughout the Baldrige criteria. All the categories, items, and areas to address relate, in one way or another, to one or more of these cardinal quality principles. It is worth repeating at this point that succeeding through the Baldrige means maintaining a balance throughout of "big picture" and "little picture." If your attention has been focused on understanding the minutiae of the criteria's areas to address, it is a very healthy thing to stand back and try to encompass the larger ideas coursing through the criteria. The Baldrige assessment process is like taking a hike in the woods. If you fail to watch your step, you can trip over a root or get your foot caught in a bear-trap. But if you do not also keep an eye on your larger target, those mountains looming in the distance, you get lost.

Having had these "15 or 20 things" that are the keys to the Baldrige Award handed to you in a velvet glove, on a silver tray, you may believe that the rest is relatively easy. Unfortunately, however, the "15 or 20 things" are really just the seeds for you to plant and cultivate as you employ your own creativity and resourcefulness at the task of improving your organization. Not surprisingly, many of the methods, tools, and techniques used by Baldrige winners to meet these requirements are similar. For example, suggestion systems are commonly used to increase employee involvement, while quality planning typically involves participation by employees, suppliers, and customers in the planning process itself. Still there is room for variation. As Curt Reimann says, "We continue to see the adaptability of the winners. Though they benchmark or copy...or steal shamelessly, they do not end up looking alike.... We have companies who have taken the trouble to shop around and tailor something to their own needs. I think that's a very important message and I think it's very traditionally an American way of going about things." You must decide what is relevant to your company in terms of each of the broad principles. Many companies often have quality practices in place but do not realize it and do not identify them as such. Sylvio deBartoli, a former "chef de village," or general manager, at Club Med and currently vice president of sales, had customer-satisfaction ratings that were off the chart but was not consciously aware that he was "doing quality." If customer satisfaction is important to you, quality should inevitably follow.

Baldrige Descriptors

The "15 or 20" Baldrige mega-concepts are critical to charting a quality improvement strategy. In analyzing their systems and preparing Baldrige total quality assessments, however, companies do not respond so much to the mega-concepts, or even to the categories or items. What they respond to are each of the areas to address. Therefore, it is important to understand what each of those areas means and what they are probing for. Descriptors are little yardsticks or hints that illustrate or help you to interpret each area. If mega-concepts are global ideas that pervade the entire Baldrige process, descriptors are minute "hints" that can be very helpful in answering specific questions.

For example, in the 1992 criteria, under the item, "Management for Quality," area to address (a) refers to ways in which the "company's customer focus and quality values are translated into requirements for all levels of management and supervision." The area to address asks specifically for "principal roles and responsibilities at each level," within units and cross-functionally, in cooperation with other units. Mark Graham Brown, a former examiner for the award, in his book on interpreting the Baldrige criteria, notes that a common response to this area is to indicate that "all employees are responsible for and evaluated on quality." In fact, he explains, what examiners look for in this area are job definitions outlining specific quality indices that are objectively measurable and a clear hierarchy of those indices that lead to overall quality measures for the company. In addition, examiners also want to know the extent to which the organization employs cross-functional management. In his list of key descriptors, Brown includes the following:

- Evidence of job definitions that identify specific quality indices over which individuals have control.

- Degree to which quality indices for various levels and functions are defined in a hierarchical fashion.

- Degree to which all quality indices for employees and managers are objectively measurable.

- Appropriateness of systems and procedures to the nature and size of the organization's business.

- Degree to which departments/functions work toward common quality goals.[2]

As a learning experience, you may want to try developing your own sets of descriptors for each area to address. At each area to address, you should stop and ask yourself: What does this point mean in our organization? In the case of the first bulleted area above, do job definitions include tasks or activities that can be called "quality related"? These descriptors would help you understand better what the areas are asking for and help you focus your data-collection process; translated into an interrogative form they are excellent questions to ask interviewees. Assessment teams can use guides such as Brown's book or other good quality-control handbooks (e.g., *Juran on Planning for Quality*[3]) that describe in detail and in highly readable form the processes referred to in the criteria. Mega-concepts, categories, items, areas to address, and descriptors are the elements, from top to bottom, implied and explicit, that make up the universe of the Baldrige criteria.

7

The First Pillar:
Leadership

The Leadership category examines senior executives' personal leadership and involvement in creating and sustaining a customer focus and clear and visible quality values. Also examined is how the quality values are integrated into the company's management system and reflected in the manner in which the company addresses its public responsibilities.

The focus of Baldrige process, as we have seen, is the concept of meeting customer needs through a process of continuous improvement. So why is it that the first category Baldrige focuses on is Leadership? Is there an inconsistency here?

Any perceived inconsistency is cosmetic. Yes, quality begins with identifying customer needs and translating them into specific product or service features. However, the process of changing an organization itself begins at the top, with the senior executives, quality values, and management systems. The Baldrige assessment is, very simply, an outline for transforming how a company thinks about and performs business. It is about changing priorities, which, quite logically, begins with Leadership.

Leadership

All Baldrige Award winners have scored very high in this category, which historically has accounted for about 10 percent of total points in the application (In the 1992 guidelines, Leadership accounts for 90 points or 9 percent of the total 1000.) As indicated in The TQM Group Leadership Pillar (see Fig. 7-1), scores in this category are based primarily on the initiative of senior executives in moving quality to the top of their own and their companies' agendas.

Quality doesn't fail solely because of Murphy's Law ("If something can possibly go wrong, it will."). According to Deming, only six percent of the "troubles and holes" in a company's quality performance can be blamed on isolated mechanical problems, service glitches, or poor workers. Ninety-four percent, on the other hand, can be blamed on problems of the system itself—and are therefore the responsibility of the system's managers and creators, contends Deming.[1]

Quality Begins at the Top

Whatever the exact ratio, the conclusion is pretty obvious: change within an organization must begin with top managers, the leaders, because they are the people with the authority to make changes. This doesn't mean that top managers are the only people who can introduce quality methods to an organization. Occasionally, people lower down in an organization—department heads, for example—will become inspired by the quality successes of other companies. They spend several months trying out various quality tools and techniques, and "talking quality up" among peers. Some become a "quality angel" to their superiors, offering inspiration and even guidance from below. But unless their bosses (and maybe their bosses' bosses) support the programs, the impact they can have will be limited. For these champions, it often feels like they're pushing a boulder up a steep incline. Sooner or later, the effort wears them out. Frontline employees and midlevel managers, working alone, do not have much chance against a large, stubborn organization. While it may be lonely at the top, it's doubly lonely and frustrating for those at the bottom.

The Baldrige criteria attacks a dimension of this loneliness by bringing managers and workers together around a common theme: quality. It acknowledges a new paradigm in business, one that stands the old top-down model on its head. In the new paradigm, the top executive is no longer the source of all knowledge, expertise, and decision rights. Today, he or she is the great facilitator, the person who encourages the flow of knowledge on improvement from the bottom up. To the surprise

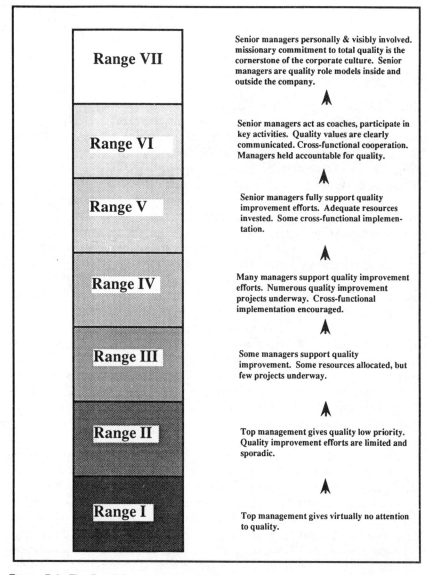

Figure 7-1. The First Pillar: Leadership (90 Points)

of many managers who have undergone the TQM transformation, this change has meant an enhancement in their stature, not a diminution.

The New View of Quality

The Baldrige Award is a major reason for the shift taking place in many companies in the perception of quality from a narrowly focused, inspection-based activity to a multifaceted, prevention-based discipline. Under this new perspective, quality is no longer a problem to be minimized, but rather, an opportunity to be exploited, a source of a major competitive advantage. Quality is the difference between a defensive and offensive strategy. Managing that transition requires a steady hand on the organizational tiller. New skills have to be learned; major investment decisions have to be made; old habits have to be broken; new behaviors have to be learned. Periods of turmoil and change like these demand strong leadership to keep everyone in the organization on course. Senior executives must demonstrate by their words and actions that they are in control and that they have a vision of where the organization is headed.

The word *ownership* is especially pertinent to leadership. It instills a sense of responsibility and accountability when the norm may be delegating authority, passing the buck, or throwing the job over the next wall. Ownership means, among other things, that problems can no longer be ignored; they must now be acknowledged. Too often managers ignore process problems or discuss them as if they occurred a thousand miles away or on someone else's watch. The Baldrige assessment is telling executives to break their 10-foot poles into 1-inch lengths, to become actively and visibly involved, as well as symbolically involved. Ownership is more than a catch-phrase. Put in place and encouraged by top management, it can make an entire organization click. As part of an assessment, the senior management team at Xerox, along with the National Quality Team, identified 500 individual areas for improvement. "The senior management team has taken ownership of all of the items," said then-CEO David Kearns, "and is going through the priority process, assigning names and dates. This is our next five-year process— to drive Xerox to be one of the best corporations in the world." In examining your organization internally using the Baldrige criteria as your assessment tool, be on the lookout for the principle of ownership over processes. Senior executives have to put quality at the tops of their agendas, both figuratively and literally. Do not be skittish about quality problems—grab them in a corporate bear hug and acknowledge they are yours. Only then can they be wrestled to the ground.

Senior Executive Leadership

*Describe the senior executives's
leadership, personal involvement, and
visibility in developing and maintaining
a customer focus and an environment for
quality excellence.*

Senior executives are the highest-ranking officials of an organization and the people who report directly to them. Where a division is applying or involved in TQM, the term "senior executives" then means division general managers and their staffs. If there is a designated chief quality officer, that person should report directly to the CEO. If you are not a high-ranking manager, however, do not skip this part of the book. Leadership is a quality that can be developed by anyone at any level of the organization. Indeed, one of the roles of senior management should be to encourage leadership at every level of the organization. As the criteria have evolved since 1988, they have come to include the leadership roles of managers and supervisors at all levels of an organization.

The Leadership category in the Baldrige criteria is made of four basic dimensions:

- The personal involvement of senior executives in leading the quality-improvement effort;
- The richness of corporate values, and the system in place to measure how well these values have been accepted by employees;
- How middle-level managers and supervisors have been integrated into the quality process; and
- The leadership role of the company in the outside community.

Personal Involvement

A key tenet in the Baldrige system is that senior executives need to be actively and personally involved in quality-related activities. Planning strategies and tactical maneuvers in the corner office is not enough. To satisfy the Baldrige criteria, you need to be down in the trenches. This is not an endorsement for micromanagement—the idea that executives should be intimately involved in every organizational task. Rather, it is a recognition that management behavior and actions often speak more loudly and more forcefully than words. The two must work together to have the desired impact. Consequently, in order for the quality message to take hold in an organization, the speeches and the exhortations

of leadership—themselves of great symbolic value—must be complemented by like-minded actions. Defining what exactly constitutes a
quality-related activity is no simple assignment, but however you do
it, the result should be rooted in the goal of developing organization-
wide customer focus and creating customer satisfaction. This connection can be indirect and still be satisfactory. One senior executive, for
example, worked closely with his engineering department in the development of a new, innovative technology, which, it was argued con-
vincingly, eventually had a huge impact on the quality of customer
service.

Serving as a role model is another way for senior executives to demonstrate leadership, motivating those around them, for example, by bor-
rowing the problem-solving techniques and process controls used on
the shop floor and reimplementing them in the executive office. John
Marous, Chairman of Westinghouse, invited the Westinghouse Productivity and Quality Center to perform a total quality-fitness audit on his
executive office. He reasoned that if it was right for the rest of the
company, it must be right for his office as well. Assuming personal responsibility for certain key clients, meeting with them to discuss business
issues, satisfaction with products and services, and opportunities for
improvement are other ways that senior executives can express their
commitment.

Motorola's Bob Galvin speaks enthusiastically of his "rediscovery of
customers." He had spent some time with customers before Motorola
began using the Baldrige criteria, but they were token, courtesy calls.
After Motorola adapted the criteria, the nature of his client interactions
changed utterly: "I set a program up in the early 80s and I went to 12
customers, roughly one a month. Spent a day at each one. Never saw
any big-shots, saw the really important people, the really good people
who wrote the invoices, made the payables, received the material on
the inspection dock. And ultimately I was able to hear something from
somebody who placed an order with Motorola. This guy says, 'We'd do
300% more business if you quit screwing up.'" The bottom line is that
quality-minded companies satisfy customers because management has
taken the time to know the customers personally. So obvious. So rare.

Participating in Teams. Roger Milliken, CEO of Milliken, often stays
late at the office, working with associates on the kinds of detailed
projects one would not think of as requiring top-level input. Rolling
up one's sleeves and participating in ordinary work teams like this
is a powerful signal. It conveys an action orientation to other workers. It signals that top managers are not statues in the park—they are
workers, just like everyone else, and they mean business. That signal has

the power to spark the entire organization. Almost as a side benefit, the project team benefits from the considerable talents and energies of senior executives.

Getting involved might simply mean spending time just talking with employees. Having breakfast with small groups or even individuals is a great way to discuss issues in an informal setting while learning details about the operation that may be contributing to poor quality. MBWA—management-by-walking-around—is another good prevention-based approach, because it gives senior executives a chance to hear first-hand what workers are concerned about and head those problems off at the pass before they become full-blown disasters. One company executive describes himself as a kind of double agent, spending almost 75 percent of his time talking to workers, uncovering problems, and then challenging his senior managers to come up with solutions. (This executive also reads exit interviews to spot patterns of employee dissatisfaction.) Management-by-walking-around is a pleasant notion, but not always a workable one. In large multisite organizations it is an impossibility. Even in large single-site organizations it can be an impractical chore with unmeasurable benefits. So what can managers do instead? Although Fed Ex executives make a practice of visiting local work sites as part of their visit to any city where Federal Express operates, the company also uses a global television network, giving its employees around the world the opportunity to talk live with senior executives. At Southeastern Freight Lines, a regional trucking company that was a Baldrige finalist in 1991, President Paul Taylor makes and distributes video messages that are shown to all employees throughout the company's network of terminals throughout the southeast. Staying in touch is not easy. It requires creativity, consultation, and the commitment of managers' most cherished assets, time and money. It is critical that quality-minded senior executives find the right way to communicate with employees, and make it succeed.

Leadership and Quality Training. Personal involvement for senior executives can also mean giving and getting education. "See one...do one...teach one," is an expression often heard where senior executives take an active role in quality training. Senior executives must understand and be able to practice the concepts and techniques they expect employees to follow. As teachers, senior executives are particularly well-suited to providing a big-picture view of company strategy, explaining why the company is pursuing TQM and giving individual employees a sense of place and purpose in the overall scheme. Training is a top-down concept, but quality education need not follow that model. Indeed, there is no correct model for the concept of quality learning. Xerox uses a "cascade" approach to education. David Kearns, according to Xerox legend, was the first at the company to learn about quality. He then taught his immediate subordinates, who, in turn, taught their employees. Fed Ex took a different approach. Everyone in the organization, from executives on down, learned quality-improvement techniques from a common vendor.

Out of the Office. Quality activities are time-consuming, and leading the charge is not an easy task. There are committees to chair, programs to review, team presentations to attend. For senior executives, the problem is not one of finding more time, but of reallocating it. For the past ten years, the first four hours of Motorola's Policy Committee's two-day monthly meetings have been devoted to quality. Former CEO Bob Galvin was known to leave meetings before discussion of financials. Why? Because he believed that profits follow when quality is high. New skills must be learned. These include basic people skills. Executives at one company took courses in learning how to listen. New attention must be given to old relationships. Old relationships must be redefined and revivified. The traditional authoritarian leadership style—the boss issues an edict he thought up over breakfast, and everyone drops everything to implement it—must be replaced by one based on coaching, consulting, information sharing, and mentoring.

To these techniques that help people to do their jobs better, are added other new technical skills, such as understanding statistics and the role variation plays in the manufacturing and service-delivery processes. Quality begins with education, and education begins at the top. Forget parking spaces reserved for executives. At Schneider National, a long-haul trucking company based in Green Bay, Wisconsin, CEO Don Schneider has reserved the best parking spaces at corporate headquarters for truck drivers visiting the home office. The Baldrige assessment is the great equalizer. In the brave new Baldrige world, executive prima donnas are an endangered species. Here quality is everyone's responsibility, and everyone is an equal participant. Roger Milliken is a perfect example of this transformation. His office not only lacks a door—it has only three walls!

Leadership Outside Company Walls. Senior executives have a role to play outside their company, as well. Just as workers dwell within a corporate ecosystem that virtually defines how they function, companies themselves are part of larger, more complicated ecosystems—cities, states, regions, and countries—that define how the company lives and succeeds. Senior executives have the task of making sure that the company understands its proper role in the larger system, and they work to nurture the system that allows their company to prosper.

Take education, for example. Many people contend that our country's educational system today is poorly managed and that we are not equipping young people with the skills they need to compete in today's global marketplace. Some high schools graduate a large number of young adults who are functionally illiterate. College graduates majoring in business often lack an understanding of basic quality concepts, tools, and methods. By contrast, you hear horror stories every day of the educational accomplishments of foreign competitors—high school students in Japan having to pass courses in statistical process control, and so on. Apocryphal or not, these stories are evidence that our schools need private sector help if the next generation is to be competitive. Unskilled people entering the workforce place a huge burden on industry. Companies like Motorola and Corning, Inc. spend millions to teach workers fundamental skills. Businesses want to know what role to play in improving the educational system. Senior executives can focus attention on the issue by speaking about quality to educators, legislators, and taxpayers.

In keeping with the Baldrige message of personal involvement in community quality affairs, executives at KPMG Peat Marwick, a Big Six accounting firm, spend a significant amount of time working with universities on curriculum development. These executives regard universities as "suppliers" of critical materials—their people. Individual businesses cannot fix all of society's woes, and the Baldrige judges do not expect them to. But a quality-minded company understands that quality does not begin and end at the company gate. Smart executives recognize that the educational process directly affects the quality of the services and products they produce. This principle is like the idea expressed by the old computer science acronym GIGO—garbage in, garbage out. Quality-minded executives are on the lookout for practical ways to improve that input.

Involvement must be just that—involved. Passive memberships in organizations do not accomplish much. Look instead for opportunities to grant interviews, serve meaningfully on boards, associations, and task forces; write articles and make speeches part of your daily agenda. Chances are that you are already involved in a variety of projects that contribute to the quality of your community. The beauty of the Baldrige criteria is that it provides a common place to pool these many activities and weigh each for effectiveness, impact, and sincerity—sincerity because quality must never be for show, whether on your company's factory floor or in the everyday life of your community.

Quality Values

Quality values are another area of intense focus and concern in the Baldrige approach to leadership. Consider the following:

The scene was boringly familiar: a hermetically sealed room in an airport hotel. The three executives, though, did not seem to care. Jackets off, shirtsleeves rolled up, they were having an intense discussion. Competition was heating up, profit margins were shrinking and putting a strain on their business. Back and forth they argued, but they could not agree on a strategy. The company they had built seemed in danger of falling apart. One of them recalled a happier time two decades earlier when, in a similar hotel room, they had plotted the creation of their company. He reminded them of the vision they had shared and the values from which that vision grew. Realizing where they had come from and the reason for creating the enterprise in the first place cast a shaft of light into the current turmoil. Finding that they still resonated to their old values made the choice of a strategy much clearer.

Like senior-executive leadership, a robust set of quality values belongs at the *beginning* of the process of creating a quality-focused organization. Values reflect what is important to a company. If values are quality-oriented, actions which improve quality will follow.

A Quality Bridge to Employees

Quality values that are never properly articulated to employees have as much relevance and power as falling snow in a sealed paperweight on a senior executive's desk. Employees need to be *shown*, not just told, that quality is paramount. The challenge to senior managers is to find ways to communicate quality's importance, above and beyond the standard operating procedures and policies that employees rely upon. Quality values must stand apart from the usual baloney. Say it like you mean it. Better yet, mean it. When Federal Express CEO Fred Smith set out to found a company and culture that valued its people, he started with a company motto—"People, Service, Profits"—that conspicuously placed people first. Then he oversaw the development of work policies, procedures, and systems that supported in actions a people-first policy. Today, it truly is a value deep-rooted throughout the company. A company's compensation and reward system is also a good place to start. How you pay and recognize workers speaks volumes about your company's values. If quality is important to an organization, then employees will be compensated, at least in part, on that basis. Employees charged with providing world-class quality products and services will logically expect something approaching world-class pay and benefits. Instilling quality values is the responsibility of top management. In the Baldrige criteria, simple communication is not enough. In addition to a transfer of information or an imperative—"Satisfy the customer!"—employees must be given the authority and the tools to achieve that goal. Values like "customer satisfaction" give employees a sense of direction and destination. A sense of empowerment gives them even more—the go-ahead to succeed. The rest—the actual day to day work of doing the work that ensures satisfaction—is up to them.

Documenting Quality Values

Values are vague, you may say—how do the Baldrige criteria verify a company's quality values? There are two tests: the form in which quality values are communicated, and evidence of their serious adoption throughout the company. The form in which quality values are communicated says a lot about their importance to an organization. To begin with, quality should be a theme woven throughout the organization's mission and policy statements. That is the bare minimum. But rhetoric alone (Quality is our number one priority) does not impel anyone to action—it costs you nothing, and commits you to nothing. It is not nearly as powerful as a quality value expressed as a goal.

Ambitious goals are called "stretch" or "leapfrog" goals. They are extremely effective ways to underscore a company's commitment to exceptional, measurable improvement. Stretch goals sound impossible at first—"zero defects," "six-sigma quality," "3.4 defects per million." Nevertheless, like hitting someone on the forehead with a two-by-four, they undeniably get that person's attention. Values can also be strongly stated as a guarantee to customers. A promise such as, "We unconditionally guarantee your satisfaction," puts your corporation's money where its mouth is. The Baldrige criteria not only asks how you communicate quality to employees. It wants to know the other half of the story as well—how your employees accept and welcome the quality challenge. Typically, surveys and interviews are used for these evaluations, and the results returned to top management for review and follow-up.

Management for Quality

Describe how the company's customer focus and quality values are integrated into day-to-day leadership, management, and supervision of all company units.

Senior executives lead. Empowered frontline personnel serve customers. But what about those in the middle of the organizational chart? What are they supposed to do? How are they linked to customer satisfaction? There are good reasons for wanting to know how midlevel managers and supervisors are integrated into the quality effort. The downfall of quality-improvement programs is often the ambivalent, ambiguous role middle managers play. If a single manager does not "buy in" or is deliberately left out of the process, all his or her subordinates are likewise excluded.

Solving the Middle Management Problem

Ask a middle manager why a company quality initiative failed: "Yeah, they blamed that on us." Ask a senior manager the same question: "We just couldn't get middle managers behind it." Somehow, your company has to bring these middle managers into the quality improvement process and keep them there. This may mean dismantling the system of finger-pointing at your company, creating an atmosphere of no blame for the uncovering of failures. It may mean creating positive incentives for meeting quality goals. It may mean communicating more effectively, hearing from managers themselves what their reservations are, and taking steps to resolve their doubts and suspicions. Besides pulling midlevel managers and supervisors into the quality process, companies need to develop systems that encourage and ensure cooperation. Cooperation among managers is essential for effective problem solving.

But cooperation cannot develop in the rigid hierarchies most companies are built on. As H. J. Harrington points out, most companies are organized along vertical functioning lines, separating teams of specialists from one another.[2] This kind of organization is sensible enough. It achieves valuable economies of scale and, usually, the individuals within each "knot" function capably as a team. The problem is that most work activities in a company don't flow vertically. They flow horizontally, meaning that managers from different disciplines need to learn to cooperate across division and department boundaries.[3] The Baldrige framework prescribes just such a system of cross-functional collaboration. It encourages teambuilding and cuts through functions and traditional lines of authority in its pursuit of quality objectives.

Linking Middle Managers to the Quality Process

What are the tools and techniques your company uses to integrate its midlevel managers and supervisors into the TQM process? What methods are used to get them to cooperate? One approach is to create new structures within an organization, that link people who need to communicate with one another. These links may take the form of ongoing cross-functional teams or interlocking quality councils. The underlying premise of this connect-the-dots approach is that an interlocking arrangement creates the conditions, or lays the groundwork, for trust, communication, and cooperation. "If you want people to cooperate," said one executive, "don't just preach about it. Create a cross-functional team and put a serious agenda on the table." The formation of teams is a clear statement about the shared responsibility of management and workers for the future of the organization.

When all managers belong to more than one council, the result is a de facto network of interlocking councils. This network can be strengthened both vertically and horizontally. Vertical communication flow is enhanced when members of the senior quality council, representing various functions, chair or serve on junior-level councils or teams. Horizontal communication improves when councils are composed of representatives of various departments or functions. Cross-functional representation is also good because it helps prevent dominance by a single point of view in the decision-making process. This freedom is so important to some companies that they bring in an outside facilitator to help conduct important meetings, to make sure that all viewpoints get equal consideration. Whatever the choice of approach, it must be deployed in the ways discussed earlier; the approach must be systematic, integrated, and consistently applied. Most especially it must be deployed in all units of the company, including those not performing up to standard.

Other Techniques for Involving Middle Management. Some companies encourage regular "internal customer" discussions, in which internal groups that supply other internal groups meet and talk out any problems that may have cropped up. Along these same lines, internal guarantees can be created, by which internal suppliers guarantee defined levels of service and satisfaction to internal customers. Nothing encourages communication between parties like a promise, especially one with the teeth to back it up. Managers can also benefit from attending quality-training seminars. These courses can be very valuable on several levels: they provide a common vocabulary, they give managers a chance to "buy in" to the quality process, and the newfound expertise boosts their self-esteem and confidence. Middle-level managers should be given the same core curriculum given other employees and senior executives, in order to ensure consistency in skills and knowledge throughout the company. Special training sessions, though, should be custom-tailored to meet their specific requirements.

Link Managers to Results! In motivating people, nothing beats old-fashioned accountability. In a quality-minded company, this means holding managers accountable for financial goals *and* quality goals. Recognition, compensation, and advancement can be linked to customer-satisfaction measures or to interdepartmental quality indicators. A common refrain is "If we could only get our people to see how serious we are about quality!" How about proving you mean it? Prove it by making quality success the cornerstone in your system of promotions. People who cast their lot with improving quality should find the quality of their careers likewise improved.

Failure to equate quality success with individual success can swamp the entire quality plan. Xerox once surveyed employees who felt that, despite the company's avowed dedication to quality principles, some managers were being promoted for reasons that had nothing to do with quality. Thoroughly dismayed at this perception, Xerox took thoughtful action, cracking down on non-quality-related promotions. The company issued standards for what constitutes a role model manager that leave little doubt about the company's commitment to quality:

1. Visibly demonstrates support and promotion of the Leadership Through Quality strategy.

2. Personally uses, and encourages others to use, the processes and tools including Problem Solving, the Quality Improvement process, Competitive Benchmarking, and Cost of Quality in all key business areas.

3. Uses customer satisfaction as a key measure in all business decisions and assures that unit activities result in an improvement in customer satisfaction.

4. Encourages formal feedback from peers, superiors, and customers on personal management behavior, and uses the feedback to modify personal style and behavior as appropriate.

5. Establishes the expectations and requirements for the Quality Plan, its implementation plan, the measurements, and the inspection process. Communicates to reinforce progress consistent with these expectations. Meets the goals set.

6. Hires and promotes people who actively practice the principles of Leadership Through Quality and works to help develop and broaden them. Counsels and instructs those who are deficient to advance them toward the role model standard necessary for promotion.

7. Recognizes and rewards the actions of individuals and teams effectively utilizing Leadership Through Quality to achieve improved business results.

8. Through regular inspection, identifies individual and team weaknesses and provides coaching and guidance in the use of the quality processes to improve.

The Baldrige criteria seek more than words and promises, of course—they also seek corroborating data. To satisfy the Baldrige criteria, a company must be able to show that it has created feedback loops that measure its progress in meeting its goals. In making middle managers part of the quality-improvement process, companies must clearly define the types, frequency, and content of reviews of middle-management involvement. Any method used to "integrate quality values into day-to-day management"—a stock phrase in the Baldrige, meaning the messages conveyed specifically to middle managers, as opposed to frontline employees—should be described. Data from these assessments—whether goals have been attained and if not, why not—can be used in your future plans.

Public Responsibility

Describe how the company includes its responsibilities to the public for health, safety, environmental protection, and ethical business practice in its quality policies and improvement activities, and how it provides leadership in external groups.

The item "Public Responsibility" will remind you of an earlier item—"Personal Involvement." It touches on the same issue of how an organization relates to the larger community of which it is a part. The difference is that "Public Responsibility" deals with company posture and policy, not just individual actions. This section suddenly gives the concept of quality an ethical or moral aspect. Should this come as a surprise? Not really. However, there are practical reasons for including social responsibility in a set of quality criteria. For one thing, the National Institute of Standards and Technology does not want to honor a company only to find out later that in its own community it behaves irresponsibly, poisoning rivers, endangering employees, and walking roughshod over local regulations. The Baldrige process is not an especially political process, but here it clearly wants to protect its own good name. But there are other reasons behind this item. First, the information in this section is used by NIST to evaluate the candidate as a "national role model"—the last hurdle on the way to becoming a winner. The Baldrige Award does not go to just any company. An award-winning company must be efficient, thoughtful, attentive, quick—and now we add *good* to the list. Second, it behooves companies as a matter of self-interest, to pay attention to the issue of public responsibility. Baldrige-quality companies say that better health and safety practices strengthen operations and public relations. Customers are more satisfied—and more loyal—knowing the company from which they purchase products and services is doing its part, for instance, to improve the environment. Promoting quality awareness to outside groups in areas like health care and education may also lead to an increase in the quality of workers available to the company.

Themes in this item encompass not only promoting quality awareness, but also real involvement in social issues. One of IBM's core principles is, "We serve our interests best when we serve the public interest." Examples of corporate community involvement are, of course, legion. As an example of its commitment to the community and the needs of working parents, IBM Rochester gave liberally to Rochester's Child Care Referral Service for the construction of an infant and toddler child-care center.

Small Company Service Options

The size of the company and its reputation will, of course, be factors in how frequently its managers and employees are requested as speakers for outside organizations. Executives of small companies typically have more difficulty getting speaking engagements than executives at larger, better-known companies. Small companies do score well in this category, however, by using a little initiative and imagination. Hosting luncheons for local civic and business leaders is a good way to build a reputation in a community. Speeches on quality can be given, along with invitations to tour the company's facility. Based on the response, companies can then develop courses, open to the community, on various quality issues, for example, statistical quality control, waste management, and so on.

A smaller company might show leadership by conducting interviews with community leaders, mapping out the most pressing community needs. From the interviews would come recommendations, allowing the company to concentrate its efforts in a few major areas that coincide with its own expertise. Programs could be developed and implemented, and follow-up surveys performed to determine whether needs are being fulfilled and where adjustments needed to be made—a great example of homegrown continuous improvement! Baldrige-quality companies invariably support their employees in a wide range of community, trade, and professional organizations, by acknowledging employee contributions in company publications, and by giving them time off from work, with pay, to engage in charitable activities.

Beyond the Expected

Companies are expected to comply with existing regulations and laws. Employees are expected to have an understanding of how health, safety, and regulatory issues affect them. Companies are expected to be responsive to employee concerns and provide a safe, healthy work environment. World-class companies, though, do more than what's expected. They go out of their way to demonstrate their concern for the environment, public health, and safety. Long before being required by law, IBM Rochester actively recruited, hired, trained, and promoted disabled people. In addition, IBM products provide many technological solutions for people with disabilities. Aircraft noise had been a growing issue, but one without an apparent solution until Federal Express, along with Pratt-Whitney, developed the technology to decrease noise levels on certain types of aircraft. The FAA approved the Federal Express/Pratt-Whitney "Hush Kit" and Federal Express is now selling it to other airlines. Some companies have charitable foundations or give a portion of their after-tax earnings to various causes. Some professional service companies (e.g., management-consulting and law firms) encourage or even require their employees to commit a certain percentage of their time to *pro bono* work. As with every other company process, processes for encouraging employee leadership and involvement in quality activities are scored on the basis of continuous improvement. Plans for improving employee leadership and involvement need to be made, indicators selected with which to measure progress, and goals set to propel the organization forward.

8

The Second Pillar: Information and Analysis

The Information and Analysis category examines the scope, validity, analysis, management, and use of data and information to drive quality excellence and improve competitive performance. Also examined is the adequacy of the company's data, information, and analysis to support improvement of the company's customer focus, products, services, and internal operations.

In the last decade of the information century, managers finally understand that reliable, appropriate data are the lifeblood of a quality-improvement system. Without systematic data collection, companies simply cannot know how their processes are performing, what progress has been made, what needs improving, or what the future holds. Without data, gains in quality improvement cannot be translated into that most elusive statistic, precise cost savings—a statistic that captivates top management and dramatizes the success of quality-improvement projects as nothing else can. In the view of many quality professionals, data analysis is the single largest deficiency in American industry today. Many companies still do a poor job of gathering relevant data, and many more do not analyze or use collected data well. The Baldrige Award's Second Pillar (see Fig. 8-1) is asking you if your company is the exception to this generalization.

This category, Information and Analysis, examines the range and variety of your company's data and information (nonquantitative data such as customer complaints, laws, and regulations may be considered important types of information); your processes for analyzing and managing them; and the role they play in your planning process. It also asks about your company's approach to benchmarking—establishing quality-improvement targets based on best practices. The usual evaluative dimensions that apply to approach and deployment apply here, especially a quantitative orientation—management by fact—and information systems that are widely deployed and readily accessible.

The Good and the Bad

Companies that score well in this category are easy to spot. They are the ones that perform frequent evaluations, that continually validate and update their data and information bases, and that actively analyze and use data to inform their planning, decision-making and improvement processes; that is, they "manage by fact," not by personal fancy, feel, or whim. These companies are also relentlessly single-minded in finding and using world-class benchmarks for performance. Companies that do not score well, on the other hand, are just as easily identified. They are the ones that do not collect or analyze data sufficiently and do not adequately utilize benchmarking in their quality-planning activities. They do not, as a rule, have much of a statistical orientation. Their management style appears to be reactive—constantly stamping out fires—rather than proactive. Too often, these companies fall back on management by opinion, not by fact.

Scope and Management

Describe the company's base of data and information used for planning, day-to-day management, and evaluation of quality. Describe also how data and information reliability, timeliness, and access are assured.

Continuous improvement requires many kinds of data—data about company performance and internal operations, customer-related data,

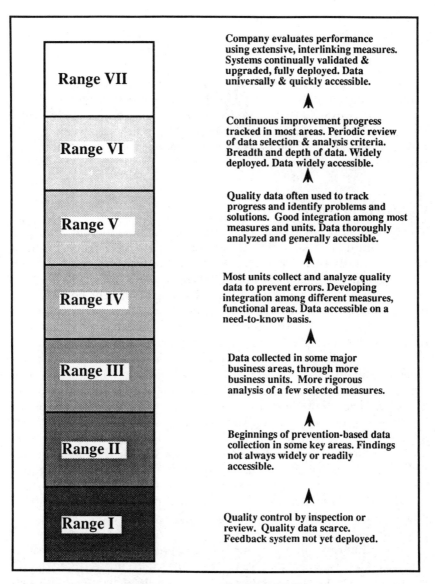

Range VII

Company evaluates performance using extensive, interlinking measures. Systems continually validated & upgraded, fully deployed. Data universally & quickly accessible.

Range VI

Continuous improvement progress tracked in most areas. Periodic review of data selection & analysis criteria. Breadth and depth of data. Widely deployed. Data widely accessible.

Range V

Quality data often used to track progress and identify problems and solutions. Good integration among most measures and units. Data thoroughly analyzed and generally accessible.

Range IV

Most units collect and analyze quality data to prevent errors. Developing integration among different measures, functional areas. Data accessible on a need-to-know basis.

Range III

Data collected in some major business areas, through more business units. More rigorous analysis of a few selected measures.

Range II

Beginnings of prevention-based data collection in some key areas. Findings not always widely or readily accessible.

Range I

Quality control by inspection or review. Quality data scarce. Feedback system not yet deployed.

Figure 8-1. The Second Pillar: Information and Analysis (80 Points)

benchmarks from other companies, and financial and cost-of-quality calculations to identify and evaluate new opportunities. Some of this data and information is time-consuming and expensive to collect and analyze. Computer-generated data, on the other hand, is often too available in the sense that there is so much of it that managers cannot wade through it all. As a manager, therefore, you need a rigorous set of selection criteria to identify exactly what data are required and which areas are most important. Once you achieve that, you have the additional task of organizing these data into their most easily accessed, most understandable, and most economical form.

What Data to Gather

The first thing the Baldrige criteria look for are the guiding principles behind your data choices. Why these data, and not those data? You must be able to satisfy that to answer the Baldrige criteria. As usual, the best rationale usually refers back to the Baldrige bedrock of customer satisfaction. You will want to demonstrate that there is a clear link between the kinds of data you collect and maintain and your quality values. If short-term financial measurements drive your company day-to-day, then measures like market value to book value and price-to-earnings multiples will dominate management reports and meetings. If, on the other hand, quality lies at the center of business strategy and planning, then a larger share of your measurement and reporting will focus on quality issues. When companies are truly committed to quality values, many data issues resolve themselves. Federal Express's "People-Service-Profit" philosophy, for example, identifies three broad areas for data collection. The "People" category includes employee-related data that helps Federal Express manage its human resources. The "Service" category includes measures related to the quality of its services. And the "Profit" category includes financial data that help Federal Express manage its financial resources and determine profitability and other key financial measures.

Federal Express's unit for measuring service performance is called a Service Quality Indicator (SQI). It is derived from twelve attributes of service quality—such as missed pickups, late deliveries, damaged packages, and other critical operating data. Together they provide the means for the company to monitor customer satisfaction or dissatisfaction. Federal Express calculates the impact of failures per day for each component by multiplying the number of daily occurrences for that component by its assigned importance weight. The SQI is the sum of the failure points for all 12 components, and it is tracked, compared against targets, and reported on a weekly basis with monthly summaries. Corporate SQI presentations are then delivered to executive and senior operational managers and evaluated using several different perspectives: root-cause analysis, understanding the flow and process of the problem being worked on, involvement of first-line employees, and results.

Wallace Company, Inc., has tailored its own criteria to determine what types of data it charts. These are its standards:

- First, the data must meet *internal customers' needs* (e.g., sales reports, branch financial statements, and inventory records).

- Second, the data must meet *external customers' needs* (e.g., on-time delivery, and supplier product quality).

- Third, the data must help improve the company's *quality leadership practices* (e.g., turnover, training, and promotion data).

The kind of data your company should collect also depends on the nature of your business. Accounting firms, for example, do not need extensive data on worker safety—their workers are not usually in physical danger. Chemical or mining companies, on the other hand, cannot afford to ignore that kind of data. The Baldrige criteria give many clues about what categories of data you should be collecting. Chief among these are data and information relating to customers, employees, and suppliers. External, independent contractors, such as market-research companies, law firms, and insurance providers, all qualify as suppliers. You must control and monitor the quality of their "goods" as carefully as you control the quality of the products and services of other suppliers. Data on support functions like accounting and internal legal services are also important and should be collected.

How should you present your data in the Baldrige application, or in your own internal assessment report? Again, you should group them into categories, that is, customer-related data, data on internal operations, supplier data, and so on, giving brief, thumbnail descriptions explaining the use and relevance of each database. You can also label data according to whether they are generated by the company itself or by outside vendors.

Complexity versus Simplicity

Baldrige-quality companies have lots of databases, and each is comprehensively segmented by customer or employee type, product or service line, location, time, and so on. In almost all cases these databases are maintained by computers, though neither computers nor computer software is absolutely required. In fact, although the sheer size and complexity of most databases can only be handled by a computer, a manual approach may be perfectly acceptable for small companies in some situations. What is important is that whatever system your company uses, you should ensure that it is tailored to your company's structure and core operating processes and to the specific needs of your customers. Off-the-shelf technology is fine as a platform, but the actual system will likely need to be tailor-made to meet your precise requirements. Federal Express, for example, the unanimous choice for the 1986 Gartner Group Excellence in Technology Award, is well-known for its use of multiple, interfacing information systems. At Globe Metallurgical, on the other hand, control charts on critical process variables are maintained by hand. "We're afraid of a little bit of computer complacency setting in," said Ken Leach, when he was Globe's vice president of administration. "We think that if the operator actually makes that point on the chart, and sees that it's out of control, then he knows that something has to be done."

Focus on Preventive Data

Spending time early on prevention will reduce the amount of time, effort, and expense you will incur later. For each process, data-collection efforts should focus on key control points, those you define as critical areas where something could go wrong, or where operational factors tend to cause variation. In services, these critical points are often called "moments of truth." They are equally important and equally revealing on the product side. A prevention-based approach to data collection means designing a measurement-control device at the earliest monitoring point in the process, to alert operators that the process is out of control. IBM Rochester uses a variety of methods—flowcharting, customer-survey results, and analysis of customer-complaint data—to spot these critical points of potential process failure. IBM found that the cost of investing in defect prevention early in the design cycle is significantly lower than the cost of detecting and removing defects during customer installation. Data prove this point.

Analysis

Describe how quality and performance-related data and information are analyzed and used to support the company's overall operational and planning objectives.

Analysis is the second phase of the data-and-information gathering and problem-solving/quality-improvement process. The aim of analysis is to comb through the raw data you have collected and to turn it into useful information for such functions as planning, performance review, design of products and services, and quality-improvement projections. The key questions in this item are:

- Who performs the analysis?
- What analytical techniques are used?
- Which data are analyzed and at what level of detail?
- How are data aggregated and how are relations between data groups cross-referenced?
- How does the company improve its analytical capabilities? (This last question relates to continuous improvement.)

In responding to this item, applicants should concentrate on how analysis, as it is performed by each major function, affects evaluation and decision-making, especially on the corporate level. An accounting firm using the Baldrige criteria as a planning tool, for example, reported that its analysis of recruiting results led directly to a decision to work with educators in revamping coursework in selected colleges and universities. Another company cited statistical process control techniques used by workers on its factory floor. The use of these tools was relevant, the company said, because they showed that advanced analytical methods had been integrated directly with internal operations.

At Federal Express, Quality Action Teams, headed by a corporate officer, apply a structured problem-solving process called FADE to each one of the indicators in its SQI system. FADE stands for "*F*ocus, *A*nalyze, *D*evelop, and *E*xecute." The Quality Action Team begins the process by brainstorming the problem, developing action grids and impact analyses. The problem is then "analyzed" using Pareto charts, fishbone cause-and-effect analysis, and so on. Solutions are then proposed ("developed") using cost/benefit and force-field analyses. Finally, the Quality Action Team "executes," implementing solutions with appropriate follow-up measurement for results and refinement.

At some companies, data undergo a preliminary review and analysis before they are passed on to senior management at a quality council meeting. The purpose of this briefing session is to give those attending a chance to review the data, analyze the data, and consider which questions senior managers will likely ask. This process ensures that very detailed data, developed at the ground level of the organization, are meaningfully aggregated before they reach top managers. The cross-functional format of the briefing session also helps ensure good root-cause analysis with supporting data.

At Wallace Company, Inc., trends in service performance, including on-time deliveries and invoicing errors, are monitored on control charts maintained by quality "cops"—Statistical Process Control Coordinators—in each district office. These trends are used to project percentage improvements. A quality management steering committee then reviews and analyzes monthly quality data to plan short- and long-range activities and to target specific processes for improvement, for example, sales performance, accounts receivable, and on-the-job training teams.

Some companies analyze data not only with a microscope, but with a stopwatch as well. At Milliken, teams meet *every single day* to review performance over the previous 24 hours. Each week, each functional area meets, then the total plant meets to review weekly performance. Milliken does big-picture analysis as well: for more than a decade, the company has been holding regular quality meetings where the top 250 managers present and review quality performance of each plant by process and by product line.

Choosing the Right Analytical Method

Baldrige winners typically employ a handful of sophisticated analytical techniques, including formal statistical analyses as well as informal tools such as "lessons learned." Choice of methodologies is important: a typical site-visit issue is whether the most suitable analytical techniques are being applied to particular types of data.

Examiners also assess whether analysis is performed systematically, whether problems are analyzed efficiently and effectively. For example, a company might perform initial small-scale analyses to determine if a problem affecting one area has affected, or is latent, in other areas of the company. The idea here is to identify a problem in one operating area, and then to see if that problem is occurring elsewhere. The company must determine what, if any, connection there is between the two problems; if there is a connection, chances are there is a basic system flaw. A good analogy for this kind of approach is keeping one's eyes peeled on the horizon for iceberg-tips—knowing something big and dangerous, threatening the entire enterprise, may loom below. A large, widespread system problem would trigger additional, more comprehensive analyses. Analyzing data in ways like this, which allow identification of system issues from among seemingly different sets of operating-group data, is the hallmark of organizations that have learned to effectively analyze information.

Trend analyses performed by world-class companies cover, whenever possible, at least three- to five-year time horizons. Data are segmented and analyzed at a level of fine detail. Frequently, the same data are subjected to a variety of analytical techniques. If you can arrive at the same conclusion through two or more methods, you know the conclusion is probably pretty good and not just a statistical quirk. "There is nothing novel about the techniques we use," said Greg Lea, Quality Consultant and Program Director-Market Driven Quality at IBM Rochester, "except in the way they are applied, and the fact that, wherever appropriate, we use more than one technique to validate results."

The complexity of some of these analytical techniques is balanced by the widespread use of the Seven Basic Statistical Tools, which are used by teams of employees, engineers, and top managers at world-class companies. These include Pareto diagrams, flow charts or process-flow diagrams, trend charts, histograms, control charts, scatter diagrams, and cause-and-effect diagrams (also called "fishbone" graphs). Root cause analysis is an especially important analytical tool. This analysis is based on the ability to trace a problem back to its source. IBM Rochester follows a disciplined approach to root cause analysis, consisting of five steps: confirming the details of the problem; probing for relevant information; analyzing the data to determine (among other things) the frequency of the problem's occurrence; correlating the information with recent actions or changes in processes or materials; and isolating the causes through statistical techniques (e.g., fishbone diagrams) and controlled experiments. Applying this method, IBM Rochester can uncover the root cause of a problem, identify needed improvements to products or processes, and in so doing, discover new ways to satisfy customers. An elegant analysis is one that enables a company to anticipate process problems and even customer dissatisfaction in advance, and to foresee and prevent problems before they occur. The theory at work here is that, by the time customers report trouble, they are already dissatisfied. Additional progress is indicated when the focus shifts from collecting and analyzing after-the-fact data on customer dissatisfaction to collecting and analyzing data on internal processes in order to identify and correct problems *before* they reach customers.

At Florida Power & Light, winner of the Deming Prize, statistical formulas have been used that predict, on the basis of past history, precisely when a failure would take place. These formulas were aimed at making aging plants more reliable, so that FP&L would not have to construct costly new plants to take their place. "The goal here," said a piece of company literature, "is not simply to be the best at making repairs following failure, but to see failure coming and prevent it."[1] At one unit, the forced outage rate was reduced by nearly half by the end of 1988. At another unit, it dropped to the best record of its megawatt class in the country. Improvements continued the following year, reaching such a level that executives could declare that safety, rather than reliability, would thenceforth be the number-one priority at FP&L.[2]

A continuous, ongoing review of the way in which data is analyzed is essential for continuous improvement. Cycle-time reduction, such as the cycle-time from design to introduction, is a major focus for improvement and a key source of competitive advantage. Which cycle-times to focus on? Those which have the greatest bearing on your business's ability to satisfy customers. Various cycle times differ in importance from industry to industry. In the fashion industry the design-to-market cycle is critical, and billing cycles may be less important. In highly competitive businesses like automobile manufacturing, the strategic planning cycle may be most critical.

Managing and Maintaining

Once your analyses are performed and your databases are assembled, you must develop methods for managing and maintaining them. In particular, the Baldrige criteria ask what specific methods and techniques your company uses to ensure the quality of your data and its rapid assimilation throughout your company.

Data Quality.   The Baldrige criteria measure data quality in terms such as validity, reliability, consistency, timeliness, and standardization. Periodic audits of the *processes* used to collect, analyze, and report data and information are a good way to ensure that the data are fundamentally sound. Some companies use cross-functional teams whose express responsibility is data-and-information management and measurement control. Outside, independent reviewers can be used to perform audits to corroborate internal findings. Because information and analysis is such a critical function, though, such audits should be aggressively monitored by senior management. Another method for ensuring reliability is to train system users in the right ways to collect and enter data. Never leave data management solely to outsiders or some corporate elite. Each function should manage its own data. Requiring each function to maintain and revise all its own operational data is a great way to establish accountability. At the same time, because the data "belongs" to that function, the people entering and using it will work to maintain its quality. Pride plays a part, as does the simple need to have one's own numbers correspond to one's own reality.

One way to help ensure data quality is to use standardized measures. Standardization means using measures that can be replicated and understood company-wide. Standardization raises to the highest level a company's ability to increase its knowledge, by incorporating information gained from previous projects, acquired over time, and shared between operating units. Standardized formats in instruction manuals, forms, and survey instruments mean that employees will all be speaking the same language. That means greater fluency in the measures themselves and less time wasted on translating one another's work. The Baldrige criteria set the data quality marker at a very high level, and expect companies using the criteria to diligently pursue attention to detail in their analyses. When changes in measurement appear necessary, for instance, extensive pretesting may be conducted to determine what kind of impact the change will have on the historic trend of the measurement. If the trend lines are affected, the company should quantify the change and make adjustments to actual historic results.

Access. Access is an ownership concept. If your data belong to relevant workers, if they have reliable access to it, the data will be entered and maintained at a higher level of quality. This concept of access must serve as the antidote to information over-centralization—data so controlled, so remote, that it ceases to be relevant, and so deteriorates in quality.

Using advanced database systems, generally driven by minicomputers or mainframes, a company can track and control a vast number of variables across even the largest organization—data about equipment, networks, software changes and upgrades. This centralization of data management creates a hub that all the different spokes of your organization can draw from, contribute to, and learn from when major changes are underway. Mismanaged, however, the centralized database can be an inaccessible monster. Companies should find a way to balance the virtues of central analytical capabilities against local data ownership—no easy task.

How computer-intensive or how high-tech your information systems are, is less important than how appropriately and how openly critical information flows to and from people who need it. Do not lock up all your data in a vault. It must be easily accessed, and easily modified. Ease of access, retrieval, and use by operating personnel greatly reduces cycle time in critical functions. "In a total quality culture," observes Frederick W. Kramer of Westinghouse Commercial Nuclear Fuel Division, "everyone has a right to know." At Milliken, databases—including product specifications, process data, supplier and raw material data, customer requirements, and safety and environmental data—are available to absolutely every associate throughout the computer network. At Wallace Company, Inc., an inside salesperson at corporate headquarters can check the inventory available at any other district office. Another type of system involves formal review of measurement reports by the senior management quality council. These reports, along with management comments, are then communicated to departmental quality councils and to each work unit and employee through quality meetings and reports displayed in each area. The frequency with which various reports are disseminated is also addressed as part of a Baldrige-inspired improvement process.

How frequently different types of data are collected, analyzed, and reported will vary. Relatively stable processes like employee-involvement programs can probably be reliably assessed annually. For more volatile process-control functions, on the other hand, data analysis may need to be instantaneous. Processes that require complex scheduling, for example—where service execution or manufacturing production involves coordinating the movement of people or equipment—demand constant attention and data feedback to prevent devastating chain reactions. At Milliken, performance monitoring is done for critical processes, and results are displayed almost immediately on monitors located throughout plants. Production associates can interact with monitoring systems and through the use of statistical methods help to stabilize and control their processes. At one management-consulting firm, data from ongoing reviews led to day-to-day adjustments in the engagements with clients, including reassigning personnel and providing additional services to clients. Many companies resist the kind of intensive management and maintenance of data that Baldrige requires, on the grounds that time spent working numbers is time not spent producing products or services. The Baldrige approach says *you* are the expert—you tell them what "just the right amount and frequency" of analysis is. But be prepared to explain why.

Comparisons and Benchmarks

Describe the company's approach to selecting data and information for competitive comparisons and world-class benchmarks to support quality and performance planning, evaluation, and improvement.

Competitive and benchmark data are so absolutely critical to quality improvement that Baldrige sets them apart from other types of data, and devotes a special section to their discussion. Vigorous benchmarking is a key indicator of external focus and an integral element in the strategic management of quality.

Stealing Shamelessly

Broadly speaking, benchmarking is the practice of searching outside one's company for new ideas for improvement of processes, products, and services. In this vein, benchmarking involves "either adopting the practices or adapting the best features, and implementing them to obtain the best of the best."[3] Many quality professionals unabashedly advise companies intent on quality improvement to "steal shamelessly" from the techniques, successes, and achievements of world-class competitors. Benchmarking also means establishing numerical operating targets for particular functions based on the best possible industry or out-of-industry practices.[4] This concept is very new for most companies, and stands in contrast to their current practices, which project the future from the company's own past trends, without any reference to what competitors and other leading companies are doing. In addition, benchmarking validates and adds credibility to the goal-setting process by its concentration on best practices. Benchmarking obliterates divisive internal debate on targets. A company can undertake a major change because "our competitor, or someone else, is already doing it." With no benchmarking data, that kind of change would be unimaginable. The key questions in this item are:

- What elements do you compare, and how do you select information for comparisons?

- What is the full scope of comparison data?

- How do you get reliable information from the companies or the industry you've selected?

- How do you use benchmark information to encourage new ideas and innovation?

And, of course, there is the inevitable continuous-improvement question:

- How do you improve the benchmarking capabilities you already have?

Right and Wrong Ways to Benchmark

Companies that do poorly in this section tend to be very episodic in their benchmarking practices—they do it, forget about it, do it again, but fail to follow up. Baldrige winners, by contrast, are ferocious benchmarkers. In 1984, Xerox used only 14 benchmarks having to do with product quality, cost, and delivery parameters. Xerox currently uses many more than that. In fact, when they reached 250 benchmark areas, they stopped counting.

The same general criteria that apply to data collection apply to benchmarking and competitive comparisons. For example, benchmarks and competitive data should relate to certain broad categories—that is, product and service quality, customers, employees, suppliers, and internal operations, including support functions. Above all, the Baldrige criteria seek assurance that a company's benchmarking activities are linked with its goal-setting process, as outlined in the category Strategic Quality Planning. (In fact, criteria related specifically to "benchmarking" were, until 1991, located in the Strategic Quality Planning category.) Benchmarking practices and even specific benchmarks should also be applied at all levels and in all units of the organization—including support functions, human resources, and suppliers. For example, at many Baldrige winners, benchmarking has been deployed into individual work groups, where it enhances employee involvement by engaging employees in defining the goals of their jobs. Accounting and legal services, both support functions, could benchmark activities such as billing, collection, accounts receivable management, the audit process, litigation management, the patent process, and so on.

Cross-industry benchmarking—General Motors learning from AT&T, for instance—can identify quality gaps that may not emerge in competitor benchmarking and that can lead to greater customer satisfaction. Consequently, the Baldrige criteria seek assurance that your company uses all available sources of comparative data. For example, a full-service resort could benchmark specific functions against (a) world leaders, (b) the best in its industry nationwide, (c) the best in its class (i.e., full-service resort), and (d) the best in the same geographic area. Xerox benchmarked its billing processes against those used by American Express; its marketing processes against those of Proctor & Gamble; and its distribution processes against those of L.L. Bean. People at IBM Rochester use benchmark data that focus on particular product features and on "full-range" competitors. They look at articles in technical journals, especially those written by competitors. They ask, Are their tools as sophisticated as ours? What kind of leverage do they have in their processes? How do they do it?

Obstacles to Benchmarking

Benchmarking is important if the United States is going to improve competitively. That does not mean everyone is happy about benchmarking. Your legal department is likely to be concerned about giving away trade secrets or about possibly violating antitrust rules by sharing information with another company. Our free market system and competitive tradition can also put insurmountable obstacles in the path of the practice. For every quality professional advising companies to "steal," there are companies who, quite understandably, do not want to be stolen from. For every Xerox, there are a dozen companies less liberal about sharing—even with "noncompetitors"—internal data that may be critical to their success in the marketplace. Still, benchmarking will not go away. Because it is a such a vital and ongoing function, it will remain an indispensable tool for companies pursuing continuous improvement.

Baldrige winners are always on the lookout for new ways to benchmark small, but important, elements of their processes—complaint handling, educational facilities, customer/salesperson interaction, and so on. Efforts should also be directed toward broadening the reliability of benchmark data, and integrating them throughout all levels of the company. Since the competition is always changing and improving, benchmarks should be assessed and recalibrated at least annually. Employees must be trained to better identify and develop appropriate benchmarks.

Benchmarking leads us to surprising new business realizations. This often can occur more readily when a competing company focuses on a competitor's processes—in addition to its products. Benchmarking has become so commonplace at some companies that they are now benchmarking elements of their own benchmarking processes! For some companies, the sweetest moment may be when your company learns that *it* is being used as the world-class reference point that competitors seek to learn from. Rather than rest on its laurels then, the company must continue accelerating its improvements to ensure that it maintains its leadership position. That is why companies like L.L. Bean continue to benchmark others—even in logistics and warehousing systems, where it is a leader—to ensure it is not surprised by a new technology or approach that leapfrogs its own winning ways.

9

The Third Pillar: Strategic Quality Planning

The Strategic Quality Planning *category examines the company's planning process and how all key quality requirements are integrated into overall business planning. Also examined are the company's short-term and longer-term plans and how quality and performance requirements are deployed to work units.*

The Strategic Quality Planning category wants to know your company's plans for quality and your aspirations for leadership in the markets you have chosen. That much is simple. However, beware of the phrase "strategic planning." It is somewhat deceptive, since this category encompasses more than the external environment. It also asks that you examine exactly *how* your goals and plans—your "tactical" objectives—are formed and deployed throughout your company. The questions you must ask in this category are:

- How do we develop our plans, strategies, and goals?
- What specific action steps do we need to take to achieve superior quality?

- How can we get everyone in the company involved in quality planning and working toward the same broad objectives?

- What are our short-term and long-term goals and plans to achieve superior quality and performance?

The Evolution of Quality Planning

Companies do not come into existence knowing how to plan for quality. It is a rigorous and evolutionary process, starting from a primitive state in which quality planning is unsophisticated and often haphazard. Like an organism that slowly evolves in response to changes in its external environment, however, the company grows, and the vague notion that it can plan to improve itself begins to assume a definite contour, a corporate face and structure. To develop fully, quality planning typically goes through four distinct developmental stages.

Stage One

In the first stage, when a company is young and relatively unstructured, quality planning is seldom much of a priority. Busy new companies have better things to do—drive sales, boost capacity, speed up production, and hire employees. Never mind that quality planning is exactly what the company needs to successfully manage its rapid growth. Demand for products or services is so strong at this stage that customers do not protest too loudly against mediocre quality. The company sees itself in a whirlwind of activity—to stop and suggest "quality planning" in such a turbulent atmosphere is tantamount to treason. Since no one has taken the time to measure the cost of poor quality, it is impossible to get top managers's attention. They may give lip service to quality in the form of buzz phrases like *"Zero Defects!"* but they are extremely reluctant to embark on what are perceived as costly, long-term quality initiatives. Instead of integrated, rigorous planning based on hard information and incremental goals, managers move erratically from crisis to crisis. Planning activities that do occur are principally focused on financial strategies and targets (e.g., sales, return on assets, etc.) and not on process capabilities, defect levels, cycle times, or other quality concerns. What managers fail to do in this first stage is to develop clearly articulated quality-performance strategies, action plans, and quantitative targets that will serve as the foundation for long-range financial success.

Stage Two

The second stage is usually precipitated by increasing competition and rising customer expectations. Individual business units, usually championed by a small cadre of dedicated individuals, develop improvement objectives, but these efforts receive only limited support from top management. Faced with reduced revenues or lowered profitability, companies without a clear strategic quality vision resort to cost-cutting or cost-containment. In the late 1970s and early 80s, for example, American auto makers blamed their problems on things like noncompetitive labor costs, when the real problem was much more fundamental—lousy product-development processes and an indifferent attitude toward customers. Instead of taking a customer-driven approach to planning, these organizations were cost-driven. Their focus was on keeping expenses under control rather than increasing revenues by increasing customer satisfaction. The market rewarded their indifference by seeking out competitors who focused on customer needs. In this second stage of planning, strategic business plans make random references to quality and other nonfinancial performance initiatives that affect the company's cost structure and profit position. However, these references to quality are not integrated within the entire fabric of the annual business plan.

Stage Three

In the third stage, which is where many companies are right now, senior management starts to get involved and a few fundamental processes are re-configured. On the whole, however, the company still reacts to market events instead of anticipating and planning for them. Quality at this stage is still mostly a defensive posture, focused primarily on internal processes and on the elimination of defects, not on aggressively identifying and planning to meet customer needs. In companies making rapid progress toward quality as a strategic operating posture, the same senior-level executives oversee both the financial and the quality plans. This helps ensure that the two sets of plans become integrated in fact—if not in format. However, where progress is slow, different sets of executives are responsible for developing the financial plans and the quality plans. This structural gap makes integrating the two plans more difficult. Too often, sensitive but vital financial data is withheld from the managers driving the quality plan. In such situations where there is an incomplete understanding of the organization's financial position, it is nearly impossible to develop meaningful systemwide performance initiatives and a comprehensive business strategy.

Stage Four

In the fourth stage, the "quality castles in the air" are finally set in cement. Companies in this stage demonstrate a disciplined process-oriented, customer-driven approach to quality planning. The marriage of financial, operational, and quality objectives is complete. This is the stage reached by only a few companies, Baldrige winners and organizations that diligently pursue quality as a central operating strategy (see Fig. 9-1). For these fourth-stage companies, financial planning and quality planning have become one seamless process. The same senior executives drive all planning and have full access to all the organization's databases. These executives recognize that financial planning and quality planning are two faces of the same critical process—a process that will influence, if not determine, the organization's success in the market and at the bank.

When a company reaches this fourth stage, everything suddenly seems to fall into place seamlessly. The strategic value of quality is now recognized at all levels of the organization. Employees know the company's short- and long-term quality initiatives backwards and forwards. Valuable data do not rot in the attic anymore. Instead, information from operating personnel on the shop floor and the sales force in the field is fed back up the organization to become part of the corporate plan. The same thing happens to input from customers and suppliers. No longer internally focused, the company is a true citizen of the marketplace, using world-class benchmarks to drive the goal-setting process. Quality plans confront and root out failure in all functional areas, including support functions. Senior executives are actively involved in mapping out strategy and linking objectives and logistical support. Interlocking quality councils at all levels of the organization speed up the communication process. The company consciously plans for continuous improvement. Episodic and narrowly focused plans are replaced by bold initiatives such as cycle-time reduction, uniform reduction of defects across the organization, and the improvement of fundamental processes. Long-term quality initiatives, such as meeting educational needs in the work force, are now undertaken.

The fourth stage sounds like business utopia and it is an enviable position to be in. At this level, the company's cost of poor quality is typically

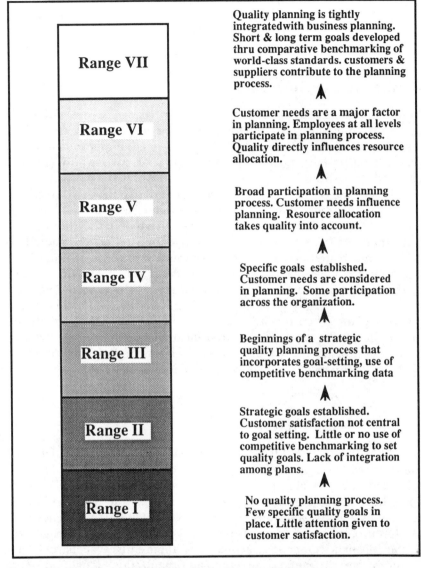

Range VII	Quality planning is tightly integratedwith business planning. Short & long term goals developed thru comparative benchmarking of world-class standards. customers & suppliers contribute to the planning process.
Range VI	Customer needs are a major factor in planning. Employees at all levels participate in planning process. Quality directly influences resource allocation.
Range V	Broad participation in planning process. Customer needs influence planning. Resource allocation takes quality into account.
Range IV	Specific goals established. Customer needs are considered in planning. Some participation across the organization.
Range III	Beginnings of a strategic quality planning process that incorporates goal-setting, use of competitive benchmarking data
Range II	Strategic goals established. Customer satisfaction not central to goal setting. Little or no use of competitive benchmarking to set quality goals. Lack of integration among plans.
Range I	No quality planning process. Few specific quality goals in place. Little attention given to customer satisfaction.

Figure 9-1. The Third Pillar: Strategic Quality Planning (60 Points)

less than that of its competitors. Competition continues to intensify, of course, but systems for continuous improvement give the company a definable edge and keep it ahead of the pack.

Quality versus Business?

In the general description of this category, the Baldrige criteria state that companies must integrate quality-improvement planning with "overall business planning." "It sounds as if quality planning is somehow different from business planning," fumed one executive, who was totally baffled by the distinction.

Part of the confusion is semantics. To most people, the word "business" is intolerably vague. What the Baldrige criteria actually mean is that quality-improvement objectives, like customer satisfaction, defect reduction, first-pass yield rates, and cycle-time reduction, should be given as much attention at the senior-executive, strategic-planning level as targets and measures to control or increase profitability. Juran refers to this re-emphasis as "enlarging the business plan to include quality goals.[1] In fact, quality goals can and should be the cornerstone of the business plan. When quality, financial, and operational objectives are not connected, it can lead to a dysfunctional organization, driven by a profusion of competing disconnected objectives. Some would call it "putting the financial cart before the quality horse."

Seeing the Big Picture

Donald M. Berwick, Baldrige judge, associate professor of pediatrics at the Harvard Medical School and member of the faculty at the Harvard School of Public Health, believes that this category, perhaps more than any other, reveals important differences between the truly world-class companies and the also-rans. Speaking at the Quest for Excellence II Conference, he noted, "As difficult as it is to move quality management to the top of a company's agenda, it is apparently even harder, and therefore rarer, to connect quality to an organization's long- and short-term strategic planning." Implicit in Berwick's words is the notion that quality planning should be rigorous and detailed, like the budgeting process. Everyone in the organization should be involved, from the senior executives on down. If you can do this, your business takes a major evolutionary step—you have inextricably linked your strategic plans (what to improve) with your operating, or process, capabilities (how to improve). "When both planning and process capabilities are done well and linked firmly together," says Berwick, "the results for market presence can be awesome. The analogy in baseball is a hitter who has a great swing, but who also has a sense of timing and 'place' to be able to hit the ball at precisely the right moment." When ball and bat come together with a satisfying whack, that is the fourth stage of quality planning evolution.

Strategic Quality Planning Process

Describe the company's strategic quality planning process for the short-term (1–2 years) and longer-term (3 years or more) for quality and customer satisfaction leadership. Include how this process integrates quality and company performance requirements and how plans are deployed.

The Baldrige criteria are your company's ticket to the fourth stage. Companies on the brink of achieving this stage give the Baldrige criteria credit for getting them over the hump. At Wallace Company, senior executives attended an MBNQA Quest For Excellence Conference. Intrigued, they studied the award criteria and discovered a crucial ingredient that had been missing from their program—strategic quality planning. "We had enthusiasm and a knowledge base. But when it got down to the nitty gritty, we weren't utilizing the process effectively," recalls John Wallace, Chief Executive Officer. "The Baldrige Award criteria provided the structure we needed and gave us a road-map to follow."[2] Ken Leach of Globe Metallurgical described his quality-planning process as sitting down with each of the 133 items in the 1989 Baldrige application and figuring out how to improve on each one. His actual, working plan was 20 pages long with 90 items for continuous improvement.

Baldrige encourages you to think of quality planning visually, as an "up, down, and sideways" kind of process, punctuated by frequent reviews that act as "reality checks."

UP: Operating personnel communicate data about customers and internal processes up the corporate pipeline to senior planners.

DOWN: At the same time, senior planners perform environmental scans, set priorities, and communicate them down the organizational chart to operating personnel.

UP: Operating personnel then feed information on appropriateness and feasibility back up to top management.

SIDEWAYS: Meanwhile, customers and suppliers contribute to the planning process laterally, in face-to-face meetings with company planners.

Short-term operational, or "tactical," plans and objectives are extracted from long-term strategic plans and goals. The Baldrige criteria, as always, encourage you to keep continuous improvement of the quality planning process itself clearly in focus.

Dissecting the Quality Planning Process

Quality planning begins by reviewing the previous period's achievements and culminates in a viable action plan and off-line review of the quality-planning process itself.

Initial Review. This review forms the basis for revising or modifying the previous period's strategic and operating goals and plans. The first question, naturally, is "Did we meet the objectives we set last period?" If so, congratulations are in order. If not, why not? It is important to look at lessons learned from past quality planning sessions and to make revisions to the current planning process. The logic, of course, is that if the process works well, good results will follow. The question you must ask is, "What did our experience teach us that will make our planning process more effective and productive?" Set specific objectives for improvement—getting suppliers more involved in the process, for example.

Situation Analysis. Here is where the company gets its current bearings, both externally and internally:

Where do we stand compared to our competition?

What do we have to do to assume leadership in our industry?

What are our current process capabilities?

Applicants who have done their homework will find a large chunk of the answers to these questions in their report for the previous category, Information and Analysis. Other answers are to be found in your company's greatest resource, its operating personnel.

Many companies are run purely by one-way, top-down decree. That management style is the diametric opposite of Baldrige-inspired companies, which thrive on the unimpeded upward flow of information through an organization. Getting this to happen is not easy and is one of the reasons why the planning function takes such a long time to evolve. It is like trying to talk a river, which has flowed one way for ages, into reversing its flow. As skill in quality planning increases with experience, however, the organization becomes progressively more comfortable and efficient in gathering information from operating personnel, who, after all, have the most detailed understanding of why a system does or does not work.

Take, for example, Motorola. At Motorola, a Corporate Quality Council performs a comprehensive quality-systems review of each business unit. Employees are asked questions covering quality performance, with emphasis on customer satisfaction and on management of the quality improvement process. Based on the answers it receives, the team quantitatively scores the unit's quality performance and the results are fed back into the strategic planning process. Each major unit is visited every two years.

Draft of Strategic Goals.   Goals are extremely valuable to an organization. It's not enough to simply point to the mountain the organization intends to climb. That gesture needs to be coupled with some sort of hint as to what the view from the top is going to be. A quality goal is a quality-improvement target. Goals describe two points: (1) This is where we are currently, and (2) This is where we want to go. While departmental quality goals pinpoint areas for improvement within functions (e.g., training needs, benchmarks, etc.), strategic quality goals are more global, and apply across all functions. Strategic goals thus reflect relatively broad areas for improvement, that is, cycle-time reduction, improved product and service reliability, across-the-board reduction in the number of defects or errors, and so on.

Goal-setting is a particularly sticky process for products and services requiring a long lead time. It does not do any good to target a level of performance and come back three years later only to find that level has changed. Goals have to be projected based upon anticipated customer needs as well as what the competition is expected to be doing when the project is completed.

In general, goal-setting should follow a pattern of incremental, continuous improvements. Set goals as a pole vaulter does, by raising the bar an inch at a time. However, well-constructed quality plans also include occasional strategically directed "stretch" or "leapfrog" goals that require quantum leaps in key performance areas. Rather than articulate small percentage improvements (1–10 percent annually), stretch goals identify improvements of major magnitude (50 percent to 100 percent annually). Stretch goals transform your business. They cannot be achieved simply by working longer hours or by investing more money. To achieve them, your organization must radically rethink and change the way it does things.

One Baldrige-quality company set a stretch goal of closing its books, at year's end, in half the time it took the year before. In their analysis, employees discovered that their existing punch-card system was physically unable to handle such a reduction in processing time. They searched for another method and learned about a bar-code technology that was already being used in other areas of the business for product tracking. Employees switched from punchcards to scanner cards. This innovative idea was subsequently adopted and the goal—a stretch goal—was reached.

An earmark of quality-driven organizations in general, and Baldrige winners in particular, is their willingness to take on these stretch goals. In 1981, Motorola established as one of its Top Ten Corporate Goals a tenfold reduction in defect rates—in both manufacturing and administrative processes—by 1986. Over the course of the five-year program, many new methods were implemented. Some of these methods resulted in quantum leaps of improvement; others resulted in more conventional "step function" improvements. Having achieved its 1981 goal, Motorola dedicated itself in 1987 to improving quality an additional 10 times over the next two years and *100 times* by 1991. By the end of 1991, the company said it would reach the legendary six-sigma capability—3.4 defects per million parts or opportunities—across all functions. This goal is the near-equivalent of the mythical "zero defects" level—99.9999998 percent defect free. The company is still pursuing its aggressive goal-setting policy, dedicating itself to tenfold reductions in defects every two years and tenfold reductions in cycle time every five years. Quality metrics will change, managers proclaim, from parts per million to parts per *billion*.

Goals are continually revised and updated as conditions change and as the progress of quality programs becomes known. Quality goals should be aligned with:

- *Quality values.* A quality goal must be consistent with a company's values.

- *Financial goals.* Quality goals should be communicated in tandem, and on an equal footing, with the company's profit/loss goals. That way they keep top management's attention.

- *Leadership requirements.* Baldrige defines quality leadership in terms of meeting customer requirements and exceeding competitors' quality levels. A quality goal reflects this standard of leadership and is informed by the benchmarking process.

- *Process capabilities.* Leadership requirements point the direction toward what a company needs to achieve. Current process capabilities indicate the distance required to reach those goals. The Baldrige is an unsurpassed tool for providing baseline self-assessment of process capability.

- *Supplier capabilities.* The quality of incoming goods and services can have an enormous impact on the goal-setting process. Quality is high at Toyota's Georgetown, Kentucky plant, but productivity runs about 10 percent below Japanese levels. Toyota blames the lag on U.S. suppliers, who are not up to Japanese standards.[3] Like customers, suppliers can also be brought into the goal-setting process early, by sharing internal measures (e.g., customer-opinion results), improvement strategies, and long-term objectives, including information about their new products and services. One company has an arrangement with its computer supplier to obtain products in advance for testing purposes. Information about the computer is then fed back to the vendor to make improvements and assure continued enhancements.

Selecting among competing goals has always been a daunting challenge for businesses. So many companies add products and services in catch-as-catch-can order—no wonder quality is mediocre, and customers are unhappy. One solution is to use an optimization process to create a company portfolio of products/services. This kind of process takes the usual grab-bag of planned offerings, evaluates each offering on its merits, and prioritizes the offerings in terms of viability. Various factors are taken into consideration to achieve this ranking—expected impact on quality, return on investment, and compatibility with the current line of products and services.

In a complex system like Westinghouse's, there are literally thousands of issues management must juggle. Keeping all the little balls in the air is hard enough—understanding the role each plays in the corporate overview is impossible. How can managers see through all the planning clutter and keep their eyes on the key issues? Managers at Westinghouse Commercial Nuclear Fuel relied on Pareto's Law, which says that in any organization, 20 percent of all management issues will control 80 percent of performance and results. With that principle in mind, Westinghouse set forth eight factors that the company felt contributed most to the division's health. Those eight factors became the focus for strategic quality planning.

At Wallace Company, senior leadership developed 16 broad strategic quality objectives that drive the quality process. All of them are directly related to the Baldrige criteria and involve such things as leadership development, information analysis, quality education, community outreach, and so on.

Review Draft and Finalize Objectives. This step is the "reality check." At Cadillac, developing a draft of business objectives takes approximately four to six weeks. The draft is then reviewed across the organization for feedback on appropriateness and feasibility of goals. Objectives are finalized by the executive staff and then shared with top union and management leaders of the company. At IBM Rochester, teams of employees develop a business strategy that includes product and business goals. The Rochester Management Committee, a cross-functional executive team, then reviews and signs off on the plan.

Development of Short-Term Operating Plans. Deploying and implementing plans, goals, and performance indicators to all work units and suppliers are complex tasks and must be coordinated across divisional and functional lines. This is where generalities must become very specific. (Some companies assign the task of deployment to special project teams.) A goal of cutting cost of poor quality by half over five years, for example, would be allocated to divisions. However, since the chief components of cost of poor quality are invariably multifunctional in nature—the barrel leaks at a dozen places, not just one—divisions often develop a series of multifunctional projects, each of which will, in due course, be assigned to a project team.

Although strategic goals are proposed at the top, managers and operating personnel lower down in the organization have the job of evaluating the feasibility of the goals, identifying the specific projects and tasks that together will meet those goals, determining the resources needed, and then communicating these needs to the next higher level. At Florida Power & Light, top managers acknowledge that lower-level employees and managers know the most about where systems fail. Teams of employees are therefore encouraged to learn as much as possible about company objectives and are given guidelines for choosing projects which they feel will do the most to improve quality. Eventually, when workers are ready for the added responsibility, they are expected to have a greater say in initiating projects. A special task force dedicated to top policy priorities is in place to foster important project ideas that employees may overlook.[4]

Goals need to be subdivided and defined in such a way that people lower down in the organization feel they can have an impact on them. One service organization set a goal of 95 percent customer satisfaction. Employees in customer service could clearly relate to this goal, but those further upstream in the delivery process—especially those in support functions—had a harder time understanding how *their* activities related to that goal. As a result, morale suffered. People cannot "do" quality unless they first understand their role in it. Communicating that role is management's task.

At IBM Rochester, manufacturing, development, marketing, service, and support teams develop so-called functional strategies, which describe in detail the human resources, capital resources, and expenses required to meet the company's quality priorities. The resources and associated expenses are compared to revenue and profit goals to balance the strategic plan. Once this package of financial goals, functional strategies, and quality priorities is approved, an operating strategy with a two-year horizon is developed and articulated. The operating plan is a detailed description of all the tactics that make up the larger strategy. It shows how revenue, market participation, profit, and return on assets are connected to resource and training needs, tools, benchmarks, and supplier improvement.

Communication and Deployment of the Plan throughout the Organization. This is where the rubber meets the road, the interface of plan and action. Communication and deployment must be done with great care. Your strategic plan is too important to convey informally at a company social function. How you communicate the plan tells a lot about the seriousness with which you yourself regard it.

In highly structured, exceedingly formal plans, the rollout from plan formulation to implementation can occur quite seamlessly, without a hitch. Materials are distributed explaining goals to be met, tools to be used, procedures to be followed, and so forth. At some companies, this transition takes place almost ritualistically, with senior managers on hand to bless the event. At Cadillac, for example, the entire business plan is laid out and communicated to all employees at the Annual State of the Business meeting in December. At Wallace, plans are implemented according to a timetable developed by the Quality Management Steering Committee; implementation is accomplished primarily through Quality Improvement Process Teams that are empowered to take the necessary steps to implement their approved recommendations and ideas.

Regular and Systematic Review. Plans are not perfect. Because customer requirements and market conditions change rapidly, your goals, and the strategies supporting them, must be reviewed on a regular basis. At Federal Express, there is a monthly system-planning meeting, in which each division's key projects are discussed and reviewed. The overall process is evaluated yearly, with progress toward achieving these goals reported monthly. When the company sees a departure away from progress, adjustments are made to get back on course. If the economy or competition produce unexpected and uncontrollable changes, the goals are reviewed and, if necessary, modified.

A final step, of course, is review of the strategic-planning process itself, with an eye toward continuous improvement. How can the process be performed more quickly? How can communications be handled more effectively? How can implementation be completed more efficiently? Like any organizational process, the planning process is always open to review and improvement.

Quality Goals and Plans

Summarize the company's quality and performance plans and goals for the short term (1–2 years) and the longer term (3 years or more).

The Baldrige assessment wants evidence of both short- and long-term planning processes. *Short-term* is nominally defined as 1 to 2 years; *long term* as 3 or more years, leaving open the possibility of extra-long-range goals. (Some pundits claim that the planning activities at some Japanese companies go well beyond the traditional 5-year horizon.) There should be no gaping abyss between the two sets of plans. They should be clearly linked and mutually reinforcing.

10
The Fourth Pillar: Human Resource Development and Management

The Human Resource Development and Management *category examines the key elements of how the company develops and realizes the full potential of the work force to pursue the company's quality and performance objectives. Also examined are the company's efforts to build and maintain an environment for quality excellence conducive to full participation and personal and organizational growth.*

A strong conviction underlies the Baldrige process: that employees are *not* simply cost factors to be minimized. Just like investment capital, human capital—the people who work in an organization—must be managed in a way that maximizes its benefit to the organization. The category Human Resource Development and Management asks how effective your company has been in developing the potential of its work force, top to bottom, and across all categories of employees. The first issue to address here is how your company's various human resource goals and plans relate to the overall quality initiatives outlined in

133

the previous category, *Strategic Quality Planning*. Keep in mind that the strategic quality plan should drive the human-resource strategy, and not vice-versa.

As with most plans, human resource plans and priorities must retain some elasticity, as trends and conditions change. Worker expectations are not set in concrete—think of the changing demands of women employees over the past 25 years. New technologies are ushered in without warning. Workforce demographics—age, education, geographical shifts—fluctuate considerably from one year to the next. To cope with this endless swirl of change, a human resource plan must be flexible and fleet of foot.

Properly explaining your company's human resource utilization processes is a complex task, requiring that you first classify them into their respective subsystems—recruiting, orientation, career development, teambuilding, rewards and recognition, and so on. The Baldrige process also requires that you describe your set of long-range goals, based on organizational objectives, and then explain how you develop incremental plans to reach them. Imagine, for instance, that your company has set for itself the goal of creating a fully empowered workforce and a state-of-the-art performance evaluation-and-recognition system, all parts of a plan to support the company-wide goal of becoming the employer of choice in your markets. Your company knows, however, it must first lay the groundwork. Accordingly, it kicks off its initiative by teaching workers basic quality concepts, underscoring the principle of customer satisfaction. So the effort is underway. Now the company installs a suggestion system and is tracking its use and setting goals for number of ideas submitted and implemented. It trains workers in problem solving skills and team dynamics. Some workers receive advanced courses in statistical process control, while others are given instruction in team building and the seven basic statistical tools. Two years later, this program is still going great guns. Eventually, according to your plan, workers will be given even greater decision-making authority and the compensation system will be restructured based on recommendations of a team looking into performance evaluation. The new evaluation system will recognize team—and individual—contributions. This is the kind of detail and linkage among systems that the Baldrige framework is seeking in human resource plans.

The Employee as Internal Customer

The importance Baldrige winners place on human resources is evident in their quality values. At IBM, "respect for the individual" is embedded in the organizational culture. People are the touchstone in Federal Express's "People-Service-Profit" corporate philosophy. "Our company always balances the needs of employees, our customers, and our shareholders, considering each in making plans or policies," say Federal Express executives. "We always consider the effects on our people first in making decisions, recognizing that if we take care of our employees, they will deliver a superior service which our customers will, in turn, utilize." One management-consulting firm takes a cradle-to-grave approach to human-resource utilization, pledging itself to recruiting the "best and the brightest," developing the highest-skilled workers, retaining top people, and maintaining long-term relationships with those who leave the company. More specific objectives are given for both the short and long terms, such as working with universities and colleges to improve curricula and developing an employee database to better match employee skills, experience, and interests with particular consulting engagements.

Companies that score well in the *Human Resource Development and Management* category, in essence, treat their employees as *internal customers,* evaluating the needs of each "segment," and translating those needs into design features for various human-resource programs. (see Fig. 10-1). The requirements of all categories of employees are addressed, including workers in sales, support, and administration as well as hourly workers. Historically, Globe Metallurgical never felt particularly inclined to include any of its hourly employees on project teams. Project teams were reserved for what the company called its "smart guys"—engineers, metallurgists, professional-level people. But there was a problem—no matter what solutions the "smart guys" came up with, they ran into trouble on the shop floor. Hourly employees resisted the ideas because they were not in on their formulation. Or they knew something critical to the plan's success that project team professionals were not aware of. "Nobody asked their opinion," Ken Leach, the former Vice President of Administration observed, "so they weren't going to help. Today we involve them very much, right up front."[1]

Companies that have difficulty with this category seldom have fully deployed human-resource systems, and what systems do exist show few signs of cross-functional cooperation. Recognition and training are episodic. Employee morale is usually low, for the ideas of developing and involving employees are foreign concepts. On the whole, these companies do not get maximum benefit from their human resources, and it usually shows in the overall quality of their processes, products, and services.

More is required of a Baldrige-winning company than simply polling workers for their opinions on company issues, of course. Communication must be two-way and ongoing, and employees must be clear on what

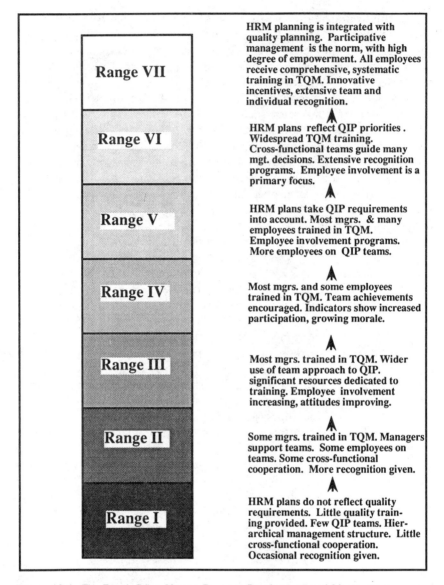

Figure 10-1. The Fourth Pillar: Human Resource Development and Management (150 Points)

is expected of them. The enemies of successful human resource utilization are indifference and inattention. Unless attention is continuously focused on expectations and responsibilities, employees and managers alike grow remote from the ultimate issue of customer satisfaction. Before long, workforce malaise and "malicious compliance" sink roots in the employment relationship. World-class companies are on the lookout for signs of apathy and alienation and are eager to eradicate them.

In the Baldrige system, there are four basic evaluative dimensions to human-resource utilization:

- Involvement (participation) in quality-improvement efforts
- Education and training
- Recognition and performance measurement
- Morale and well-being

Obviously, each of these areas is linked to the others: recognition reinforces participation and morale, training facilitates participation, and so forth. That is why the four areas are common to all mature human-resource management systems. To score well in this category, therefore, companies must demonstrate that they have a comprehensive "people vision" and that, like IBM Rochester, they "enable, empower, excite, and reward" their employees.

Human Resource Management

*Describe how the company's overall
human resource development and
management plans and practices support
its quality and company performance
plans, and address all categories and
types of employees.*

Relax. Baldrige does not require that your company have a full-blown human-resource department, a Vice President–Human Resources with a corner office, a renowned team of training and education specialists, or a multimillion dollar educational facility. There is certainly nothing wrong with these things, and they may even be considered appropriate if a company is large, or if a company's skills and knowledge base are highly specialized. A Big Six accounting firm, for example, is not going to rely on an employment agency or classified ads for qualified applicants; it will have its own recruiting specialists and training experts to conduct ongoing professional education.

If a company is small, a dedicated on-site quality training center is probably out of the question. However, quality training objectives can still be accomplished in other ways—through nearby schools, for instance, or by contract. If the company is a small but vital supplier to a large business, that business may pick up the tab for quality training or even provide the instructors. Motorola and Ford, along with a number of other progressive companies, have developed close relationships with key suppliers, whom they address in training and recognition programs.

Statistics—in the form of employee-survey data, skill evaluations, suggestions per employee per year, and overall quality—will together indicate whether or not a particular approach works. At Globe Metallurgical, training was deliberately kept simple, according to Ken Leach. Everyone in the company was given six hours of basic training in statistical process control, including the creation, maintenance, and interpretation of control charts. "Using your own data works better than using abstract concepts like a distribution diagram of the height of all people who entered the army," said Leach. "So we used real data that employees were already familiar with, that they themselves captured out on the shop floor. To satisfy Ford's requirements we brought in an outside vendor and for specialized training, we send people offsite. As we learn more, the coursework gets more sophisticated."

Ultimately, what emerges from the *Human Resource Development and Management* category is a picture of your company's efforts to mold an energetic, intelligent, and motivated workforce or, at the very least, to pull the workforce away from the adversarial or indifferent mindset that characterizes companies in trouble. The information requested in the category also documents your company's capacity for continuous improvement in each of the four major areas.

Employee Involvement

Describe the means available for all employees to contribute effectively to meeting the company's quality and performance objectives; summarize trends in involvement.

The underlying ethos in this section of the Baldrige criteria is an optimistic one. Jaded managers may even say it is a naive one. It is that employees want to contribute to their company's success and do good work and that, given the tools, the training, and responsibility, they will respond with intelligence, innovation, and native wit. This view is a 180-degree shift from Taylorism, a management philosophy and approach developed around the turn-of-the-century, which holds that managers should plan and direct every aspect of every job, down to the finest detail. For their part, workers are assumed to be "cogs in the machine," not expected to think about anything except the next paycheck.[2] Taylorism epitomizes the engineering mindset toward human-resource management. In their book, *Working Together,* John Simmons and William Mares characterize Taylor as having an engineer's faith that technology defined the nature of the job and that human beings were secondary to technology. "In the past," they quote Taylor, "man has been first; in the future the system must be first."[3]

The Baldrige Vision

One might suppose, given its focus on processes, methodologies, and measurement, that the Baldrige process would advocate scientific management—Taylorism. But much to its credit, the Baldrige correctly perceives that neither the tasks nor the workforce are the same as they were during Frederick Taylor's day. The turn-of-the-century labor force was often immigrant, largely uneducated, and unskilled. Production tasks were relatively straightforward: moving objects, assembling mechanical devices, adjusting machinery, and using sheer physical energy. By contrast, the modern labor force often engages in complex and intellectual tasks, using advanced technologies. Front-line workers and operating personnel are a company's top experts on where things bog down, back up, and fall apart in the system. The Baldrige criteria propose that companies utilize this wisdom, these insights, abilities, and goodwill by giving workers as many opportunities as possible to contribute to quality improvement.

Teams and Suggestion Systems

Employee involvement is a major buzzphrase of our times. But how does one get beyond the slogan to practical reality? There are many methods for getting workers to participate, ranging from companywide suggestion systems to policies encouraging employees to rearrange their work stations. Increasing empowerment—giving employees greater decision-making authority and responsibility in their jobs—is another way to deepen worker participation and understanding. Two of the most common, and potentially the most powerful, mechanisms for involving employees are *teams* and *suggestion systems.*

Basically, the team concept gives groups of workers, supported by supervisors and technical personnel as required, the chance and the authority to identify problems and opportunities, find out where and why processes go wrong, develop and test proposed solutions, and implement those that work. Teams also give individuals the opportunity to help solve problems that they could not solve on their own. Ideally, quality action teams address only those problems whose solutions contribute in a big way to quality improvement—like evaluating the usefulness of an "800 number" phone line to handle customer complaints and inquiries. In practice, though, many companies, especially those in the early stages of their quality-improvement program, are less strict and give their teams the freedom to tackle lesser problems, too. The effect of these idea teams is to jump-start the organization by providing a stream of "quick hits." In this way, team members develop an increased sense of motivation, involvement, and commitment to TQM.

At IBM, teams form spontaneously in response to problems that employees themselves identify. Spontaneous teams are usually small ones—two or three people. No special permission is needed for employees to work on a problem this way. This impromptu system works because employees have achieved a high level of comfort and empowerment and are familiar with the company's broad quality objectives. This approach is especially interesting because teams are formed cross-functionally, not along narrow functional lines. Management also has the option of creating more conventional teams to investigate problems that might otherwise be overlooked.

Semiautonomous work groups are the pattern at Xerox. The company uses a network of district partnerships throughout the United States. Each one, consisting of three partners, from sales, service, and administration, operates without a general manager. These partnerships are empowered to make decisions that promote customer satisfaction. For example, they are free to swap advertising dollars for sales manpower, or customer-engineer allocations for administrators. If teams do not achieve a given level of customer satisfaction, funding is curtailed, no matter how well they do profit-wise.

Suggestion systems are another device for involving employees. For many, the suggestion box sitting empty in the employee cafeteria or outside management's door will leap to mind. But for suggestion systems to be effective, they must be more than a passive receptacle for employee ideas.

- First, companies must be ready to read and respond to employee suggestions while they are fresh.
- Second, employees need to be coached and trained how to identify problems and develop solutions.

- Third, suggestions for small improvements must be as welcome as suggestions for big improvements, since small improvements are an important part of the overall environment for continuous improvement.

- Finally, management should commit to implementing as many suggestions as possible. Suggestion systems with low implementation rates soon lose momentum because employees become skeptical that their ideas will be acted upon.

Other Involvement Techniques

There are many ways to involve employees in the vital activities and processes of the organization. Here are just a handful at random:

- Mentoring systems, in which lower-level employees are assigned to and counseled by senior-level managers.

- Corporate "town meetings"; call-in TV opportunities on the corporate television network (Federal Express does this).

- Company newsletters that solicit and publish comments, letters, and articles by employees.

- "Open door" policies, and "skip-level" programs that give employees a chance to take their ideas over the heads of their immediate bosses. Federal Express's Open Door Policy is considered a model for any industry. Employees write up their concerns, which can address any concern or issue of a systemic nature in which the remedy might affect not only the individual but the corporation as a whole. Concerns are then sent to the Employee Relations Department, which monitors the whole process. The employee concerns are delivered to the management member who can best resolve or address the issue. Resolution is required within 14 days of receipt. One example of corporate response to open door concerns was a task force formed to address opportunities for station personnel to move to full-time from part-time positions at stations in desirable locations.

- Customer partnerships, in which individual employees or teams of employees work directly with customers, are powerful ways to boost employee participation and customer satisfaction simultaneously. Employees learn first-hand about the quality of their company's products and services, and customers enjoy the individual attention.

- Quality council meetings and periodic quality forums open to all employees are other mechanisms for increasing involvement.

- Vendor-quality feedback reports, in which employees rate the quality of goods and services they receive from suppliers, are still another way of getting employees to participate in and work toward company quality objectives.

Whatever technique is used, the Baldrige judges will want evidence of process and continuous improvement—of a systematic effort to perpetually *increase* employee participation in quality-improvement efforts. Every method you employ should have its own set of indicators and be tracked to ensure that stated objectives or benchmarks are being met. The idea is to monitor the system and measure its effectiveness. In work team formation, for instance, you should know how many teams have been implemented. With a suggestion system, you should have an idea of the number of suggestions per employee per year, and what percentage of those suggestions get implemented.

The Power of Empowerment

Unlike plain-vanilla involvement, empowerment programs give employees more control in actually running the company, by giving them more decision-making authority and responsibility in their jobs, along with the skills they need to perform their jobs better. Empowerment can mean giving specific employees more freedom to respond to unexpected problems (a hotel desk clerk refunding $50 to an irate guest, for instance), or it can be a general, companywide effort to shift decision-making authority further down in the organization, like a policy allowing marketing managers to choose an advertising agency on their own without first getting permission from the most senior executives.

Empowerment is an extremely effective management tool. First of all, it is superb training. It creates a pool of managerial talent by training frontline employees in problem solving and decision making. By making decisions where the impact of the decision is not likely to be lethal, low-level managers and frontline employees get valuable decision-making practice with little downside risk. This prepares them for assuming greater authority as they rise in the organization and gives them a sense of "ownership" over the areas in which they work. Empowerment also leads to better customer service during critical "moments of truth." Think of that dismaying moment when the clerk says to you, "I'll have to get my supervisor's approval first." If that clerk or cashier or salesperson were empowered, service response would be almost immediate. In addition, empowerment frees up your company's regular managers. It reduces their decision-making burden, giving them more time—and the psychological space—to concentrate on overall corporate objectives. Finally, empowerment shortens the chain of command and encourages a feeling of individuality and motivation. Employees can see the result of their actions firsthand, and therefore they take a greater interest in and responsibility for those results. By contrast, the conventional status of "disempowered" employees, who never have the green light to make decisions on behalf of the company, creates a gulf of indifference that can harm company-wide performance.

A company's commitment to empowerment shows up in other places besides the item on involvement. In the Baldrige item on "Employee Performance and Recognition," applicants are asked "how the approaches ensure that quality is reinforced relative to short-term financial considerations." The question is intended to uncover situations in which employees are encouraged to stop a process if they detect a problem that may compromise quality. Federal Express, for example, encourages its employees to be innovative and take risks. The anecdotage from this rule is impressive: One employee chartered a plane, and another rented a helicopter, to get their packages delivered on time.

A system to encourage empowerment gives certain types of employees (like customer-contact personnel) basic decision-making skills, lays down some rough guidelines (like customer reimbursements up to $75), and promotes a general policy that employees do not necessarily have to seek managerial permission to act on behalf of quality or customer satisfaction. Empowerment does not mean employees run the show. Many companies insist that employees report decisions they make, or discuss them with management, to see whether the decision was one the individual or the organization can learn from. A good system for empowerment will also require tracking and evaluation, perhaps based upon scores of internal-survey questions such as, "My manager listens to my ideas" or "I have a lot of decision-making authority in my job."

Employee Education and Training

Describe how the company decides what quality-related education and training is needed by employees and how the company utilizes the knowledge and skills acquired; summarize the types of quality education and training received by employees in all categories.

What kind of training should quality-minded companies furnish? In his book, *The Quality System,* Frank Caplan says that all the training most companies provide is on-the-job training. On-the-job is all there is, because it is easy—it requires a minimum of facilities, resources, and preparation. However, notes Caplan, it is the most variable in terms of results, the most susceptible to "sloughing off," and the least likely to provide proper "quality indoctrination." To be effective, Caplan notes, on-the-job must be combined with other, more formal training methods.[4] But planned, formal training of everyone in a company requires a substantial investment. Indeed, it is often the biggest upfront cost in a quality-improvement effort. To ensure that education in concepts, tools, and techniques is cost-effective and of the highest caliber, companies must be extremely systematic in their approach. Like all systems in Baldrige, education and training consist of a cyclical pattern of assessment, goal-setting, application, and evaluation.

What Kind of Training Do You Need?

Needs are determined by assessing employees' technical know-how, conceptual knowledge, and skill levels, and by monitoring changes and trends in the environment outside the company. Accounting firms, for example, are constantly monitoring changes in tax laws and regulations to determine how their educational requirements may be changing. In gathering ideas, be open-minded. Information and ideas on training needs can come from anybody—supervisors, suppliers, training experts, quality professionals, even customers. The types and amounts of quality training will vary from one type of employee to another. However, the general approach involves increasing new employees' quality awareness through quality orientation, providing everyone with basic quality tools and concepts, and giving advanced quality-skills training to key "process" individuals and specialized training to appropriate employee groups. Unsure what your priorities are? Let customer satisfaction be your guide. Think about giving top priority in recruiting, training, and recognition to those employees who serve customers directly. That is the best place to invest money and effort.

Quality Orientation

Some kind of quality orientation for all new employees is a must. This orientation should describe the company's view of quality, introduce the concepts taught in basic quality courses, and outline opportunities for employees to contribute, such as suggestion systems and teams. The broad goal of orientation must be to lay the groundwork for a shift in your company culture, from a product-driven focus to a customer- or market-driven focus. In most cases, this reorientation involves "inverting the pyramid." The old organizational pyramid has customers at the bottom of the pyramid, employees in the middle, and management at the top. In that configuration, everyone—including the customer—"worked for" top management. In the new pyramid, top management is really at the bottom, working with employees, teaching them to see their jobs in terms of serving external customers, who are and should be enthroned at the top.

Special Modules

Special educational modules can be developed for inspector and tester training, training in health and safety issues (e.g., handling of dangerous materials, safe work practices), and so on. In one company, instructors themselves go through two weeks of annual skills updating (training the trainers) during which they return to the work area and perform the job they train others to do.

At Federal Express, all managers receive the company's Total Quality Advantage and Quality Action Team training seminars. The training takes four days and covers topics such as the meaning of quality, cost of quality, customer-supplier relationships, and continuous improvement. The second half of the training develops skills in problem solving. Front-line managers then train employees who have not gone through the formal training processes.

It is not easy for new employees to "hit the ground running." Consider creating *transition work groups* to ease newly trained employees into your company's regular work cycle. Each employee might be given actual work at a pace appropriate to his or her growing skill level. The emphasis here should be on quality, not speed. Employees remain in this special transition unit until both they and their supervisors feel they are ready for the regular work unit.

Education and training goals and methods have to be well thought out. Which methods you use will depend on what stage of quality improvement your company is at, and who exactly is being taught. Executive education, for example, often relies heavily on case-study instruction and group interaction. A lecture format is more suitable for other types of learning. Some companies are now experimenting with interactive computer and video training on quality. Consider using multiple approaches. Instructors in one company's training program use materials that are keyed to either verbal or visual learning styles. Do not be afraid to bring in outside help. Baldrige-quality companies often rely on educational/training professionals to establish precise training objectives and the most effective teaching methods and curricula.

Evaluation

Training without evaluation is pointless—you will not know what your training accomplished. The data gathered at the end of the education-and-training cycle should be used as the basis for future goal-setting and improvement efforts. (A series of evaluations, lasting up to a year after a course has been concluded, may be used to determine how students respond to certain types of training.)

In one company, a training project included a provocative, computer-based tutorial performed during class. Results of participant and instructor evaluations showed that the tutorial would be more effective if performed *before* the course, using class time to reinforce concepts and answer questions raised in the tutorial. The quality action team decided that the change was a good idea, and the course was restructured accordingly. Baldrige-quality companies also assess the ablility of students to *transfer* their knowledge to the shop floor and to retain it once there. *Reinforcement* of ideas learned in training is also accomplished by performance evaluations, by consulting with supervisors, through interacting with other workers on quality-action teams, and by a company's array of rewards and recognitions. Try scheduling "class reunions," generally three months after the conclusion of a training course, in which participants are encouraged to discuss lessons learned in implementing action plans they themselves designed as part of the class.

Both qualitative and quantitative measures should be used for evaluation. The data may be drawn from student surveys, customer surveys, test scores, and the like. Ample opportunities exist to put the students to work here—ask them to fill out evaluation forms, rating the course content and the quality of the instruction. Training evaluations serve to improve the delivery techniques and effectiveness of the instructional staff. With these kinds of data in hand, quality action teams can develop future training objectives. Education-improvement strategies should be formally presented to your company's senior quality council.

Performance and Recognition

Describe how the company's employee performance, recognition, promotion, compensation, reward and feedback processes support the attainment of the company's quality and performance objectives.

Recognition and performance-measurement systems, handled badly, have the potential to do more harm than good—hurting morale rather than helping it, destroying teamwork rather than enhancing it. Yet properly acknowledging the achievements of employees is essential to the continuous improvement process; even quality skeptics admit its fundamental value within an organization. Recognition plays a key role in promoting employee involvement; it reinforces quality objectives, and it encourages employees to cultivate initiative and creativity above and beyond the expectations of their formal job descriptions.

On the down side, it is hard to develop fair systems that somehow balance individual and group recognition. One of Deming's harshest criticisms is that traditional employee recognitions are random; that recognition systems fail to account for naturally occurring variability in the broad spectrum of employee talents and aptitudes; and that the good effects of recognizing one individual are nullified by the ill effects of overlooking another. Others complain that "hokey" recognition programs treat employees like children and ask them to get emotionally involved in packaged hoopla and preprinted excitement. "We get tired of balloons, gift certificates, and associate-of-the-month awards," grouse some employees. At a minimum, these employees would like to see quality achievements tied to increased pay.

Baldrige winners have accordingly approached recognition and performance in a variety of ways. At Federal Express, operational employees are treated differently from management and staff employees. For operational employees, individual recognition and rewards emphasize proficiency, dependability, and safety. There are a variety of contests (safe-driving rodeos, etc.) and short-term incentives that target specific topics and reward individual achievements. For management and staff employees, however, individual pay is merit-based; performance evaluation is less standardized. All managers and most professional staff participate in a bonus program based on management-by-objectives. Objectives are focused primarily on individual responsibilities, but also take into account team contributions. The pool of funds from which individual bonuses are paid is tied to the performance of managers as a group. As a result, the program rewards individual accomplishments proportionate to overall team success.

There is no real reason why a company's teams cannot develop their own recognition and reward systems. Indeed, employee involvement is the best way to ensure that the pat on someone's back is the pat that employees want and perceive to be meaningful. An example is Federal Express's Publishing Services Group, in which an employee panel makes "Perfect Standards" awards for error-free work, "Perfect Service" awards to internal/corporate clients, and "Perfect Solution" awards for innovative ideas.

Picture a company where teams composed of a cross-section of employees, from different grade levels and departments within a particular function, get together to create their own performance measurement system, using indicators like "quality," "quantity," "timeliness," and "customer satisfaction." A management task force then reviews the proposed system, checks it for consistency with companywide goals, and weights each performance indicator according to its importance. This kind of homemade system has one advantage that no other can have: top management knows that its reward system is what employees want, because employees themselves designed it. It certainly goes beyond conventional systems, in which employees win "employee of the month" certificates for doing X amount of work in Y amount of time. The winners in that kind of system are indeed good workers, and they deserve their certificates. But they may be rewarded for the wrong things: volume and speed. The right things are the things this book has been talking about all along—activities and awareness that lead to, create, or enhance customer satisfaction.

Globe Metallurgical was pleased with a dual system it had instituted to reward hourly workers. It involved both monetary and nonmonetary rewards. The company quickly experienced a downside, however. It discovered that individual rewards led to disappointment in workers, who felt that their ideas were worth more than $1000, and created jealousy in co-workers, who felt that they should have shared in the pot. Globe changed its system to profit-sharing that pays each hourly worker exactly the same amount.

Recognition programs can be structured or stratified in a number of ways:

- By status of the award (from a president's quality award on down)
- By leadership, teamwork, or individual
- By contribution (e.g., technical competence or service to external or internal customers or to suppliers)

A particularly good idea is to reward *first-time* participation or achievement in a quality activity. Catching people the twentieth time they do the right thing suggests you have not been paying attention. Catching them the first time shows the company is alert and eager to show new employees that they are members of the team. Awards should be presented so that fellow employees are made aware of the recognition and so that honored employees receive appropriate accolades from management. Finally, something to look out for: while it is important and good to extol the virtues of customer service representatives, do not forget to share some of the glory with employees in less glamorous positions (e.g., receiving, credit evaluation, etc.). After all, their work helps run the business—do not make them feel like second-class citizens.

Employee Well-being and Morale

Describe how the company maintains a work environment conducive to the well-being and growth of all employees; summarize trends and levels in key indicators of well-being and morale.

A healthy, happy employee is apt to be a productive employee. That sounds like it should be stitched in needlepoint on a Baldrige Award seat cushion, and it suitably describes the ethos behind this examination item. Health and safety issues are examined here, along with professional growth and support services like counseling and recreational offerings. Most importantly, this item seeks to assess how a company defines *employee* satisfaction, and how it uses these findings to improve the quality of worklife.

Federal Express takes an extraordinarily active and prevention-based approach to promoting employee well-being. It was the first company, for example, to set standards for transporting infectious substances like blood. The first thing each new manager learns about is Federal Express's "Safe Practices" program. Employees learn how to work safely through training in a variety of safety issues: dangerous goods handling, lifting methods, and safe driving. Federal Express publishes its safety statistics every month, broken down into categories such as back injuries, ankle injuries, and so on. These reports lay the groundwork for root cause analyses by spotlighting most frequent injuries and accidents. One safety quality action team won an award not long ago for coming up with an on-line system to report employee injuries. Data from this improved reporting system helped reduce the number of employee injuries.

Employees value job security as much as job safety. The year before it won the Baldrige, Federal Express was praised for keeping 1300 employees on the job when its ZapMail service collapsed. The company was given "The Employer Responsiveness Award," one of six Corporate Conscience Awards given by the Council of Economic Priorities, for its policy of no layoffs. Likewise, Federal Express's Guaranteed Fair Treatment Procedure is generally recognized as world-class. The procedure affirms the employee's right to appeal any issue through a systematic review by progressively higher management levels. It provides feedback to senior executives regarding policies and operations as well as statistics for trend analysis on employee concerns. One example of a major human resource policy change was to standardize minimum job requirements to ensure fair assessment of employee qualifications in job applications.

11

The Fifth Pillar: Management of Process Quality

The Management of Process Quality *category examines the systematic processes the company uses to pursue ever-higher quality and company performance. Examined are the key elements of process management, including design management of process quality for all work units and suppliers, systematic quality improvement, and quality assessment.*

The *Management of Process Quality* category looks at a company's operating systems—specifically, the processes directly involved in producing and delivering the goods and services that have been selected through the organization's strategy formulation as outlined in the category *Strategic Quality Planning*. This chapter will consider how the processes that contribute to the production of the organization's wares are managed and improved.

The major questions in this category are:

- How are products and services designed to meet customer requirements?

- How are manufacturing or service-delivery processes controlled?
- How is the quality of systems, products, and services assessed and improved?
- How is the quality of business processes, support services, and suppliers ensured?

Companies that score well in this category (see Fig. 11-1) are strong in "process thinking." They have evolved beyond managing products or departments in isolation to managing the processes that combine activities across departments. Customers, suppliers, and the company are brought together in a common alignment. High-scoring companies develop comprehensive sets of measures to continually monitor the quality of their processes. They regularly evaluate the "fitness for use" of all their processes, practices, products, and services, with the never-ending, single-minded purpose of improvement. The quality of support services, business processes, the new product/service development cycle, and supplier quality are all ensured, assessed, and improved.

By contrast, companies that perform poorly in this category spend most of their time correcting mistakes rather than preventing them. Interfunctional cooperation is low; product/service concepts are "thrown over the wall" from marketing or the executive suite, first to engineering and then to manufacturing. Control and assessment processes are loosely regulated. There are no evaluation-change cycles; communication with support functions and suppliers is minimal.

Management of Process Quality is mostly about the prevention of errors. It provides a foundation for building quality into production by eliminating errors at the source. This is a huge category, covering a great deal of ground. It starts with the conversion of customer requirements into design features and then winds its way through process-quality assessment and control, and the quality of support services and suppliers. Naturally, there are many stops along the way to check for continuous improvement.

Design and Introduction of Quality Products and Services

Describe how new and/or improved products and services are designed and introduced and how processes are designed to meet key product and service quality requirements and company performance requirements.

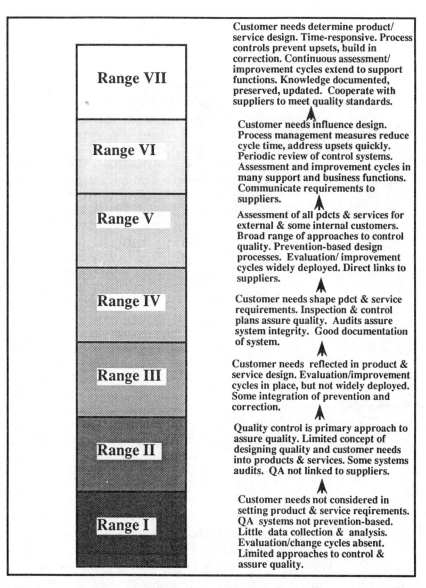

Customer needs determine product/ service design. Time-responsive. Process controls prevent upsets, build in correction. Continuous assessment/ improvement cycles extend to support functions. Knowledge documented, preserved, updated. Cooperate with suppliers to meet quality standards.

Customer needs influence design. Process management measures reduce cycle time, address upsets quickly. Periodic review of control systems. Assessment and improvement cycles in many support and business functions. Communicate requirements to suppliers.

Assessment of all pdcts & services for external & some internal customers. Broad range of approaches to control quality. Prevention-based design processes. Evaluation/ improvement cycles widely deployed. Direct links to suppliers.

Customer needs shape pdct & service requirements. Inspection & control plans assure quality. Audits assure system integrity. Good documentation of system.

Customer needs reflected in product & service design. Evaluation/improvement cycles in place, but not widely deployed. Some integration of prevention and correction.

Quality control is primary approach to assure quality. Limited concept of designing quality and customer needs into products & services. Some systems audits. QA not linked to suppliers.

Customer needs not considered in setting product & service reqirements. QA systems not prevention-based. Little data collection & analysis. Evaluation/change cycles absent. Limited approaches to control & assure quality.

Figure 11-1. The Fifth Pillar: Managing Process Quality (140 Points)

There are no shortcuts in quality design. The creation, testing, and modification of products and services requires a very structured, disciplined approach. Companies can luck their way to market success, once or twice, without a clear design-and-introduction plan. But a systematic approach, with a learning feedback loop, will ensure that errors are not repeated from one product or service launch to another. More importantly, a systematic approach will improve the quality of the designs themselves and reduce the length of the cycle time between design and introduction. Companies that frequently develop new products, such as those that produce consumer package-goods, need to have finely tuned design-and-introduction procedures. Even if a company does not frequently develop new products or services, it should have a process for continuously improving or enhancing existing ones.

Baldrige, quite appropriately, has created a separate item to deal with the important issues in this phase of quality assurance. The design-and-introduction process starts with the verification of the need for a new product or service and culminates with full-scale production. In the best companies, the design-and-introduction phase is characterized by extraordinary teamwork and cross-communication. Designs are reviewed and validated to keep the process on track and headed in the right direction.

Market Research

In the first stage of the design-and-introduction process, qualitative and quantitative market research must be performed to determine the need for a new product or service. Tools and techniques for determining market potential include informal talks with customers, customer-focus groups or "roundtables," customer surveys, attribute studies, and forecasting studies.

Customer requirements and expectations must be researched in depth to determine the best possible mix of product or service features. Possible designs are then reviewed by a task force—a multi-functional one, if possible—made up of people from marketing, manufacturing, engineering, finance, sales, human resources, and other relevant departments.

Issues related to health, safety, process capability, and supplier capability must also be addressed. Teamwork at this stage is essential to ensure that the constraints and ideas of all departments are taken into consideration. Suppliers and customers can also be brought into the process at this point in order to correct oversights or uncover flaws that might be overlooked or ignored by company personnel.

Analysis of Benefits and Costs

Next, all the benefits and associated costs of providing the product or service are evaluated. A proposal detailing product/service specifications, business risks (i.e., obsolescence or competition), and constraints (i.e., availability of resources to develop the project) is submitted to the person or committee with approval authority. This proposal sets forth a timetable for developing and testing the product or service, identifying key people who will be involved in the process, and outlining plans for introducing the product or service.

All "downstream" production and delivery factors should be thought of as elements in the design process. Each phase of the development process has a specific schedule. Each significant resource requirement is incorporated into overall planning, in order to ensure timely funding and availability. Customer education, employee hiring, procurement of facilities, documentation updates, software development, preparation of advertising materials, and other factors are all taken into consideration. A control plan is also developed. This plan details how the processes used to manufacture the product or deliver the service are to be measured and controlled and sets performance standards for each key variable of the manufacturing or service delivery process.

The human factor must also be taken into consideration. Training needs for operating personnel are evaluated simultaneously with other production and delivery factors. In response to a new legal requirement, for example, companies can develop a guide and train experts on the new requirement very early in the design process. These experts would then be available to answer technical questions from practitioners in the field.

The Need to Validate

Validation constitutes the next phase of the design-and-introduction process. It consists of verifying that external and internal product/service requirements have been met or, alternatively, establishing proof of process capability. Validation is extremely important; as Deming observed, inadequate testing of prototypes is one of the key obstacles to quality.[1]

Validation takes place at least twice during the design-and-introduction process: once during the "prototype" stage, which requires that new products and services be test marketed in controlled pilot programs, and once after the service or product has been fully rolled out. The determination of a test market is based upon questions such as, "Will test results from a local market indicate whether or not the service or product is likely to be accepted nationally?" The performance data collected from these pilot programs are used to validate and modify the prototype until each performance requirement is routinely met or exceeded. The data include a financial analysis, which helps to determine the potential return on investment and profit margin of the product/service. Feedback from customers and internal operators is used to fine-tune its features. Customer input is collected in the same way it was at the beginning of the development process—from surveys, focus groups, customer-contact employees, and so on. The impact of the new product or service on existing ones is then assessed. The data collected at this point provide a basis for monitoring the service after introduction.

Considering customer satisfaction with the new service or product, the company's capability to consistently deliver, and the financial impact, the product/service is either introduced in a phased rollout (a continuance of the testing phase) or in a general rollout to all customers. Monitoring and measuring is continued with the initial introduction and general rollout. Steady improvement in the quality of the design-and-introduction process is indicated by advances such as cycle-time reduction. Program timing-and-process bottlenecks are identified, and significant variances or delays are reviewed by operating personnel and project managers.

Cadillac's Design-and-Introduction Process

Cadillac uses an approach called simultaneous engineering to coordinate the many diverse tasks involved in conceptualizing, approving, producing, and continuously improving its cars. In the first phase of the program, vehicle concepts are developed, taking into consideration the needs and expectations of customers, business-plan objectives, and future product and process technologies. Vehicle teams study the concepts and convert them into actual production plans, which include a marketing strategy, vehicle criteria, manufacturing objectives, and so on. The exterior and interior designs are sent to Cadillac's "Customer Clinics" to test their acceptability. Process and product technologies are then identified and the concept receives official approval. In the next phase, "Product/Process Development and Prototype Validation," part characteristics and process requirements are described, vehicle prototypes are built and validated, and the manufacturing and assembly design is completed. Once the program is given final approval, it moves to the phase of "Process Validation and Product Confirmation." Here pilot vehicles are built from actual production tools. Once the assembly facilities are ready for production, and sale-and-service programs have been completed, the project enters the final phase, "Production and Continuous Improvement."

Product and Service Production and Delivery Processes

Describe how the company's product and service production and delivery processes are managed so that current quality and requirements are met and quality and performance are continuously improved.

Delivering customer satisfaction is a goal that is greatly emphasized but not always achieved. What dynamics stand in the way of customer satisfaction? If your company fails to follow through on its intended goals, it is quite likely that your processes are inherently incapable of meeting customer needs, as if you were using the Pony Express to deliver overseas mail. Or your customers's needs may have changed—suddenly, they want something better, faster, different, newer. Still another possibility is that your customers's perception of your company's products or services, compared to those of the competition, may have changed. Or your process may be capable of meeting customer needs but something, somewhere, is preventing that from happening.

If your processes are malfunctioning, you must fix them. Identify the root causes of your problem, make the correction, and bring the process into a state of *control,* in which goals or standards are consistently met. In this way, the quality of the output, whether it be goods or services, is maintained. The concept of control weighs heavily in the Baldrige criteria for two reasons. First, effective systems need to be maintained to prevent existing quality from unraveling. There is no immutable law of nature stating that once processes reach a high state of quality they will remain that way forever. In fact, the opposite is probably true. A good first law of quality control might be the second law of thermodynamics, which states that the natural tendency of things is to decay from order to chaos.

Likewise, it is necessary to bring processes under control, or into conformance with plans, before making systematic attempts to improve them. Factors that cause wild swings in variability and force a process to go "out of control" are like static from a radio receiver. It is impossible to understand the speaker or, in statistical terms, to judge the capabilities of the process. Therefore, nonsystemic factors ("static") must be eliminated and the process brought into conformance before systemic problems are attacked. Only then will it be possible to tell whether changes have the desired effect. This procedure is similar to eliminating the static on a radio and then adjusting the bass and treble to increase the quality of the sound.

Note, however, that some processes may not warrant improvement. A process that is "in control" and produces widgets to within 1/1000th of an inch, for example, may be perfectly acceptable if your customers are unwilling to pay for improvements that would yield tolerances on the order of 1/10,000th of an inch or better.

There is a classic, logical order to quality control. First, the objectives of the process are defined and product manufacture (or service delivery) commences. Next, the actual performance of the process is evaluated by measuring the most critical variables—in other words, those that have the greatest impact on the quality of the output. If problems are detected—that is, if operating standards are not being met—the problems are analyzed to determine the ultimate, or "root," cause(s) of error. Cause-and-effect, or "fishbone," diagrams are useful for identifying sources of error far "upstream" in the process. Solutions are then proposed and the best ones are implemented. Critical performance variables are checked again to ensure that standards are being met. If they are, the output of the process is once again predictable and the process itself has been returned to a state of control.

An excellent example of this quality control sequence is demonstrated by the following paraphrase of a Federal Express report detailing how a QAT (quality action team) evaluated persistent causes of customer dissatisfaction. This is a real case of a real problem, but the methodology is universal in its usefulness:

1. A problem statement was written so that all QAT members understood the task at hand.

2. The problem was analyzed to determine root causes. These causes were then categorized by type and by geographical location.

3. A Pareto diagram was drawn to identify the location that was the source of the greatest number of customer complaints.

4. Team members then visited the worst location to further analyze the problem and to begin formulating potential solutions.

5. An optimal solution was developed and tested at this worst location. For the next month, the location was monitored and trend data were collected.

6. Within one month after the final solution was implemented at this location, customer complaints had decreased significantly.

7. Consulting the Pareto diagram, the QAT identified the next four worst geographical locations relating to persistent customer dissatisfaction. The solution implemented at the former worst location was then implemented at these other locations.

8. This process continued until all locations within the country had been covered, and the corporate service-quality indicators reflected the improvement.

Product versus Service QA

The principles, tools, and techniques for process control can be found in almost any quality control handbook. For many processes, these techniques are quite straightforward and obvious. However, in the case of complex services such as consulting or health care, whose processes are often more complex and less amenable to quantitative analysis (and benchmarking) than are manufacturing processes, the path to control becomes less distinct.

Why the disparity? Manufacturing processes are often more measurable. Interaction of customers is a much more predictable affair. The transformation of raw materials is sequential and routinized. In services such as consulting, by contrast, processes constantly fluctuate in response to new information. Five bad parts per million in the manufacture of screws is a nice, neat concept. But how do you define five bad parts per million in advertising, investment banking, or hairstyling? Nevertheless, it is possible to set up *tolerance variables* against which to measure the acceptability and quality of a service, even if such measurement is based only on the subjective perceptions of customers (such as customer satisfaction or dissatisfaction).

A New York-based sales-training organization, TBA Resources, Inc., uses an approach to controlling service quality that is a model worth examining in some detail. TBA employs a "stepladder" of six training goals together with six measures of effectiveness. The first of these is participant satisfaction, and the top rung on the ladder is return on investment. TBA designates "critical success factors" (CSFs) that accompany each step. For instance, instructor charisma and market relevance are considered CSFs for achieving participant satisfaction, and management coaching and feedback are considered CSFs for on-the-job skill application (the fourth rung).

Achieving progressively higher performance goals requires greater commitment by a TBA client, who is free to choose a program that satisfies his or her particular need. Standards and measurement techniques change as training goals become more rigorous. For a client to qualify for level 6 (ROI), for example, a number of issues need to be considered: Is ROI a legitimate goal given the scope of service being provided? (ROI is measured for specific projects only and not for overall corporate performance.) Does the client have the skills to implement system recommendations? Will the client work with TBA and accept technical recommendations? (Client companies must accept TBA's recommendations for complete system changes, if necessary.) In addition, control groups must be made available for validation.

TBA uses conventional quality assurance techniques to keep its program on track. In the initial stages of project definition, the company and its clients work together to determine the exact training solution, types of skills desired, expectations, measurement systems, and completion dates for implementation and evaluation. These criteria then serve as the basis against which the success of the project is judged. During each phase of the project (every two months or as often as the client desires), TBA asks for written and verbal feedback from client representatives charged with evaluating the program's progress. A cross-section of participants, their managers, and project administrators are selected to form the Quality Assurance Steering Committee, which provides independent assessments. Evaluation questionnaires are *custom-designed* to the level of expectation previously agreed upon, and they reflect the respective roles and responsibilities specified at each stage of the project relationship. The questions allow for both numerical rating and written commentary, observations, and appraisal. TBA's approach works well for the kind of business in which it is engaged. Moreover, with a bit of tweaking and adapting, it is a good model for other service companies to use when creating their own quality assurance programs.

Quality Assessment

Describe how the company assesses the quality and performance of its systems, processes, and practices, and the quality of its products and services.

A company cannot simply mount the quality podium and announce, "Henceforth, we shall do this." Quality-minded companies must first consider whether it is *possible* to execute their quality-improvement plans and whether, in fact, they are doing so. Determining true capabilities and actual performance requires conducting a process review or assessment. The Baldrige criteria lay out an assessment strategy by questioning, "Who, what, when, and how?"

- *Who* performs the evaluation? Is it an employee, a team, or an outside auditor?
- *What* exactly is being evaluated and what type of evaluation is being performed?

- *How often* are measurements and assessments performed? It is useless to look at some data only at the end of every 12 months because you miss crucial fluctuations. You must check indicators frequently— daily, weekly, and monthly (some companies check *hourly*). Consider flowcharting and standardizing each production step or process. Conduct measurements three ways: first, on a routine basis (if you are a line manager, periodically sample actual transactions or batches of work); second, on a "surprise" or unscheduled basis; and third, in response to noticeable deterioration in any process measurement variable (e.g., response times, customer-inquiry rates, etc.).

- *How* are the accuracy and reliability of measurement or assessment tools ensured? For reliability's sake, you should independently verify market research studies performed by an outside vendor. For instance, you might want to call 10 percent of the customers surveyed to determine if the interviews were actually performed and to make sure the survey accurately conveyed the customer's response. Have an outside auditor check to ensure the accuracy of service measures.

When assessment findings indicate problems, root causes need to be identified and corrections made. In one company, whenever an assessment indicates a problem, the appropriate line manager investigates. Simple quality failures caused by explainable lapses in procedure or communication are resolved immediately. More complex quality failures are examined by quality-action teams. Senior managers are involved as needed and corrective actions are referred to the appropriate line managers. The teams follow up to verify that assessment findings are acted upon and that corrective actions are effective.

Remember that audits should be *customer-focused*. Output should be evaluated from your customer's point of view, since company personnel often overlook certain product or service design flaws. Frequent users of a company's products and services may also accept suboptimal quality as part of the price of doing business. To avoid these pitfalls, try bringing selected customers into the assessment process for their direct personal input.

Business Processes and Support Services

Describe how the company's business processes and support services are managed so that current requirements are met and quality and performance are continuously improved.

Other topics of concern in the *Management of Process Quality* category are the quality of internal business processes and support functions. These items are often the most neglected components of quality programs, but they are certainly not the least important. Business processes and support services include many disparate activities and operations: finance and accounting, software services, sales, marketing, information services, purchasing, personnel, legal services, plant and facilities management, research and development, and secretarial and other administrative services. Companies need to develop strategies, methods, and plans to increase and improve the participation of support services in quality activities. In general, you continuously improve support services by using the same tools and techniques that you use to improve your primary business processes: root-cause analysis, quality action teams, and the like.

Each support service should have its own quality-related policies, procedures, and manuals; formal training in quality tools and techniques; and quality audits, reviews, and surveys. Each support service should be represented in an executive-level quality council. In addition, each support service should be required to prepare an annual quality plan detailing how the service measures and monitors quality to its users, how it trains its personnel, what its goals are, and so on. A learning feedback loop should also be in place to ensure continuous quality improvement.

Supplier Quality

Describe how the quality of materials, components, and services furnished by other businesses is assured and continuously improved.

Supplier quality also plays a critical role in overall quality assurance. The use of outside goods and services can occur at any stage in the production and delivery of a company's products and services. The "old way" of obtaining outside goods and services was to play one supplier off against another, to negotiate on the basis of price, and to inspect incoming goods from top to bottom. However, this was a time-consuming and expensive procedure that did little to improve supplier quality. Baldrige-winning companies, by contrast, work closely with suppliers to establish precise quality standards. One prerequisite is that the supplier must share the company's customer-satisfaction philosophy. Supplier-quality techniques include requiring vendors to provide a control chart with each shipment of parts or materials to verify their conformance to the buyer's requirements.

Some companies require fully implemented quality procedures at vendors' facilities, including inspection of incoming material by the supplier, control measurements during each phase of manufacture, and final inspection prior to shipping. One tactic to consider is sending relevant company personnel a questionnaire requesting feedback about individual vendors and asking for suggestions on how to improve supplier quality. A relatively new technique is to require a guarantee, shifting the cost of defective goods and services back to suppliers and giving them a financial incentive to improve and sustain quality. Companies can also require their suppliers to provide access to facilities, equipment, personnel, and records as a way of ensuring quality. Vendors can also be required to allow the buyer's quality action teams to conduct performance assessments of supplier operations that involve the buyer. Some companies even assign a permanent on-site representative to monitor supplier quality. In turn, vendors are brought to the customer's facility to see its operation firsthand.

Some companies get intimately involved in the *design* of the supplier's products and services. Other companies include representatives from outside suppliers on their quality action teams. An "early-ship" program with vendors gives many top-notch companies the opportunity to develop training materials and obtain the latest technology prior to general availability. Documentation of supplier equipment failures and turnaround times should be available when future purchasing decisions are made. Vendor goods may be evaluated before purchase by interviewing actual users at another company. Some of the most effective supplier-quality programs work through incentives such as establishment of national accounts and supply agreements for long-term relationships.

Although a university is not a "vendor" in the same sense as a parts supplier—the university is independent, with its own separate agenda and mission, and its services are not "for sale"—it still benefits companies to work with institutions of higher education for better bilateral communication. As providers of critical material—in this case, trained personnel, research, and a forum for communications—universities should be recognized, rewarded, and otherwise made to feel "connected" to the fortunes of the companies they assist. Gifts, grants, scholarships, internships, and research funding are sometimes given to colleges and universities by professional-service firms who see these institutions as especially critical suppliers.

Companies must work with not only suppliers but also with distributors and dealers to set and achieve standards of quality. In the old days, companies had a hands-off attitude toward the level of performance at sales outlets and showrooms. Today's competitive atmosphere, however, breeds active involvement. Cadillac's field reps counsel dealers who have below-standard evaluations and work with them to implement action plans for improvement. Dealer performance is also regularly gauged through the GM Customer Satisfaction Index, which measures the degree to which customers are satisfied or dissatisfied with their dealership sales and service, the vehicle itself, and their overall ownership experience after six months.

Documentation Issues

Documentation control involves the creation of programs that preserve and transfer knowledge regarding customers, production, distribution, procurement, and the like. There are many kinds of documents: operating manuals, bulletins, newsletters, checklists, sign-off forms, applications, flowcharts, questionnaires, electronic mail, cassette tapes, manuals, computer printouts, charts, labels, placards, and so on.

Most companies produce too much documentation. The mountain of paperwork grows until no sane employee wants to tackle it. Documentation also has an unfortunate addictive effect on some individuals. Such people don't dare answer a question "off the top of their heads." They must look up the response in manuals and reports. Soon they are no longer able to think for themselves; the answer must be found in the documentation. We all know colleagues who "do everything by the book"—their creativity died a long time ago.

On the other hand, documentation is sometimes necessary. Without it, employees can be forced to improvise in tight situations. The wheel is reinvented again and again. Analysis is replaced by guesswork, and inconsistency and sloppiness cause expensive errors and even legal problems. Accurate documentation is also necessary as a source of information about raw materials and goods-in-progress. For example, manufacturers who want to know which parts are to be used for which equipment and who want to avoid mixing repaired items back into lots of unrepaired items need to keep accurate and easily accessible records.

In documentation, you should strive for simplicity. Documents should be sufficient in scope and detail to meet operational requirements, and they should be concise, clear, and up-to-date. A key consideration is the educational and interest level of the user (e.g., service technician). Remember that the user of this documentation is your customer (either an external or an internal one). Take a few moments to consider his or her needs!

Documents may be handwritten or computerized, although computers offer the advantages of easy input and retrieval. Many companies with 1–800 customer service numbers, for example, rely on automated databases for "boilerplate" responses to frequent inquiries. Important, time-sensitive publications can be distributed by electronic mail to geographically dispersed business units. Standard forms, once issued as hard-copy documents, can be incorporated into computer-based data files, easily accessible by employees using microcomputers and laser printers. Procedures for recording, filing, viewing, amending, canceling, or printing customer data can be designed in standard screen formats for easy on-line computer viewing. Companies such as USAA, a national insurance company, are using state-of-the-art image-processing techniques to facilitate document transfer and move toward the paperless office.

Documentation that is not accessible is useless. On the other hand, all documentation needn't be at everyone's fingertips every second. At the 1990 Quest for Excellence III Conference, Paul Vita of Wallace recalled with amusement how a site-visit team member, before he went back to the hotel for the night, asked for current charts updating the information regarding on-time delivery performance that Wallace had submitted with its application. As the examiner was speaking, Wallace's lead SPC coordinator silently rose from the table, went to a computer in the room and, in less than two minutes, before the examiner had finished asking for all the things he wanted the following morning, handed over three charts. "What are these?" the examiner asked. "These are the charts you just asked for."

12

The Sixth Pillar: Quality and Operational Results

The Quality and Operational Results
category examines the company's quality
levels and improvement trends in quality,
company operational performance, and
supplier quality. Also examined are
current quality and performance levels
relative to those of competitors.

Except for customer-service systems (described in the next and final category), most of your systems and processes thus far have been covered in the criteria. If your quality program is on track, your systems and processes should meet all the requirements outlined by Baldrige for "approach": they should be *prevention-based; appropriate* in terms of tools, techniques, and methods; *systematic;* and so on. Each system should be *deployed* to all relevant areas of the company. In other words, you should be completely and thoroughly process-oriented, and all of your quality-improvement efforts should aim at preventing errors upstream in the production or service-delivery process. High-quality goods and services will follow naturally. So—if processes are everything and you have assessed and improved processes throughout your organization— why does Baldrige care about your results?

The Importance of Demonstrating Results

Your results are your bottom line. It is hard for examiners to know from your descriptions alone how good process improvements are. Saying one improvement sounds wonderful and another sounds pretty good are subjective judgments. Who can say precisely how good a system is from a mere description? This is where results are valuable. Quantified results make it easier to judge system quality. If a particular system produces good results, chances are that it is a good system. Recognizing this, the application gives more weight to Quality and Operational Results than to any other category except Customer Focus and Satisfaction. As a general rule of thumb, the Baldrige criteria have weighted the scoring system so that about 50 percent of all points are allocated to questions inquiring about approaches and systems and the other 50 percent are allocated to items seeking data and results.

Results neatly summarize the passage of quality improvements from approach, to deployment, to final outcomes. In fact, some examiners skim the results category first and then read the sections where the relevant systems are discussed. This might be likened to a financial analyst whose eye immediately tracks to the bottom line of a profit-and-loss statement to review profits before carefully inspecting the revenue and cost structures. If the system looks good but results are bad, the examiner will look for some sort of explanation: the economy, new regulations, poor implementation or deployment of the system, environmental factors, and so on. If the system does not look all that good but the results are stellar, examiners must consider what is causing the results: Is it plain good fortune, or, upon further examination, is the system more effective or innovative than it appeared on first inspection?

Internal data also verify progress toward customer satisfaction. Indeed, quality results of the kind requested in this category are usually strong predictors of customer satisfaction. If there is a gap between the two, the company and examiners can look for reasons why.

Finally, results show you mean business. A well-documented set of results indicates that a company is laying the groundwork for continuous improvement. To assess progress, results are compared against goals. Results also demonstrate that the company is measuring and tracking its systems. Since you cannot "manage" what you do not measure, well-documented operational and quality results are evidence that you are attempting to manage your processes and systems. If there are gaps in the result trends, learn why, and devise corrective actions. If results show steady progress and improvement, the systems are probably in control and producing the desired effects. Press on, perhaps setting even more ambitious plans and goals for improvement.

Showing quality results is not an easy business, but by carefully organizing them they are easier to address. The Baldrige criteria group results into four sections: product and service quality; business processes and support-services quality; operational results, including financial data; and supplier quality. Note that process results are also requested in other categories like Human Resources and Customer Focus and Satisfaction. In scoring this category, a company must pass muster in five separate areas: absolute quality levels, improvement trends, benchmarks, competitive comparisons, and company goals. The company also has the chance to note and explain any adverse trends or "blips" in its data. What examiners do not want to see is volatility. A steady, sustained upward course is the surest indicator that continuous improvement is underway. The longer the period of results, the better; there should be at least three years of trend data. If only short-term data is available, say so; you can phrase it something like:"...nevertheless, on a month-by-month basis...."

Signs of Success and Failure

Companies that do well in this category (see Fig. 12-1) demonstrate achievements in most major areas, sustained over the past three to five years. Results are directly related to quality practices and data are presented for all major quality indices. Companies that do poorly can be detected in a variety of ways. They typicaliy show isolated, spotty examples of improvement, often in core operations. These same companies almost always fall down trying to show that their business processes and support services are improving. If companies have indifferent or arms-length relationships with suppliers, it quickly shows up in their results—or their lack of results—in this area. The quality of competitive and benchmark data is generally poor. Leading quality indicators are not identified. Vague narrative descriptions, sometimes known as "weasel wording"—for example, "...our canning process shows significantly better results than those of our competitors...."—are substituted for hard, demonstrable data.

Rules of Thumb

If you want to win with Baldrige, you must be able to demonstrate quality and operational results. In presenting data, ask yourself, "What form is going to make it easy for examiners or managers to read and understand?" Several guidelines can be followed to present information in this category as strongly as possible. They can be boiled down to four rules of thumb: be selective, provide comparisons, be clear and specific, and explain adverse trends. Discussing them one by one is useful.

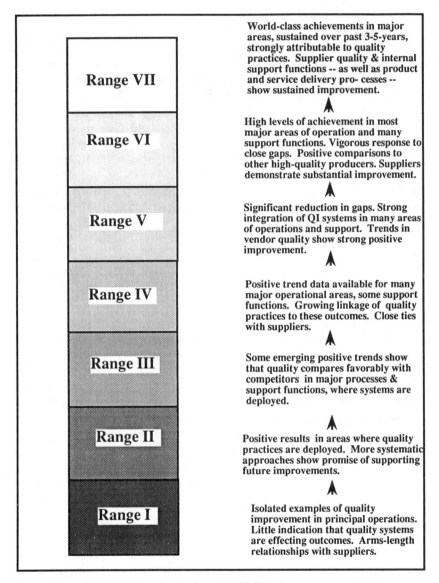

Figure 12-1. The Sixth Pillar: Quality Results (180 Points)

Be Selective. Baldrige examiners realize that the appropriateness of a company's metrics (how many and what kinds) depends on factors such as company size, types of products and services, and competitive environment. Explain clearly which key quality measures you are using. Don't overdo it. Measures can easily number in the hundreds. Because of limited space in a Baldrige assessment, companies need to be selective, narrowing the number down to an elegant few, concentrating on the most important quality indicators, and summarizing the rest. Eliminate the haystack and reveal the needle. This is critical. Companies that fail to winnow their data down to a manageable number of precise, prioritized measurements are missing the whole point of Baldrige's call to focus and alignment. They are saying, "Look at all this data, and tell us we're not excellent." The examiners' response will be, "No, you show *us* the measures that properly demonstrate your excellence." Demonstrate that your strategies, goals, and measures are tightly interconnected and aligned as one system. Then an examiner can feel comfortable that the results data you have gathered reflect an organization that is properly functioning and aware of how well (or how poorly) it is performing at any given moment.

When describing product and service quality results, stress those features that most directly influence customer satisfaction, and those that address critical quality requirements—reliability, accuracy, durability, timeliness, and so forth. When describing intracompany quality results, stress those characteristics that represent quality and effectiveness in meeting requirements of customers in other company units (i.e., your internal customers). The quality of data received by the accounting department, for instance, would be a critical variable for most companies. When describing supplier quality results, stress the impact of quality-improvement initiatives outlined in the item "Supplier Quality" in the Management of Process Quality category.

In its 1990 application summary, for instance, Cadillac stated that, since the 1987 implementation of its Targets of Excellence program, the number of new production parts approved on schedule had increased by 21 percent. The number of suppliers delivering just-in-time had increased by 425 percent since 1986.

Provide Comparisons. Without some point of comparison, either from competitors, world-class performers, or internal goals and reference points, there is no way for examiners—or the company, for that matter—to assess how well or how poorly it is performing. Competitive data, benchmarks, and goals provide the frame of reference examiners need for evaluating results, and they also lay the foundation for continuous improvement. As with other results, you should describe your company's competitive comparisons, benchmarks, and goals in terms of the key quality indicators outlined in the overview of your business and throughout the rest of the application.

The number and quality of comparisons is a key factor in scoring this category. Applicants will note that there is an extremely close relationship between this category and the "Benchmarks and Competitive Comparisons" item in the "Information & Analysis" category. In that item, the scope, source, and frequency of measure of major competitive comparisons and benchmarks were described. This data should be tightly cross referenced with the "Results" section.

Be Clear and Specific. All information in this category should be clearly and concisely presented. Accompanying explanatory text should relate strictly to the interpretation of data—something along the lines of, "Inventory data accuracy improved 14 percent in twelve months after switching from centralized APICS system to local networked PCs." Rhetorical expressions ("... our performance is world-class....") are acceptable, but they should be credible and should be sparingly used. Do not use adjectives you cannot back up with numbers and other types of hard data.

Data does not all have to be numeric, incidentally. Claims of superior performance can also be supported by citing major awards and recognition. Some results can be stated without numeric evidence, for example, "delivery data are on-line and continuously updated; the report is so accurate that our three largest customers have stopped tracking our performance independently and now go by our own delivery reports." For reasons of space and easy readability, as much data as possible should be presented in the form of charts and graphs, accompanied by a brief explanation of what the numbers represent and the significance of the results. Exhibits should be clearly labeled and backed up with explanatory text. If possible, put the text and accompanying exhibit on the same page. Data should be scaled, not binary. "Satisfactory" and "unsatisfactory" ratings do not count for much. Indeed, in the world of continuous improvement, where progress is measured incrementally, results need to be calibrated very carefully.

Explain Adverse Trends. Examiners do not expect every trend to be positive every year. However, adverse trends do need to be explained, and countermeasures given. For example, the acquisition of a poorly performing business unit, if it led to poor results, could be explained in terms such as: "The acquisition dropped our average trend for a year, but we expect the unit to turn around as quality systems are installed." Bad things do happen to good companies, and there may be a very plausible explanation for some adverse trends. If a company installs an

800 hotline to field customer comments, for example, it can expect a jump in the number of complaints. Make points like these clear in the written report.

Carefully documented results can spur a company to intelligent action. One professional-service company, when confronted with slippage in its service-quality trend indicators, took forceful steps to turn the situation around. The firm identified those units that accounted for most of its unsatisfactory ratings, and developed special training programs to reverse the negative trend. It also screened all its clients to determine whether any of them had unreasonable expectations about the level of service the firm was able to provide.

To those who wonder why the Baldrige framework is so concerned about processes, the fixation with results may seem a contradiction. But to those who have worked the Baldrige criteria and seen the usefulness of results in gauging the success of a total quality plan and its supporting processes, results are indispensable.

13

The Seventh Pillar: Customer Focus and Satisfaction

The Customer Focus and Satisfaction category examines the company's relationship with customers and its knowledge of customer requirements and of the key quality factors that determine marketplace competitiveness.

The Baldrige saves its most important category for last. Customer Focus and Satisfaction tops every other category in point value—300, to be exact, or 30 percent of the total. Getting to this spot in the assessment framework is not easy. It requires companies to move beyond the narrow internal definition of quality ("conformance to internal specifications") and to define quality afresh, from the customer's point of view.

A mistake many businesses make is thinking of Customer Focus and Satisfaction in too isolated, too discrete a form, as if it were merely a category, merely a "pillar" to pass on their way to achieving other business objectives. That kind of thinking is too constricted. Customer Focus and Satisfaction must become the culmination of all your quality improvement efforts. Think of the customer relationship as a living sponge might think of sea water. It should be so familiar, so ubiquitous a concern, so much a part of every moment of business life, that it cannot possibly be seen as external or incidental. "Satisfaction" is a very broad concept—it involves understanding everything that matters to external customers (internal customers are addressed in the Management of Process Quality category) and considering every aspect of their relationship with the company from the moment they purchase a good or service to the moment when, as customers, they have a complaint and come forward demanding compensation. Customer satisfaction in the simple sense of the phrase is just the beginning. For companies to meet the broad criteria of Baldrige, their "customer sat" processes and results have to go on to provide feedback for the continuous improvement of each preceding item in the Baldrige scheme—Leadership, Information and Analysis, Strategic Quality Planning, and so on.

Baldrige winners know better than anyone how central customer satisfaction is to their winning. They are on record, company after company, as establishing customer satisfaction as the cornerstone of their quality strategies. Federal Express's Customer Satisfaction Policy states, "The most fundamental service objective of Federal Express is to have a satisfied customer at the conclusion of each transaction." In like spirit, Cadillac's mission statement concludes, "...Cadillac will continuously improve the quality of its products and services to meet or exceed customer expectations...." Other Baldrige winners, too, take the concept of customer satisfaction as their personal mantra.

Essentials of Customer Satisfaction

The most salient characteristic of companies that do well in this category (see Fig. 13-1) is that they are relentless in collecting data on customers. They are knowledgeable about competitors' customers, and they compare their customer-satisfaction ratings with those of the competition. Companies that score well in this category are also experts in cultivating long-term relationships with customers and giving them easy access to comment, seek assistance, and even complain. These companies create "safety nets" in the form of comprehensive warranties and guarantees. Companies scoring well in Customer Focus and Satisfaction also show innovation in their use of tools and techniques. Wallace uses a technique called Failure Mode and Effects Analysis (FMEA) to evaluate all its customer-service processes as a way of anticipating problems and preventing errors. FMEA, which was originally used in manufacturing settings, is a way of prioritizing processes in a company by looking at three factors: severity of the effects of a process upset on customers, how often it occurs, and the probability of detecting an error *before* it affects customers. Each factor is rated on a 1 (inconsequential) to

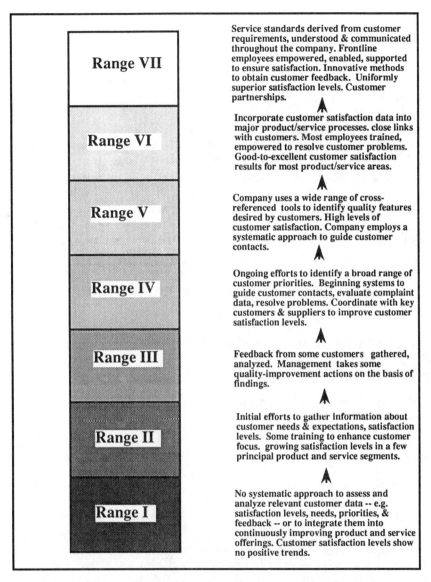

| Range VII | Service standards derived from customer requirements, understood & communicated throughout the company. Frontline employees empowered, enabled, supported to ensure satisfaction. Innovative methods to obtain customer feedback. Uniformly superior satisfaction levels. Customer partnerships. |

Incorporate customer satisfaction data into major product/service processes. close links with customers. Most employees trained, empowered to resolve customer problems. Good-to-excellent customer satisfaction results for most product/service areas.

Company uses a wide range of cross-referenced tools to identify quality features desired by customers. High levels of customer satisfaction. Company employs a systematic approach to guide customer contacts.

Ongoing efforts to identify a broad range of customer priorities. Beginning systems to guide customer contacts, evaluate complaint data, resolve problems. Coordinate with key customers & suppliers to improve customer satisfaction levels.

Feedback from some customers gathered, analyzed. Management takes some quality-improvement actions on the basis of findings.

Initial efforts to gather information about customer needs & expectations, satisfaction levels. Some training to enhance customer focus. growing satisfaction levels in a few principal product and service segments.

No systematic approach to assess and analyze relevant customer data -- e.g. satisfaction levels, needs, priorities, & feedback -- or to integrate them into continuously improving product and service offerings. Customer satisfaction levels show no positive trends.

Fig. 13-1. The Seventh Pillar: Customer Focus and Satisfaction (300 Points)

10 (severe) scale. For example, a process upset that could result in death or injury of a customer rates a 10. Similarly, any process upset that could occur at any time might rate a 10 on the frequency scale. A risk-priority number for each process is determined by multiplying all three numbers. Speaking at the Quest for Excellence II Conference, Paul Vita, Wallace's director of National Accounts and Chairman of its Customer Service Quality Strategic Objective Team, called FMEA "Wallace's best quality tool." Vita said that he wished they had discovered it earlier in their quality-improvement effort when it would have helped prioritize their entire program.

Companies that do poorly in this category usually do not understand that performance ratings of their products and services differ widely by market segment. They do not do a very good job of segmenting the market and differentiating their products or services. They generally take a very short-term view of customer relationships, and they do not have systems, like complaint resolution, to collect and aggregate post-transaction data. As a consequence they deprive themselves of an extremely rich source of market information.

Determining Your Customers's Future Requirements and Expectations

Describe how the company determines future requirements and expectations of customers.

The first, most vital step on the road to customer satisfaction is to identify customer requirements. Since most companies offer a range of products and services, analyses should be structured to obtain information that is as specific as possible to particular product or service features. The information you obtain on customer requirements is absolutely critical. It is not only useful in itself, but it helps ignite other categories. Information gathered at this stage is fed back into Strategic Quality Planning, where priorities are assigned to various quality initiatives, and into "Design and Introduction," where requirements are translated into specific product and service features.

There are three areas of concern in this item: how customer data and market information are determined, including the process for collecting market information directly from customers and competitors's customers by surveys, interviews, or other means; how the company projects into the future what products, services, and special features customers will require; and how the company evaluates and improves its processes for determining customer requirements.

Successful Market Segmentation

Although the Baldrige does not specifically address strategy issues, such as what business your company should be in, the segmentation criteria touch on the importance, to your company and to market profitability, of properly identifying important customer groups. Segmentation is what people mean when they talk about market "niches"—satisfying the needs of particular customer segments, each of which perceives your company's products and services differently. The message here is, "One size does *not* fit all." If you are not being precise in meeting customer needs, you are leaving yourself wide open to competitors who can.

Financial impacts of market segments, considering customers' perceptions of quality levels, are quantified as part of the segmentation step. A frequently used technique is Pareto analysis, which groups customers according to who contributes the most profits or revenues to a business. A Pareto analysis might show, for instance, that 20 percent of the customers account for 80 percent of the sales, or profits. Obviously, those customers must be the primary target of your company's drive to provide satisfaction. The Pareto analysis is not to be used as an excuse for ignoring the remaining 80 percent—they are important, too, and must be attended to. However, Pareto analysis points clearly in the direction of your business's greatest self-interest.

Customer requirements and profitability are not the only factors that vary from one segment to another. Competition, economic stability, and even the methods used to sell products and services—all can vary by customer segment, geographic region, industry, and business. It becomes very complicated very quickly. To appreciate these differences, information from each step of the segmentation process has to be analyzed to develop criteria for the next level of segmentation until you have enough data to assess a market opportunity.

One Baldrige Winner's Segmentation Approach

At IBM Rochester, the segmentation process begins by gathering data from around the world. Sources for this data include government demographic information, consultants' reports, university studies, economic forecasts, and feedback from owners of IBM equipment. IBM Rochester then segments each geographical area into six industrial classifications: process, health, finance, manufacturing, distribution, and miscellaneous. Each of these is subdivided into small, medium, and large business establishments, subindustries, and specific "application-opportunity" segments. For instance, the distribution industry can be divided into businesses of various sizes, as well as wholesale, retail, and specialty subindustries. The retail subindustry is divided into specific opportunity segments—drug stores (small, medium, and large), auto parts (small, medium, and large), and hard goods stores (small, medium, and large). With the aid of industry consultants, academic experts, and its own market planners, IBM Rochester evaluates each market segment, taking into consideration its growth rate and whether the company's products and services fit that market. This analysis is performed using a decision-support tool called Analytical Hierarchy Process that mathematically compares the relative strengths of each market segment with IBM's ability to serve it. From this analysis, target markets are then selected.

Having selected customer segments that represent the most viable opportunities, IBM then identifies specific product and service features in detail. Tools like conjoint analysis are used to evaluate features within four strategic categories: product, software applications, service and support, and marketing channels. Product/service features are ranked by relative importance within each category, weighed against the resources needed to achieve those goals, and prioritized into short- and long-term plans—the same operating plans developed as part of IBM Rochester's overall strategic quality plan. Operating plans are validated and adjusted, if necessary, through a wide variety of means—customer councils, feedback from the field, and cross-comparisons with informal data such as complaints.

Segmentation at Federal Express

Other Baldrige winners take similar approaches to identifying and prioritizing customer requirements. Federal Express, for example, uses a two-step market-research process to identify product and service quality features and the relative importance of these features to customers. From this information, it projects future needs. The process starts with extensive qualitative research—customer-focus groups or in-depth unstructured personal interviews—that help identify the general features of the service and help the company understand just why these features are important to customers. Federal Express then conducts research to quantify customer preferences for features of the product or service being considered. Questions are developed to measure the relative importance of these features. For example, in its Collect-on-Delivery study, customers evaluate 22 features of service and are asked to rate their importance on a five-point scale, ranging from "very important" to "not important at all." Cross-comparisons using complaints, gains and losses of customers, and service-level performance data help refine the service design. A systematic, ongoing internal review process, including management review and dedicated quality-action teams, ensures continuous improvement of surveys and analytical techniques. In addition to all this, Federal Express maintains a constant stream of communications with customers through comment cards, surveys, market studies, and recorded conversations with customer-service personnel.

Other Segmentation Approaches

Cadillac prides itself on the thoroughness of its customer orientation, exploring every avenue to identify, understand, and meet the requirements of its customers. Their determination extends to even the smallest details such as the design of license plate holders. Through a series of segmentation schemes and other market-research techniques, Cadillac first determines who its customers are, what their wants and needs are, and what criteria they use in making a purchase decision. The division diligently explores every possible product feature for improvement. Simultaneous Engineering teams then translate data into technical specifications, and this information is used in making decisions about product design and content priorities. Cadillac validates new vehicle concepts by collecting feedback in product-and-feature clinics and customer councils, which bring current vehicle owners and team members together to talk about product satisfaction and areas for improvement.

Wallace Company uses an unusual constellation of segmentation techniques. One is its network of outside salespeople, which Wallace links together as "listening posts" to report on customers. Wallace also uses four different kinds of customer surveys, ranging from "one-minute" questionnaires for assessing customer requirements and satisfaction to annual "blind" surveys conducted by a third-party market-research firm. Wallace has also created "partnering" relationships with some of its industrial customers to give both sides the chance to learn every pertinent aspect of each other's operations. Wallace also came up with the concept of a "Tri-Level Task Force," a group that brings different constituents together so that all the elements of a complete distribution sandwich— manufacturers, distributor (Wallace), and end users—are represented. The task force idea enables primary suppliers to hear, first hand, and all at once, the needs of their end-user customers.

Whatever the approach used in this section of the criteria (and a dedicated market research department is not always necessary), companies need to consider the *quality* of customer-related data as well as *quantity*.

Customer satisfaction is, after all, enormously complex. The rule of thumb here is that the more sources of high-quality data a company uses, the clearer its customer portrait will be, the faster the company will be able to adapt to changes in the marketplace, and the better it will be in anticipating needs before its customers—or its competitors—can articulate them.

Customer Relationship Management

Describe how the company provides effective management of its relationships with its customers and uses information gained from customers to improve customer relationship management strategies and practices.

What is the ideal customer relationship most like? In a 1983 article published in the *Harvard Business Review,* Theodore Levitt likened the relationship between a seller and a buyer to marriage.

> The sale...merely consummates the courtship, at which point the marriage begins. How good the marriage is depends on how well the seller manages the relationship. The quality of the marriage determines whether there will be continued or expanded business, or troubles and divorce.[1]

Levitt's insights on relationship management have enormous implications for customer retention, as well as for the strategy of a quality-minded company. As he points out, products and services are too complicated, repeat negotiations too much of a hassle and too costly, and markets too competitive, for buyers and sellers to just walk away from each other after the first transaction. "The era of the one night stand is gone," Levitt intones. "Marriage is both necessary and more convenient."[2]

Baldrige as Marriage Counselor

Sellers are obviously interested in making the first big sale. Customer loyalty and resale opportunities, however, depend on staying in touch with buyers—keeping abreast of changes in their business, how those changes will affect sellers, and how competitors might try to break up the "marriage" with new products, improved features, and better prices. Sellers must not permit themselves to be distracted from the great goal of business, which is customer satisfaction. Their appetite for new and more detailed information about customers must be insatiable and obsessive. Unlike customers, sellers should never be satisfied with the relationship. Sellers should always seek to know: How does the customer feel? What is the customer thinking? What will the customer want tomorrow? Is performance up to the customer's expectations? Has the relationship changed in some way without the company realizing it?

For their part, customers are also interested in what happens after a transaction takes place. They are understandably preoccupied with after-sale issues, such as installation, learning how to operate the equipment or use the product, parts availability, maintenance, and so forth. David A. Garvin of the Harvard Business School notes that, as customers have become more quality-conscious, price has given way as the preeminent purchase consideration to total life-cycle costs, including expenditures on service and maintenance over time.[3]

In other words, in a healthy customer-supplier relationship the two parties are yoked together because they need one another. In a proper relationship both the buyer and seller will benefit or the relationship will not last.[4] But the marriage analogy isn't perfect, because the partners are not quite equal. The seller carries the greater burden of responsibility for continuing satisfaction.

Historically Baldrige has had only one item titled "Customer Relationship Management." But the commitment is broader than that. In truth, three concepts—customer-service standards, commitment, and complaint resolution—all have relationship management as their general theme. These three combined form a comprehensive set of criteria that companies can use to judge the quality of their customer relationship-management systems, as well as subprocesses for assessment and continuous improvement. (Alternatively, a company can treat these concepts as a set of tools for setting up a relationship-management program.)

Going the Extra Mile for Customers

How important are relationships to the Baldrige? Every winner can point to the genuine partnerships it has formed with its customers. Wallace's "partnering" meetings were discussed earlier in the context of determining customer requirements. However, these relationships also include problem solving and work sharing. These efforts are very valuable to customers—if Wallace is expediting product delivery and providing status reports, then partners don't have to waste time continually checking their orders. In addition, because there is no way to get 100 percent error-free service if customers make mistakes, Wallace helps partners resolve problems at the receiving end. Many of the creative ideas from partnering teams are improving processes for the entire customer base.

Federal Express truly sees itself as part of a "quality partnership," and it devotes considerable resources toward improving service and helping customers. For example, Federal Express once agreed to make multiple pick-ups at a customer's docks. Federal Express also generated custom, preprinted airbills for each of a customer's locations. It set up a special computer sort just for that customer so that all airbills were identified by department, which helped the customer with its internal billing. Setting up this individual arrangement took a little extra effort from Federal Express, but once it was set up, it ran smoothly. Going the "extra mile" made a profound impression on the customer and set a high standard for service throughout the company.

One of the first customer-relationship management systems in which companies should invest is one that makes it as easy as possible for customers to seek assistance and to comment. By the same token, companies need to set up procedures for executives and employees to follow-up with customers to determine satisfaction with recent transactions and to seek data for improvement. This two-way flow of information creates an interdependency that benefits both buyers and sellers.

Use the Telephone

Baldrige winners rely most heavily on telephone systems—like twenty-four hour, seven-days-a-week, toll-free "hot lines"—to ensure easy access. Federal Express even has a toll-free number for the hearing-impaired and an automated call distribution system for smoothing out demand peaks, relaying calls to the first available agent at any one of its 18 call centers. Cadillac, never to be outdone, has 21 different toll-free numbers that customers and dealers can use. All employees are invited to listen to recorded calls to acquire a sensitivity to what customers are telling the company about its products.

At IBM Rochester, the Customer Partnership Call process thanks customers for purchasing AS/400 systems. Calls are made 90 days after systems are shipped, and customers are asked what they like about the system, what they dislike, and what suggestions they might have for improvement. These comments are then compiled into a database, analyzed, and distributed regularly to engineering, programming, marketing, manufacturing, and service teams to guide them in their work.

Have you tried requiring your employees to call customers on a regular basis? Even when customers are not complaining, call them anyway. Get inside their heads, let them know that you are thinking about them.

Senior management should be involved, too—they should be spending time, via phone or in person, with the company's top customers, letting them know that their needs are important. (Does that ring a bell? Talking with customers on a regular basis was one of the requirements discussed in the very first category, Leadership. Now, in the final category, it appears again.) Each customer contact should be logged and described. Write-ups should be reviewed by senior management and circulated throughout the company, so employees in all areas are aware of the customer's relationship with the company. Depending on the frequency and nature of transactions with a particular customer, the company should consider assigning primary and secondary account representatives to make sure all areas in the customer's total relationship are covered.

The Importance of Training

Of course, when a company commits to this kind of intensive communication with customers, training and support for customer-contact personnel are of paramount importance. These people, after all, are the first, and sometimes the company's only, line of contact. To your customers, they *are* the company, and the entire organization is judged according to their performance. The Baldrige criteria go into great detail on human-resource requirements for this very select group of employees: hiring, training, career path, evaluation, logistical support, reward and recognition, and so on. Just as pilots have to demonstrate their proficiency every six months, so customer-contact employees at Federal Express must take "recurrency training" annually. (This also helps to determine their merit increase or, if they are at the top of their range, what their bonus will be.) Federal Express even gives a two-day behavioral and training workshop to managers who assess the company's customer-service agents and their interactions with customers. Empowerment, discussed in Human Resource Development and Management, is an especially important concern for customer-contact personnel who must work through recovery situations.[5] Cadillac dealers can use their own judgment in warranty disputes. At Federal Express, some customer-contact employees are empowered to make refunds of $250 or more. And at Motorola, the amount is as much as $1000.

Customer Service Standards

Empowerment picks up where customer service standards leave off. Indeed, at the heart of successful customer-relationship management must be a set of rigorous, well thought-out standards. What are service standards? They are measurable levels of performance that define the quality of interaction, that is, direct contact between a company and its customers. Some examples of this are measures of response time (e.g., to customer queries and complaints), accuracy, and the conduct and dress of customer-contact personnel.

Cadillac is very diligent in the area of setting service standards. For example, the company pits itself against 261 standards in its annual dealer service evaluation, measuring dealers' customer satisfaction and service-operation effectiveness. Cadillac also offers a rigorous certification program honoring dealers who meet and maintain stringent service and customer satisfaction standards. In filling in the service standards section in the application, ask these questions:

- Does your company have a system for tracking compliance with service standards? Are results publicized throughout the company? Federal Express uses its internal television network, FXTV, to communicate standards and performance on standards. (Remember to report historical trend data in the Quality and Operational Results category.)

- Does your company benchmark and use competitive comparisons when it sets standards?

- Are appropriate standards deployed to all relevant units?

- Are standards objectively measurable?

- Are standards assessed and upgraded periodically? Customer contact-personnel should be involved in developing, evaluating, and improving the standards that they are required to meet. Customer service agents at Federal Express asked to have the data item "customer-handle" time removed from their productivity ratings, so that they could concentrate on the *quality* of customer interaction, rather than the amount of *time* it took. It was a good idea, and management implemented their suggestion.

Technology—databases, on-line computer libraries, computer networks, and so on—can be used very effectively to track conformance to customer-service standards. Wallace Company uses an on-line paperless expediting system to provide delivery status to customers, a material-test report scanning system to instantaneously retrieve data that gives the exact chemical composition of pipes and valves, and a generic part-numbering system to provide almost immediate response to customer requests. Federal Express uses extensive computer systems and a proprietary "SuperTracker" technology to help its thousands of customer-service personnel track packages and letters. Automatic devices track packages and provide information directly to customers at their sites. Computerized customer-account information gives employees quick answers to basic account questions. Wallace Company utilizes a sophisticated customer-profiling system, containing the minutia on customer accounts such as number of invoices required, part numbering, and tagging requirements.

Commitment to Customers

Describe the company's explicit and implicit commitments to customers regarding its products and services.

Promises to customers—warranties and guarantees—are extremely effective quality-improvement tools. When meaningfully deployed, they compensate customers for service and product failures, and they also provide valuable data on product and service failures that can be put to use improving quality. Wallace stands out among pipe/valve and fitting distributors because it is the only one offering a written money-back, service-performance warranty package that goes beyond the usual terms of the manufacturers for which it distributes. Wallace's warranty promises partnering customers that on-time delivery performance will not drop below 98 percent. The industry average for all products in distribution is 86.3 percent; Wallace's direct competitors are averaging 78 percent on time. Federal Express is famous for its Money-Back Guarantee, which refunds or credits customers full transportation charges if the shipment is even 60 seconds late. Cadillac has extended warranty coverage on the total car to four years or 50,000 miles. On the Allante, it is seven years or 100,000 miles. None of Cadillac's warranties requires the customer to pay a deductible. (Incidentally, Cadillac's warranty costs for the first 12 months or 12,000 miles actually decreased more than 29 percent between 1986 and 1990!)

Companies can express their commitments in other ways, too—through the kinds of partnering relationships discussed earlier and through free, supplementary services. Federal Express installs POWERSHIP, an automated shipping device, free for its customers. It also provides, free to customers, assistance in designing packaging materials for objects that are difficult to pack, saving some customers up to $1500 a day in fees that would have to be spent for the services of an outside laboratory. The bottom line is that quality means assuming greater risks on your customer's behalf. However, the risk is coupled with a tremendous payoff in customer loyalty and retention.

Complaint Resolution

Complaints used to be treated as necessary evils that companies had to endure. Today they are eagerly sought after as golden opportunities to learn and to improve the system (so-called "golden nuggets"). This is why Baldrige winners systematically collect, analyze, and track trends in customer complaints, why they very aggressively use this information for cross-comparative purposes, and why they even measure customers' satisfaction in terms of complaint handling.

IBM Rochester performed a study in which it measured three complaint variables: customers' perception of problem resolution, the likelihood of their recommending an IBM system to others, and the likelihood of their purchasing an IBM system in the future. Ninety-two percent of those who had problems, but who were satisfied with the resolution, said they would purchase an IBM system in the future. Ninety-four percent said they would recommend an IBM system to others. Of those who had a problem and who were still dissatisfied, only 46 percent said they would purchase in the future, and only 48 percent said they would recommend a system. The study concluded with a classic good news/bad news scenario. The good news was that satisfied customers would tell three other people. The bad news was that dissatisfied customers would tell seven other people. The key to satisfaction was that customers needed to know that the company was responding to their problems and spending time communicating with them. After processing this data, IBM Rochester looked at its own forecasts, current customer base, and current satisfaction levels and made a remarkable calculation. They estimated that if they could increase overall satisfaction by a mere 1 percent, they would increase revenue by $257 million. There are few more convincing statistics for the power of incremental improvement!

IBM Rochester also uses a complaint-management process that links marketing and service teams to development and manufacturing teams. The complaints are managed by a Customer Satisfaction Management Team working with the branch office closest to the customer in question. An investigator is assigned to look into the specific details of the complaint, which must be resolved within two weeks. Feedback from the process is collected by the Customer Satisfaction Management Team, which dutifully records and correlates the information for use in reports to the Customer Satisfaction Council. This council puts the reports to practical use in fine-tuning customer satisfaction processes.

Complaints represent only a fraction of actual dissatisfaction. Federal Express knows that only 3 percent of the customers who experience a late delivery call to complain. Therefore, they take each complaint seriously, coding and analyzing it by category. The company has set a standard for itself of 24 hours in which to respond to each complaint.

At Wallace Company, every complaint is handled by a special "customer response associate" with training in complaint resolution. (Wallace's theory is that an unbiased decision can be made only by taking the employee most directly involved out of the situation.) If the problem is not resolved within 60 minutes, customers can choose what they perceive as a fair and reasonable solution to the problem. The customer response rep and a statistical process coordinator then perform root-cause and FMEA analyses, identify whether the problem was a special cause (probably won't happen again) or common cause (could occur again and again), and, if it is the latter, assign it to a team that investigates and makes recommendations to the Quality Management Steering Committee. This committee oversees the entire complaint process, reviewing all reported problems weekly. This is a lot of work, but it is all about information sharing, which is then applied to process improvement, in the most important of all Baldrige categories.

Customer Satisfaction Determination

Describe the company's methods for determining customer satisfaction and customer satisfaction relative to competitors; describe how these methods are evaluated and improved.

You have reached the end of the rainbow. Now you can ask yourself, "Is there any gold in the pot?" Results are your bottom line here. Either your efforts have paid off in a measurable way or they have not. Customer-satisfaction results are reported in the same manner as the product-and-service quality and operational results asked for in the sixth category. In particular, downward trends in satisfaction measures and trends in negative indicators (e.g., complaints, litigations, etc.) should be noted and explained. Just as in product-and-service quality, you are required to compare your results with those of competitors, that is, how customer satisfaction stacks up against that of competitors in your key markets, against industry averages, against industry leaders, and against world leaders. If you have accomplishments you are just bursting to share, now is the best time to do it.

> Overall satisfaction with our products, as measured by our customer satisfaction index, has improved 8 points since 1986 and currently stands at the highest level of domestically produced electronic equipment, and is competitive with the best in the world.

> We are very proud that our customer retention rate over this three-year period was 100%.

> Independent consumer surveys conducted in 1990 and 1991 ranked us #1 in six separate categories of product quality, and among the top three in eleven others.

> Percentage of on-time delivery increased at a rate of 5% annually during the period from 1987–1992.

> Complaints increased in our retail stores in the last two years of our survey, but improved complaint resolution procedures resulted in a 43% growth in the percentage of complaining customers who, when questioned 30 days after the complaint, characterized their degree of satisfaction as "very good" or "excellent."

> From 1987 to 1990, our sales grew from $52 million to $90 million. In the same period, market share rose from 10.4 percent to 18 percent.

The Baldrige criteria are strict, but if there is one loophole among its many categories, items, and areas to address, it is that you can never go too far or say too much in the name of customer satisfaction.

14

The Future of Baldrige

Whither Baldrige? This is a question many people in business and government are asking. Being a changing and continuously improving set of criteria, the Baldrige framework is not perfect, and it never will be. But what are the system's failings and inadequacies, and how serious or irremediable are they? Are its faults "fatal flaws" as its detractors claim, or do they simply signal the taste of sour grapes? Will the Baldrige criteria focus American business on long-term strategic quality improvement, or is the Baldrige approach itself part of the problem, another "program of the month" gussied up for corporate consumption?

The Passion of John Hudiburg

If there is any hero to the tale of the establishment of the Malcolm Baldrige National Quality Award, it is John J. Hudiburg. It was he who set the example of what an American company could achieve in the name of quality when the company he ran, Florida Power & Light, won Japan's prestigious Deming Prize in 1989. Florida Power & Light was the first non-Japanese company ever to win the prize. It was a splendid example of a quality loop coming full circle; an American consultant (Deming) inspired Japan to unheard of levels of quality improvement, and then the vision of quality slowly made its way back to the land of its origin. However, the story has a catch. By the time Hudiburg was honored for his achievement, he had been stripped of power.

Hudiburg was a full-fledged, total quality zealot. He and his predecessor at FP&L, Marshall McDonald, were avid admirers of the 1984

Deming Prize winner, Kansai Electric, the utility for the Osaka, Japan area, which went through an entire year once without a shutdown. FP&L customers endured about an hour and a half of power outages yearly; Kansai customers suffered through only seven minutes. Therefore, in 1986 Hudiburg decided to bring in Japanese consultants and "redo" FP&L to match the Japanese model. The method was, if anything, even more exhaustive than Baldrige-style TQM. Processes were identified, measurement systems were put in place, and quality was made the centerpiece of the utility's strategic plan. During this time Hudiburg became the patron saint of industrial quality. It was he who planted the germ of the idea for a national quality award in the ear of his own congressman. Hudiburg served as the second chairman of the Baldrige Foundation. "I feel," he once said, "like the little kid at the top of the mountain who kicked a little rock off, and it turned into an avalanche." However, instead of standing at the top of the mountain, Hudiburg was buried at the bottom. FP&L had problems that Hudiburg's *kaizen* approach was not solving—specifically an errant nuclear plant at Turkey Point. Financials stepped to the fore—profits were down due to some unwise diversification; the stock price was drooping; and the morale of people inside and outside the company was at a low point. In 1990, the new chairman of FP&L's holding company stepped back from Hudiburg's vision of a highly-structured, Japanese-styled approach to total quality management. Within months, Hudiburg was history. The patron saint of quality in this country had been deposed.

Does this story mean that American business must think twice before instituting Japanese-style quality management systems? That a long-term vision of quality has not yet attained the importance in business of short-term financials? That quality awards mean little in a world fixated on return on assets? The Baldrige process is, more than any other single thing, a process of learning from mistakes. In its short history, the award has already been subject to a number of controversies, miscalculations, and misunderstandings. If the Award is not managed well, it can become a joke, or irrelevant, or both. What are some of the challenges facing the Baldrige Award, and what can the Baldrige Award do to remain a force in American business?

Complaints about the Baldrige

By and large, Baldrige has been the object of broad enthusiasm, both in corporate circles and in the business press. Nevertheless, there have been occasional mutterings of displeasure with the way the award process has gone to date. These complaints[1] tend to center on seven areas.

The Suspicion That the Award
Is Just Not Fair

Do the big companies buy the award? Xerox is said to have spent $800,000 cultivating the prize, tapping the talents of 500 employees in preparing the assessment. Xerox does not back off from its commitment. "The real value was what we learned about ourselves," one spokesperson said. "You can't put a price tag on that." Other companies have spent just as much, proportionately, without winning anything, and they are not complaining, either. Small companies such as Globe won on a dime. Still, the impression persists that the big rollers have an "in" on winning.

The Award Is Superficial,
Marketing-oriented Fluff

The view that the award is not what it seems to be was conveyed in a critical front-page *Wall Street Journal*[2] article blasting the advertising overkill of Baldrige winners such as Cadillac and IBM Rochester. "The award is considered such valuable public relations, the winners haven't waited for the formal ceremony to start promoting their success," the *Journal* observed in 1991. "The morning after its award was announced on October 10, GM's Cadillac division unleashed a barrage of advertisements carrying the message that Cadillac is the first and only auto maker good enough to win the award."

There Is Something Amiss
in the Criteria

Many companies feel that the award is not well thought-out. In the early rounds, the Baldrige process appeared to discriminate against service companies. The questions simply did not appear to have a bearing on these kinds of processes. The people at The Paul Revere Insurance Company were miffed at one question in particular: Which problem-solving techniques did you use for each problem? The Paul Revere people looked at the examiner and wondered, "Who gives a damn?" Companies that vow never again to submit to such questioning may not appreciate the fact that lunkhead questions get weeded out year after year.

The Award Process Is Permeated
with Conflicts of Interest

The Baldrige competition has attracted criticism recently because some examiners also work as consultants on Baldrige assessments (though never consulting with companies they are also examining). Out of approximately 200 senior examiners and judges, only a small percentage list themselves as independent consultants or employees of consulting firms. The implication of these connections, say some, is that the examining process may have conflict-of-interest problems. Common sense helps NIST steer clear of obvious conflicts, but suspicions linger. As Curt Reimann says,"We wouldn't let someone in the automobile industry judge in the manufacturing category, if their company were running, or if their company's competitors were. However, if the auto company for which that person consulted didn't apply, and no other companies from the auto industry applied, he or she would be allowed to judge in the manufacturing category."[3]

Something Is Amiss in the Application and Judging Processes

No one wants to sound like a sore loser, but United States Automobile Association (USAA) has gone on record about its frustration with making it to the Baldrige finals three times, yet never winning. How can they be so good and continuously improving, but never worthy of the brass ring? Again, USAA felt that the examiners the Baldrige administrators sent to them were asking off-the-wall questions: What percentage of women is there in the organization? What percentage of your executive group is retired military? Conversely, as author and training expert Ron Zemke asked in an article in the March, 1991 issue of *Training,* how is it that Cadillac won the award, despite fairly mediocre car ratings by consumer groups? Given the wild variety of experiences applicants have, is Baldrige really anything more than a crapshoot?

The Award Is Held Hostage by Its Winners

The thought here is that as soon as one winner fails publicly, the award's prestige will be shattered. During the recession of 1991, the business world had one eye on the Baldrige Award, and another on the prospects of a few of its winners. Wallace Co., in particular, was laid low by the recession. What would happen, people wondered, if a Baldrige winner were to go bankrupt? What impact would that have on the claim so many quality gurus appear to make, that quality improvement inevitably leads to improvement on a company's bottom line? Or that quality—to grossly simplify the Baldrige mentality—somehow armor-plates companies against everyday business realities and economic cycles? The

Cadillac award also prompted many raised eyebrows throughout American industry. What will happen to the glitter surrounding the Baldrige award when Cadillac announces the recall of 100,000 cars for steering problems? That has not happened, but skeptics wonder if Baldrige examiners ask companies every question under the sun *except* questions whose answers might someday come back and haunt the award. Loss of credibility is the number one threat to the Baldrige Award's success.

Winning the Baldrige Award May Be Its Own Punishment

You can see it in the faces of the quality managers at companies that won the award. You get the feeling that they would like to be left alone for half an hour, to do some regular work. Many of these people, from middle management all the way up to the top offices, have been doing the work of twenty since the award was announced, sponsoring symposia, leading tour groups, talking to reporters, and so on. Winning entails many responsibilities that do not let up even two or three years after winning. Is it possible that all the attention can distract a company from its mission of continuously improving the quality of its goods and services? Is the publicity an albatross around the necks of winning companies?

Keeping the Baldrige a Model for Ongoing Improvement

Ron Zemke, Tom Peters, and other critics have made many useful suggestions on how to improve the award. Among them are the following:

- *The wording of the criteria is still much too elliptical.* Books, consultants, articles, and so on, help, but much work remains to make the language more understandable to everyday people.

- *Allow more time to complete the application.* Currently the entire process is crammed into a few frantic months. Lengthen the process, and perhaps the circus atmosphere surrounding the application will die down.

- *Put a lid on how much winners can commercialize the award.* Call winners to remind them of their educational obligations as winners. Great that GM proper cannot take credit for the award. Better if Cadillac were required to explain what the Award meant, instead of just beating its chest about having won it.

The feeling among people who run the Baldrige program is that these questions are all legitimate, and that critics are quite right—the Award is not perfect, any more than its winners are perfect. Curt Reimann himself acknowledges that.

Let the Baldrige be the Baldrige. Every year the award is streamlined, overhauled, reexamined, and reverse engineered. New concepts and requirements are introduced, highlighted, and brought into focus. Our suspicion, confirmed by Reimann, is that the biggest changes are behind us. However, if there is a major flaw still running through the Baldrige criteria, wait around for a while, and it will be fixed.

A Nonprofit Baldrige?

There is discussion even of the Baldrige award broadening its mandate beyond industrial and service companies. The Commerce Department is said to be taking very seriously the proposal that Baldrige be enlarged to include a category for nonprofit organizations. The proposal is aimed at rewarding institutions such as hospitals, universities, and other nonprofit organizations that have achieved a distinguished level of excellence. Behind this movement is the National Coalition for Health Care Reform, an advocacy group based in Washington, D.C., which sees the Baldrige Award as a carrot to urge its membership on to better management. Education wants in, as well. "The management concepts are the same," a representative of the American Association of School Administrators told the *Wall Street Journal*.[4] "We're all working with people. We're a service business."

Curt Reimann is on record as being cool to the idea. Expanding the award too much, he said, would place considerable strain on the NIST's ability to examine and judge. Not to mention the fact that the Award began with the specific objective of making American industry more competitive. Expect to see this issue remain on the table and for controversy to continue. Yes, education and healthcare are processes susceptible to the same kind of rigorous monitoring, measuring, and continuous improvement as making cars or selling insurance. Yes, a Baldrige-equivalent award would be a valuable spur for institutions seeking to become the best they can be. But should they be made to stand under the Baldrige umbrella? The Baldrige Award never intended to be the final word on all quality throughout the universe. Nonprofits should be encouraged to start their own award, for their own purposes, based on the Baldrige model. To lump awards for universities, hospitals, and—who knows?—governmental agencies together and to make them all eligible to compete for the Baldrige award is to dilute the vision of a powerful business tool.

Is That All There Is?

The Baldrige Award probably begins as a dream within senior management to bring out the best in a company's people and processes. Thousands of hours of work, meetings, late night think-sessions, reams of thrown-away first drafts, broken pencils by the score—all these things go into the assessment process. The experience is at once humbling and exhilarating. Xerox identified over 500 "warts"—our euphemism is "improvement opportunities"—as a result of its Baldrige assessment. So humbled by the process and by all it learned was Federal Express that the company placed its likelihood of winning only between 20 and 50 percent. After the intensity of the self-scrutiny and the competition, winning is a bonanza of the first magnitude. Companies that have won have, in different degrees, all gone wild celebrating it, both internally and externally. Given out by the President, the award vaults a company into the very first ranks of American business with the likes of Motorola, Xerox, Westinghouse, Globe, Federal Express, Solectron, Zytec, and Marlowe Industries. The Baldrige Award has become the canonical agent of American business excellence. Winning is like going to heaven without first having to die.

And yet, winners wistfully signal that business is not quite the same after winning. Baldrige conveys a level of self-consciousness that many find wearying and distractive. Quality leaders and executives, already committed whole-heartedly to improving internal processes, suddenly must wear the additional mantle of cheerleader for the rest of the world. Visitors troop through their factories and offices, sniff at the ordinariness of it all, and wonder what the big deal is all about. Reporters expect them to drop everything and attend to their needs for the umpteenth generic article about the award. Carrying the banner of benchmarking, their competitive adversaries smilingly request information about their quality results. Ten years ago executives would have laughed them out of their offices, or worse, dummied up a bunch of funny numbers and sent them away. Today, there is an eerie atmosphere surrounding winners that their processes have somehow entered the public domain. It can be unnerving.

Nevertheless, the line of companies wanting to give up their awards is noticeably short. Indeed, Motorola and other winners have vowed to reapply for the award when they become eligible after the passage of five years. Others, like Xerox, IBM, and Milliken, continue to apply the Baldrige assessment criteria to themselves even as they reign as Baldrige winners. This commitment to the assessment criteria themselves—above and beyond the "Award"—affirms our conviction that the greatest benefit of the Baldrige process is derived undergoing the process on one's own, for the purpose of true improvement—not just to grab the brass ring. No matter how a company decides to use the Baldrige criteria, the pluses obtained through them vastly outnumber the minuses. For a small application fee—in 1992 it was $4000 for manufacturing and service companies and $1200 for small business—the Baldrige is one of the best bargains around. It adds a whole second battery of incentives to companies that want to do well—a second bottom line, so to speak, the first being traditional financials, the other being a cogent and measurable system for continuously improving processes.

The Baldrige process is, above all, a *motivator* that breathes spirit, energy, and an extraordinary passion for excellence into people and entire organizations. In so many different ways it makes things happen that would otherwise not happen. It changes the way that entire organizations think about goals, about their reasons for doing business, and even about what their true business is. As Roger Milliken said, "In the pursuit of total quality management, we recognize that good is the enemy of best, and best the enemy of better." For those companies that apply the Baldrige criteria to themselves, regardless of whether they actually step into the formal national competition for the prize, the rewards lie in the journey. By committing to continuous improvement, customer satisfaction, and everything else that the Baldrige criteria represent, these companies have already set foot inside the winner's circle.

PART 3
The Baldrige Toolkit

15
Executive Exercises

Vision Statements

There is an old saying that "if you don't know where you're going, any road will get you there." The same is true of organizations setting out on their quests for excellence. If they don't know where they are going, any road will get them there. Yet, many roads headed toward quality can prove to be circuitous and filled with potholes. That is why organizations who are expert at "managing quality" take great care to articulate their mission and their vision of where they are going in an increasingly competitive global marketplace. The creation of a clear mission/vision statement is a critical first step in blazing a trail through the land of total quality management.

It is no surprise that the Baldrige criteria plumb this issue. In Category 1, the Baldrige criteria explore the ways in which senior executives can communicate their quality vision and values throughout an organization. Baldrige examiners, when conducting a site visit, frequently ask to review the organization's mission and vision statements and seek additional evidence that employees throughout the organization embrace this vision in the field.

A vision statement is nothing mysterious. Quite simply, it is a declaration of what a company wants to become in the future. Depending on the industry in which they compete, some organizations' vision statements extend between 3 and 15 years into the future. Good vision statements embrace an organization's key values and clearly articulate, in easy-to-understand language, how the company wishes to make its mark.

Strong vision statements help guide an organization's planning and decision-making processes. Characteristics of an effective vision statement may include:

- Captures the essence of winning; describes being the best in one way or another
- Defines the desired leadership position (world, regional, local, industry, etc.)
- Inspires performance; has meaning for everyone in the organization
- Stretches an organization's current capabilities and resources
- Provides consistency and stability; guides short-term action, leaves room for taking bold initiatives as they emerge
- Communicates an achievable goal

Does your organization or operating group have a clear sense of where it is going and where it needs to be in order to achieve success? Has this future been articulated in a summary statement or policy guideline that is easily communicated throughout your work unit? If not, you might consider using the following executive exercise with your team. The objective of this exercise is for a management team to formulate a clear and motivating vision statement for its operating unit. This exercise can be used by senior executives who are thinking about a company or strategic business unit or by mid-level managers and front-line employees who are articulating the operating vision of a department or work group.

Developing a vision for a company can be a messy and artistic process. Tom Peters states in *Thriving on Chaos,* "The process of developing a vision, though it represents the 'highest level of abstraction,' is quintessentially a trial-and-error process."[1] Don't expect that you'll get it right the first draft through; and certainly don't expect that everyone will embrace the vision after a first work-session draft.

Step One

To help busy managers, who customarily spend most of their work hours focused on current operating issues and may have difficulty envisioning a future beyond next quarter's operating summary, you might consider the following scenario: You have just been transported to the year 2010. Using the first person, and the present tense, compose one sentence—or at most a few sentences—to serve as a description of your organization or operating unit. In other words, "What does the organization look like in the year 2010?" (Don't labor over wording and punctuation. Focus on the key elements you use to describe the organization in the future.) Use the form in Fig. 15-1 to guide and record your thoughts and initial ideas.

Use this worksheet to organize your initial thoughts and ideas.

What are the future products, services, markets?	Define the desired leadership position.	List the core values needed to support the vision.	What are the hallmarks of excellence—the differentiators?	List the stretch goals that would help fulfill the vision.

You have just been transported to the year 2010. Using the first person, present tense, compose a description of your organization.

Figure 15-1. Vision Statement Worksheet

Step Two

Each manager participating in this executive exercise should now record his or her vision statement on a flip chart and "read" it to the other team members. (There will be no discussion of the different vision statements at this point. If ten or more people are involved in this process, it is advisable to break into smaller discussion groups of five or six.)

Step Three

Each team should designate a facilitator. Through a process of consensus, the team facilitator should work with the group to identify the common elements of the individual vision statements. The team members will then consolidate their thoughts and ideas into one vision statement. (If more than one vision team is involved in this process, the consolidation process must be repeated.) The final product will be a "draft" vision statement for the organization or work group. Shortly following this vision work session, the draft vision statement should be refined by a designated individual or office and then distributed for review, amendments and approval by the group.

Role Model Behavior and Managerial Effectiveness

What do Xerox and Federal Express have in common? In addition to the fact that both are Baldrige Award winners, both corporations understand the importance of managerial behavior. Consider the following facts:

> Xerox will not promote managers unless they are deemed to be "Role Models" for quality. To support this, the company has developed eight standards for "Leadership Through Quality" Role Model Managers. Role model managers "encourage, recognize, reward, and support" others. This decision to require managers to "walk the talk," made in the late 1980s, sent a powerful message to managers who were not team players or coaches.
>
> Federal Express's company motto is "People, Service, Profit." All management is, accordingly, held accountable for having a people-first attitude, displaying impeccable service to internal and external customers, and achieving a reasonable profit, which can be used both to reward employees and to reinvest for company improvement. If management does not live up to this credo—as it is measured through a leadership index on the annual employee opinion survey—no one in management receives any bonus.

There is no more powerful tool with which to communicate the total quality process than management behavior. Consequently, one of the greatest challenges managers face is setting an appropriate and compelling example for their employees. That example should be clear, visible, and constant. In short, management behavior should embody the stated values of the organization.

Many organizations find it helpful to examine the management practices that constitute role model behavior. Following is a team-based exercise that can help managers and work-group participants explore what types of actions and behaviors would be considered "role model" or exemplary in your organization. The objectives of this exercise are to:

- Understand how management behavior serves as a communication tool

- Consider the link between management behavior and organizational values

- Review what constitutes role model behavior in your organization

Step One

Each participant should fill out the Role Model Behavior Individual Worksheet (Fig. 15-2) for each of the six activity areas. Each activity area represents a place where a manager might have an impact through his or her actions. Record those management programs, processes, actions and practices that you believe should be held up in your company as exemplary or "role model" behavior (Fig. 15-3 is a sample worksheet that has been filled; it is provided to help fuel participants' thoughts).

Step Two

Using the worksheets each participant has just completed, discuss your organization's practices with other team members. Your objective is to identify outstanding practices for each category. Typically, different managers will develop different approaches and practices for each activity area. Consolidate your group's "best practices" in each of the six activity areas. Then each manager should consider these questions:

1. How do employees view your behavior?

2. How do you use quality practices and tools to improve your management behavior?

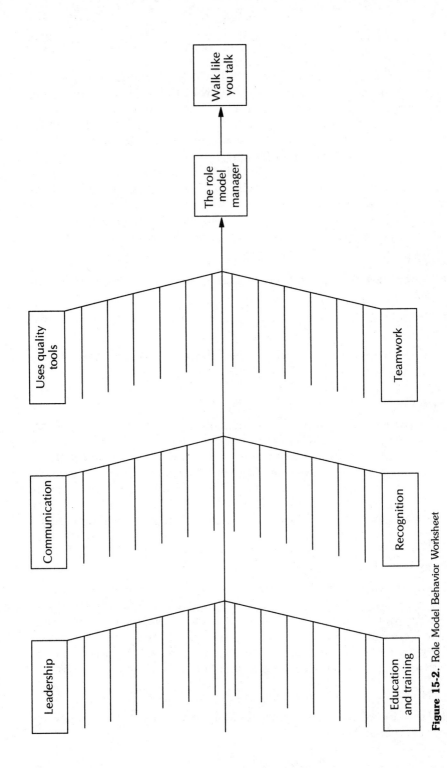

Figure 15-2. Role Model Behavior Worksheet

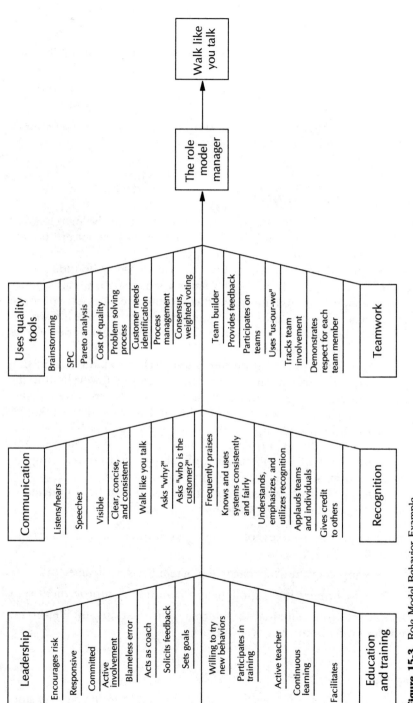

Figure 15-3. Role Model Behavior Example

3. How does your organization reward individuals that exemplify role model behaviors?

4. Are the behaviors rewarded in your organization consistent with the stated values and highest level goals of your organization?

5. In what ways might you change your own behavior to become more of a role model manager?

Sharing Success Stories

"Don't let your search for the great idea blind you to the merely good idea," advises inventor Bob Metcalfe. "Reject everything except for the very best and you'll end up with nothing."[2]

Successful quality initiatives build on the existing foundation of strengths in an organization. Total quality management involves more extensive action than just finding and correcting weaknesses; you must also propagate new strengths and expand existing ones. Sharing success stories provides a look at your strengths that will reveal opportunities for performance improvements.

The Approach/Deployment/Results framework, developed for the Baldrige total quality assessment process, is a proven tool for evaluating the thoroughness, consistency, and sustainability of any initiative, quality or otherwise. Here is a way to apply this tool in your department or work group to help build upon the foundation of excellence that your people have already put in place. Managers often comment that this fundamental shift in the perspective of management—enhancing the successes as opposed to limiting the problems—is refreshing.

The objectives of this executive exercise, which can be conducted in small- or large-group settings, are to:

- Understand the sources of your organization's or work group's strengths
- Practice applying the Approach/Deployment/Results framework
- Explore the implications of following a continuous improvement cycle
- Demonstrate the potential of internal benchmarking by identifying and deploying your own best practices

Step One

Working in small groups, each participant should recall a success story from his or her own area of operating responsibility. Every person should then take a few minutes to describe his or her success story to the group. Each presentation should cover the following points:

- What is the success story?
- What started it; how were actions triggered?
- What were the most important results, and were they the ones expected?
- How were results measured?
- What were the cause-and-effect relationships between actions and the results?
- To what extent did everything go as planned?

Step Two

Each team or work group should select a success story to analyze in depth, based on which success seems to have had the largest impact on end-customer satisfaction or on internal waste reduction. (The potential depth of analysis is more important than which particular story is analyzed.)

Next fill out the worksheets (Fig. 15-4) and use the simplified Baldrige scoring guidelines (Fig. 15-5) to score the approach, deployment, and results of the success story. Be sure to answer all of the summary questions.

Step Three

As a group, discuss the success story and your answers to the worksheet questions. Work toward a consensus concerning what score you would give the success story in terms of its approach, its deployment and its results. Lastly, identify ways that you could make this success story even more successful, through both process improvements and further deployment.

Managing the Employee Development and Retention Process

Imagine what your organization could accomplish if all its employees were as motivated as Elizabeth Mauras, a room service operator at the Crystal City Marriott Hotel in Arlington, VA. While on duty, Mauras

Sharing Success Stories
Analyze Approach
Group #:
Success Story:

Is the approach based on solid information?   Y / N

What is the objective or goal? _____

Is it consistent with other initiatives and high
level goals?   Y / N

Is it consistent with your business strategy/plan?   Y / N

Does the design of the approach include
a measurement system for performance tracking?   Y / N

If yes, how effective is the measurement system?   _____

Are individual responsibilities assigned for
all actions?   Y / N

Does the approach include appropriate
implementation milestones or targets?   Y / N

Were the required resources clearly specified?   Y / N

What possible obstacles were identified during planning? What
contingency plans, if any, were made? _____

What evaluation and improvement cycle has been incorporated in
the approach? _____

Approach Score (0% - 100%) _____

Figure 15-4. Success Story Worksheets

Sharing Success Stories
Analyze Deployment
Group #:
Success Story:

(Do not answer if not applicable to the story chosen.)

Were all the intended processes, activities, or
transactions included in deployment?   Y / N

If not, what percentage of target was completed? _____

Were all the intended people included in deployment?   Y / N

If not, what percentage of target was completed? _____

Were all the intended departments included?   Y / N

If not, what percentage of target was completed? _____

Were all the intended facilities or sites included?   Y / N

If not, what percentage of target was completed? _____

Were all the intended products or services included?   Y / N

If not, what percentage of target was completed? _____

Deployment Score (0% - 100%) _____

Figure 15-4. Success Story Worksheets *(Continued)*

Sharing Success Stories
Analyze Results
Group #:
Success Story:

Were the intended results reached?   Y / N

What were the results? _____

_____

Were the intended results surpassed?   Y / N

If so, by how much? _____

_____

What measures were used to evaluate this successful initiative?

_____

_____

What evidence demonstrates the results were caused by your
actions? _____

_____

Do the results bring your organization closer to your
long-term strategic objectives?   Y / N

If so, how? _____

_____

Are the results significant?   Y / N

Are the results sustainable?   Y / N

Results Score (0% - 100%) _____

Figure 15-4. Success Story Worksheets *(Continued)*

Sharing Success Stories

Group #:
Success Story:

Please discuss and respond to the following summary questions.

What lessons that might be of lasting value can you derive from this success? _____
_____
_____
_____
_____
_____

What opportunities exist to enhance further this success? _____
_____
_____
_____
_____
_____

What actions can be taken to build on this success? (For example, create more systematic procedures for using the practices involved, deploy more extensively in the same department, deploy extensively outside of the department.) _____
_____
_____
_____
_____
_____

Figure 15-4. Success Story Worksheets *(Continued)*

Score	A/D/R Characteristics
100%	• Undisputed world-class organization
60-90%	• World-class contender
50%	• Good company • Notable systems and results
10-40%	• Some systems, integration incomplete • Preliminary results
0%	• Anecdotal • No system evident

Figure 15-5. Sharing Success Stories: Scoring Guidelines

received a call from a guest canceling a dinner order she had placed a few moments earlier. The guest seemed distraught and Mauras asked if she was okay. Mauras discovered the guest had just been informed that her mother in California had suffered a massive stroke and was not expected to live. The guest had called the airlines to book a reservation and was told there was only one flight that night, leaving in 35 minutes. Assuming that she couldn't get to the airport in time, she had made a reservation for the next morning. Because she was too upset to eat, she was canceling her room service order. Mauras jumped into action. She called the restaurant hostess, briefly described the problem, and had the room service phones forwarded directly to the hostess. She then went to the guest's room, greeted her with a hug, and said, "Start packing. I'll make sure you get on the plane tonight." As the guest packed, Mauras called the airlines to change the flight, called the front desk to prepare the account, and contacted the bellstand to have a cab standing by and a bellman sent up to help with the bags. Because of Mauras' actions, the guest was able to arrive at her mother's bedside before she passed away that evening. That guest will never forget Elizabeth Mauras and the Crystal City Marriott.[3]

Managers struggle with the challenge of how to inspire exemplary performance levels in their employees. How can they encourage every employee to act with the speed, sensitivity and thoughtfulness of Elizabeth Mauras? The total quality management framework shifts management's focus. Total quality managers don't wonder what they can say or do to make their employees smarter, better, and more productive. Rather, they inquire what they can do to develop and improve the process and systems that produce employees who are loyal, involved, empowered, and contribute value to the organization and its customers. Employees who embody each of the points of the star in Fig. 15-6 will shine throughout the organization.

Recruiting, developing and retaining value-contributing employees is increasingly viewed as a process management challenge. The processes and systems to be managed are "people systems," such as recruitment, orientation, and career development. How do you manage the process of employee recruitment, development and retention? Leading-edge organizations have begun to wrestle with this issue by mapping the life of an employee as he or she enters and advances through the organization. This process begins with recruitment and progresses through orientation, training, career development, outplacement and alumni relations (see Fig. 15-7). Managing the employee process means managing the many systems and sub-processes that compose each step of this process.

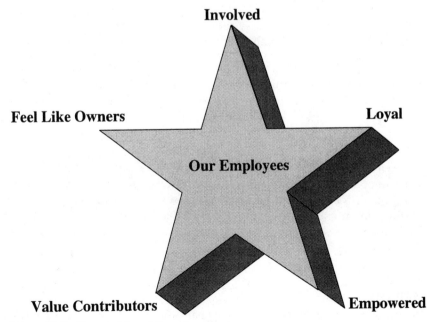

Figure 15-6. Characteristics of Exemplary Employees

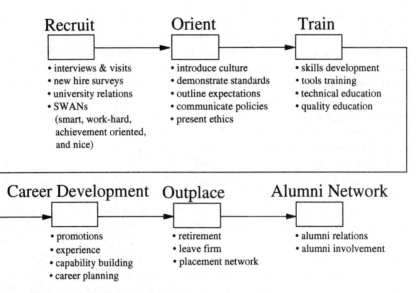

Figure 15-7. The Life of an Employee

Think about the life of an employee in your organization. In this exercise, managers examine their organization's people systems. The objectives of this executive exercise are to:

- Explore and understand a systems approach to managing employee development and retention
- Assess your own organization within the Baldrige framework
- Learn how other organizations in your industry are approaching this issue

Step One

Have each member of your management team fill out the Employee Development and Retention Individual Worksheet (Fig. 15-8). Record those programs, processes, and systems that exist to encourage employees to perform in an exemplary manner. Should you have any trouble identifying systems to fill out your worksheet, review the completed fishbone diagram sample (Fig. 15-9).

Step Two

Working from the Worksheets each team member has completed, discuss your organization's employee development and retention practices.

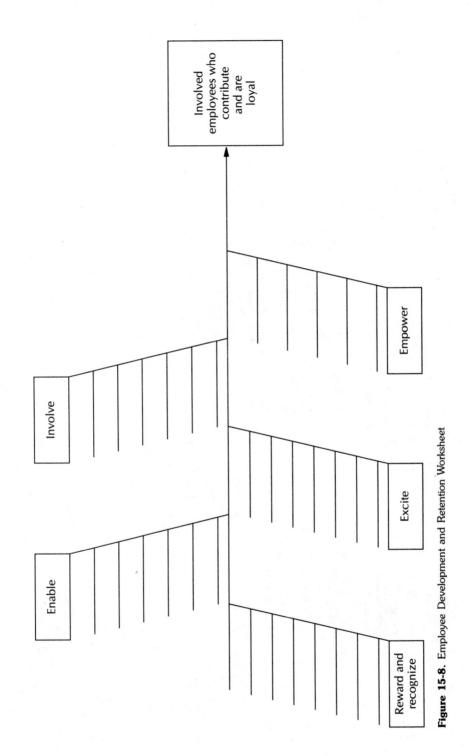

Figure 15-8. Employee Development and Retention Worksheet

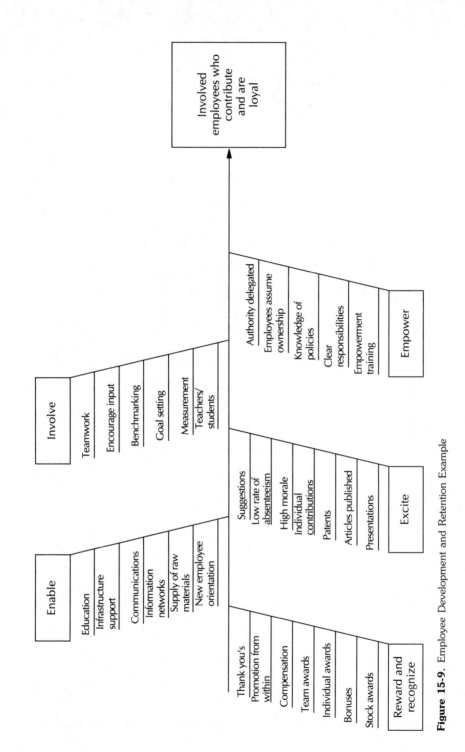

Figure 15-9. Employee Development and Retention Example

Identify as a group the most outstanding practices for each category. In many companies, it is typical that different departments and operating groups develop different approaches and practices to these different processes.

Step Three

Consolidate the group's identified "best practices" on a group worksheet. During your group's work session, consider the following questions:

1. What is the extent of deployment of these best practices in your organization? How can you fully deploy your best practices throughout your organization?
2. How do you measure employee development?
3. In what ways are employees encouraged to contribute to their work environment?
4. In what ways is your organization committed to employee development and retention?
5. What areas in the career path of an employee in your organization are noticeably lacking systems to totally support and develop the employee?

Managing for Customer Satisfaction

Managing for customer satisfaction begins by developing a systematic approach to listening to your customers throughout the total service or product life cycle: design, delivery, and so on. It is not surprising that those organizations most renowned for high levels of customer satisfaction are also very good at listening to their customers and understanding their customers' interests, needs and expectations. Consider a few examples:

- Managers at L.L. Bean routinely orders packages from their company and from their competitors to determine how Bean, when viewed from its customers' perspective, stacks up against the competition.
- IBM created a customer council comprised of representatives from IBM's top fifty clients. It meets regularly to provide input on the development and design of future IBM products and services.
- When servicemen from Hewlett-Packard visit customers, they gather information about competitors' products (what the customer likes,

dislikes, etc.). This information is then used to develop new products and enhance existing ones.

A critical first step in managing for customer satisfaction is to identify the steps in your customer delivery process; next, ask yourself what methods are available to listen to your customers at each step in the process. These methods are often called customer listening posts. Each listening post is just one point in the customer communication process; it is the means by which information is received. Each listening post represents only one piece in what should be a comprehensive and coordinated strategy for capturing and utilizing customer communications. Customer satisfaction managers also closely examine the frequency with which they gather customer information, the types of information gathered, and the organization's relative position when compared to the competition (Fig. 15-10).

This executive exercise is designed to help managers think strategically about how their organizations can capture, consolidate and use customer information. In short, the objectives of the executive exercise are to:

- Identify how, where, and when your organization listens to its customers

- Compare your organization's customer listening approaches to industry standards

Customer Process

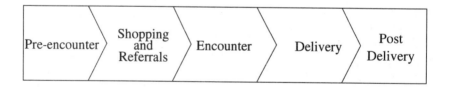

| Pre-encounter | Shopping and Referrals | Encounter | Delivery | Post Delivery |

| ← Listening Posts → |
| ← Frequency → |
| ← Information Gathered → |
| ← Competition → |

Figure 15-10. The Customer Communication Process

- Consider how the system can be improved and better integrated to optimize performance

Step One

Each executive or work team member should fill out the matrix labeled Managing for Customer Satisfaction: Part A (Fig. 15-11). Identify and record those programs, processes, and systems (formal or informal customer listening posts) in place to capture customer information. Try to identify at least one listening post for each step in the service delivery process. Think broadly about the formal and informal ways customers communicate with your organization. A completed matrix containing some possible responses is included to help spur your thoughts (see Fig. 15-12). Once you have identified the listening posts, fill in the frequency with which you employ these listening posts and note what types of information are gathered at each post.

Step Two

Using the Managing for Customer Satisfaction: Part B worksheet (Fig. 15-13), consider your organization's practices as compared to industry standards. Is your organization below, at, or above industry standards? Next identify what additional listening posts you would like set in place by the year 2000 if you were to build a world-class system to manage for customer satisfaction.

Step Three

As a group, discuss what your organization is doing today, and what you would like to see it doing in the year 2000. Consider the following questions:

1. How do you use this information?
2. Does your organization effectively aggregate, analyze, and use the information gathered from different sources?
3. At which step(s) in the customer delivery process does your organization have the greatest impact on customer satisfaction?
4. What types of information do you gather at each source?
5. Which listening posts are you not using to full potential in terms of gathering information? How can you successfully use these listening posts?

Customer Process	Listening posts	Frequency	Types of information gathered (Check if applicable)					
		(monthly, quarterly, annually, ongoing)	Overall satisfaction	Needs and expectations	Technical ability	Improvement ideas	Future needs	Complaints
Pre-encounter								
Customer shopping and referrals								
Encounter								
Delivery								
Postdelivery								

Figure 15-11. Managing for Customer Satisfaction: Part A

Figure 15-12. Managing for Customer Satisfaction: Part A, Example

Customer Process	Listening posts	Frequency (monthly, quarterly, annually, ongoing)	Types of information gathered (Check if applicable)					
			Overall satisfaction	Needs and expectations	Technical ability	Improvement ideas	Future needs	Complaints
Pre-encounter	Client service teams	Ongoing	X	X			X	X
	Focus groups	Annually	X	X		X	X	
	Surveys	Quarterly	X	X	X	X		X
	Customer councils	Quarterly	X	X		X	X	X
Customer shopping and referrals	Surveys	Annually	X	X	X	X		X
	Customer referral analysis	Monthly	X		X			
	Interviews	Quarterly	X	X	X	X	X	X
	Competitor assessment	Annually	X	X			X	
Encounter	Frontline feedback	Ongoing	X			X	X	X
	Customer complaint line	Ongoing	X	X	X	X		X
	Customer response cards	Ongoing	X			X		X
	Competitor assessment	Annually	X	X	X	X	X	
Delivery	Frontline feedback	Ongoing	X			X	X	X
	Mystery shoppers	Quarterly	X		X	X		
	Customer response cards	Ongoing	X	X	X	X		X
	Customer complaint line	Ongoing	X			X		X
Postdelivery	Customer service inquiries	Monthly	X	X	X			X
	Telephone interviews	Annually	X	X	X	X	X	X
	Customer complaint line	Ongoing	X	X		X		X
	Customer surveys	Quarterly	X	X	X	X	X	X

Customer Process	How do you rate yourself compared to industry average? (below – at – above)	Your organization in the year 2000 (What listening posts should be in place?)
Pre-encounter		
Customer shopping and referrals		
Encounter		
Delivery		
Postdelivery		

Figure 15-13. Managing for Customer Satisfaction: Part B

Key Indicators of Quality Excellence

What constitutes "world class" performance? This is one of the leading management questions of the 1990s. Senior executives wrestle with this issue when they engage in strategic planning and goal setting. Department heads and key function leaders contend with it when they review and assess their operations. Quality improvement teams tangle with the question when they inquire how they can improve internal performance or when they undertake competitive benchmarking studies in order to understand what performance levels other organizations have attained. Malcolm Baldrige National Quality Award examiners have been known to quiz site-visit finalists about how their organizations can demonstrate or provide tangible evidence that their practices are world class, worthy of serving as a national role model.

As a growing number of companies apply the Baldrige criteria to their operations, some important characteristics of organizational excellence emerge. The traits that characterize high-performing companies are called *key excellence indicators*. No single company—not even the Baldrige winners—embody all these characteristics, but, taken together, these indicators of excellence help to identify what constitutes world-class performance in each of the seven Baldrige quality categories.

Many executives report that the Baldrige criteria become much more meaningful and powerful when real company examples are used to illustrate Baldrige concepts. The tables at the end of this chapter identify characteristics of excellent companies, including high scorers on Baldrige assessments. These key excellence indicator tables are intended to help managers understand what merely good companies are doing and what some really excellent companies are doing along various key dimensions highlighted by the Baldrige criteria. These key excellence indicator tables, though not meant to be comprehensive, are intended to:

- Illustrate important Baldrige concepts through the use of "real world" examples
- Give substance to the concept of "world class"
- Encourage you to begin to think about your own organization in terms of the Baldrige assessment criteria

The key excellence indicator tables are divided into four columns. Moving from left to right, the columns contain:

- The Baldrige category and corresponding key excellence indicators
- Characteristics and operating descriptions of a "good" company in each topical area

- Evidence and anecdotes of excellence drawn from the Baldrige winners and a wide range of other "excellent" organizations

- A blank column for you to consider and sketch what your organization would look like if it were to pursue a total quality initiative and if by the year 2000 it were to establish a world-class benchmark for each of the relevant excellence indicators.

Many management teams have found it illuminating to go through the group process of discussing each of the key excellence indicators and relating it to your organization. The following instructions can be used to help guide a management team through such a discussion.

1. *Select a team facilitator.* Each management team or discussion group should select a team leader who will be responsible for facilitating discussion and for summarizing the group's observations and findings.

2. *Read each category's key excellence indicators. Focus on one category at a time.* Quickly read through a single category of key excellence indicators. Pay particular attention to the differences between the examples of excellence and the descriptions of the practices from merely good companies.

3. *Discuss the assigned category's key excellence indicators.* As a group, consider the following questions:

- What activities can you identify within your organization that might apply to or provide evidence for the relevant key excellence indicators? (Describe the current situation.)
- What other examples of excellent performance can you identify from your own experience both inside your organization and external to the organization?
- What rating would you give your own organization on a scale of "poor," "good," "excellent" in each indicator area?

4. *Develop a vision of excellence for your organization for the year 2000.* Imagine that your organization has successfully pursued and advanced your total quality management efforts for two or more years. Address the following questions:

- What behaviors, systems, characteristics and processes will you see in your highly successful organization in the year 2000?
- What improvements are desirable? What improvements are feasible?
- What are the key excellence indicators of a world-class organization in this area in the year 2000? How high will the bar measuring performance excellence be raised in the next few years?

5. *Summarize your team's vision for the year 2000.* Consolidate your discussion, comments, and observations into an executive summary describing your vision of what your organization would look like in the year 2000 if it were to become the "world class benchmark" in each area. Your executive summary should include:

- A summary of your current situation
- Your team's evaluation (poor, good, excellent) of current practices
- Your team's view of the future

Key Excellence Indicators

Excellence indicator	Good company	Excellent company	Your organization
Category 1: Leadership *Missionary*	Management verbally supports quality improvement efforts and occasionally takes action. Organization leaders occasionally attend conferences and seminars about quality. Leaders speak about quality issues before groups within their industry but do not proactively look for opportunities to speak and rarely speak outside the industry.	John Marous, Chairman of Westinghouse invited the company's Productivity and Quality Center to perform a total quality fitness audit on his executive office. Each year, Bill Marriott, Jr. visits 80% of the company's hotels and eats at company restaurants as often as five times a week. He is known for walking around his hotel at all hours, surveying breakfast preparations at 6:15 A.M. or looking over rooms for the slightest imperfection. For the past ten years, the first four hours of Motorola's monthly Policy Committee meeting has been devoted to quality. Bob Galvin, CEO, has been known to leave meetings before the discussion of finances. At Federal Express under CEO Fred Smith, all senior management's MBO incentive bonus is tied to reaching quality goals measured through the company's SQI (Service Quality Indicator) scores. If the *company* does not meet its goal, no one in management receives any bonus money, as much as 40% of a corporate officer's annual salary.	

Stretch goals	Management supports efforts that ensure products and services meet or exceed industry standards and averages.	Motorola CEO, Robert Galvin, expressed in 1987 the long-range quality goal in this way: "Improve product and service quality 10 times by 1989; and at least 100-fold by 1991. There is only one ultimate goal: zero defects, in everything we do."
	Managers focus on and project small incremental improvements in quality.	Milliken & Company has established goals of tenfold improvements in 4 years.
	Long-term quality goals tend to be qualitative rather than quantifiable improvement goals of major magnitude.	Federal Express has a "Five Year Goal" of reducing failures by 90% while maintaining a 20% annual volume growth rate.
Strong cycle-time driver	Service delivery systems are designed to focus on reliable and timely product or service delivery.	Motorola has set a tenfold annual reduction goal for all cycle times. James E. Norling, Exec. VP, says, "In services, cycle time is often more important to customer satisfaction than it is in manufacturing."
	Attention to cycle time is focused on select critical processes.	At Globe Metallurgical, customer inquiries from anywhere in the world must receive a response within 24 hours. Formerly, response time ranged from several days to over a week.
		Xerox has cut its new product design-to-market cycle by 50%.
		Westinghouse Nuclear Fuels reduced manufacturing cycle time by 40% through its TQM efforts.

(Continued)

Key Excellence Indicators *(Continued)*

Excellence indicator	Good company	Excellent company	Your organization
Clear, easily remembered values	Quality vision and values have been developed but are not deeply rooted in the organization. Often employees and managers cannot cite from memory all the core values.	Federal Express's company motto is "People, Service, Profit." All management is held accountable for having a people-first attitude, displaying impeccable service to internal and external customers, and achieving a reasonable profit, which can be used both to reward employees and to reinvest for company improvement. Motorola has given all employees a wallet-sized card printed with their quality policy: total customer satisfaction.	
Flat organization	Authority is commensurate with responsibility; changes are suggested at the bottom and approved by higher management. Empowerment is a novel concept. The organizational chart looks like a large pyramid. Mid-level and senior management ranks are often top-heavy.	Milliken prides itself on having reduced the number of middle managers from 52,000 in 1981 to 31,000 in 1988. John Rampey, a senior executive, claims that the more layers eliminated, the better the company understands the expectations of the customer. Remaining associates benefit from self-management and the creativity and problem-solving that result from more direct interaction within the company. At General Mills' cereal plant in Lodi, CA, self-managing teams schedule, operate, and maintain machinery so effectively that the factory runs with no managers present during the night shift.	

"Non-denominational"	Managers subscribe to and are well-versed in the tools and approaches of one quality "guru" or "school of thought."	Xerox recognized early that no single approach to quality would work, so it developed its own quality process called "Leadership Through Quality." Westinghouse Nuclear Fuels developed a "Pulse Points System," that looks at more than 60 critical junctures that affect the quality of its product.
"We can learn from everyone"	Managers seek out performance information from their own industry. Some managers subscribe to the philosophy that "if it ain't invented here, it can't be any good."	Milliken employees are encouraged to "steal shamelessly." The strategy is to borrow good ideas from other organizations and implant them in your own. To develop the AS/400, IBM Rochester went outside for guidance. Executives met with 250 customers to ensure that the product was designed correctly the first time. It adopted Milliken's teamwork approach, Toyota's short-cycle product development system, and Motorola's six-sigma defect prevention program. Xerox is known to be a world leader in benchmarking. It sets internal standards by identifying world-class examples of critical business processes and then strives to achieve those standards. For example, Xerox studied L.L. Bean for improvements in distribution, P&G for marketing, and American Express for expertise in billing.

(Continued)

Key Excellence Indicators (Continued)

Excellence indicator	Good company	Excellent company	Your organization
Contact with customers	Managers deal directly with a small number of customers on a periodic basis. Customer contact is not a uniform requirement of all management. Customer contact depends primarily on how close to the customer the individual manager is.	Motorola managers wear pagers to ensure that they are available to customers at all times. They also regularly visit customers to find out what they like and dislike about Motorola's products and services. Brand managers at Procter & Gamble spend several hours per week answering the 1-800 customer lines. They hear and respond to customer complaints, problems, and suggestions. J. Willard Marriott, the founder of Marriott Hotels, is said to have read every single customer comment card for the entire 56 years of his leadership.	
Managers as coaches	Development is emphasized through job-related training and promotion to progressively more demanding jobs. Focus is on the development of upper and middle levels of the organization.	CEO Jamie Houghton of Corning Glass says, "Clearly, total quality leaders understand that their personal success is derived from group success." Xerox will not promote managers unless they are deemed to be "Role Models" for quality. To support this the company has developed eight standards for "Leadership Through Quality" role model managers. Role model managers "encourage, recognize, reward, and support" others. This decision sent a powerful message to managers who were not team players or coaches.	

Category 2: Information and Analysis *Quantitative orientation*	Information is regarded as a resource for estimating and planning for internal quality control. Quality data are used to track progress and identify problems and solutions. Some areas of the organization, often internal support functions, are less rigorous in collecting and using quantitative quality data. Often volumes of data are collected but not effectively used.	"In God we trust, everybody else please bring data" is a favored Milliken saying. One area identified for improvement in Milliken's 1988 application was its use of statistical tools. Between 1988 and 1989, the company underwent a major training effort in which every Milliken manager, including the CEO, received training in how to use statistical tools to support the company's quality efforts. Federal Express's Service Quality Indicator (SQI) consists of 12 key components that the firm has determined to be the most important dimensions correlating with customer satisfaction. Each component is measured and compiled into an average daily failure point score based upon actual failure occurrences. Each component is assigned a weight (determined by customer perception). Weekly SQI scores are posted firmwide, and the management team looks at the scores daily.
Integrated external and internal measurements	Integration exists among different measures and among functional areas and units. However, the link between internal and external measures of quality is often not direct and not well understood.	Federal Express's SQI tracks the 12 service and operational components that were determined through extensive market research to correlate with customer satisfaction. Federal Express does not just track these elements internally. It continues to conduct external surveys and hold focus groups and interviews with customers in order to validate the components it currently measures and determine the effect its efforts are having on customer satisfaction.

(Continued)

233

Key Excellence Indicators *(Continued)*

Excellence indicator	Good company	Excellent company	Your organization
Widely deployed, readily accessible data	Data are readily accessible to the top executives of the organization and generally accessible on a need-to-know basis to other employees. No proactive efforts to educate the organization on the quality data that are being tracked. Data are not collected for all internal operations. Data such as projected completion times and employee attitudes are frequently omitted.	The Westinghouse Quality and Productivity Center performs Total Quality Fitness Reviews for operating units or departments. Approximately 100 requests for internal reviews are received per year. The center conducts interviews and analyzes all levels of the organization and surveys customers. The results are translated into a total quality score. The center then works with SBU's to improve their scores. Westinghouse also distributes quality plans to every employee. L.L. Bean tracks customer feedback/complaints by product, tallies them daily, and places them in a "problem file," accessible to all employees. At Milliken, electronic scoreboards glow in many plants, tracking quality progress by the hour. Big charts and readable graphs are also on display in accounting, personnel, and data processing departments. Federal Express has developed a computerized tracking system designed to tell the customer where any package or document is at any time in real time from pick-up through delivery. Drivers carry handheld computer/scanners to record important routing information. Delivery trucks contain on-board computers to provide drivers with up-to-date information.	

Category 3: Strategic quality planning *Strong linkage between business and quality plans*	Strategic and business planning functions take some quality issues into account, but the organization does not employ a fully formed strategic quality planning process that systematically prioritizes quality improvement initiatives and coordinates them with other business and strategic planning functions. Often quality plans and goals are not set by senior management.	Cadillac has so tightly integrated its quality planning and business planning processes that the organization now has only one plan that marries all business and quality initiatives. At Globe Metallurgical, senior managers, who are equity owners in the company, are responsible for setting both business and quality plans.
Benchmarks and comparative measures	The organization conducts extensive competitive analysis within its own industry to identify areas for improvement and strategies to close gaps. However, the data are limited to a few characteristics, and little benchmarking is conducted outside the industry. Sometimes multisite organizations neglect to identify and deploy the best-demonstrated practices within the company.	Xerox's benchmarking process has been deployed down to the work unit level. They benchmark more than 230 indicators, always asking "what is world class?" L.L. Bean routinely orders packages from itself and from its competitors to determine how Bean stacks up against the competition. GTE Telephone Operations benchmarks "best-in-the-world" performance for more than 65 processes in 10 critical management areas. IBM Rochester benchmarks 148 processes against 55 companies.

(Continued)

Key Excellence Indicators *(Continued)*

Excellence indicator	Good company	Excellent company	Your organization
Identify short-term and long-term priorities	Specific quality goals for the organization as a whole have been established. These goals have been converted to department-level goals in some cases, but not all. The organization responds to environmental changes that may influence quality requirements. Quality is viewed as a key differentiator, but customer satisfaction is not always central to short- and long-term goal setting.	Cadillac's quality planning process identifies annual improvement priorities and long-term priorities that span a 15-year planning horizon. Federal Express's five-year goal is for the company's SQI to have only one-tenth of the actual failure points that the company had at the beginning of the first year, despite an annual volume growth rate of approximately 20%. Additionally, quality projects and initiatives are assessed, reassessed, and prioritized on a monthly basis. In 1987, Motorola CEO Robert Galvin expressed the long-range quality goal in this way: "Improve product and service quality 10 times by 1989; and at least 100-fold by 1991. Achieve six sigma capability by 1992. With a deep sense of urgency, spread dedication to quality to every facet of the corporation and achieve a culture of continual improvement to assure customer satisfaction. There is only one ultimate goal: zero defects, in everything we do."	

| **Category 4: Human resource utilization**

Employees are internal customers | The organization speaks about employees as an important resource, but often pays less attention to them than to external customers.

Technical staff such as legal, accounting, and R&D departments sometimes fail to recognize their colleagues as their customers.

Ongoing processes to track and improve the satisfaction of employees are weak or do not exist. | Federal Express's "people" objective is also tied to the company's management-by-objectives incentive program. If the employees do not rate management leadership at least as high this year as last year on the organization's annual employee survey, no one in management receives any bonus money for the entire fiscal year.

GTE Management Education and Training offers an unconditional guarantee on all courses offered. If for any reason a program "does not satisfy the participant's expectations upon completion" the full tuition will be refunded.

Metropolitan Life developed a comprehensive program to measure all its customers' expectations, including internal customers (i.e., employees). Met recognizes that only 25% of its employees have daily contact with outside customers.

Marriott Hotels in Portland, OR and Chicago guarantee the quality of cafeteria meals to employees. If you don't like the food, or if it is more than one day old, you don't have to pay for it. |

(Continued)

Key Excellence Indicators *(Continued)*

Excellence indicator	Good company	Excellent company	Your organization
Comprehensive training and education	Most managers and many employees are trained in the basic concepts, practices, and tools of total quality management. Quality education may be limited to quality tools targeted at specific work groups. Training in concepts beyond the immediate responsibility of employees is not an ongoing process. Advanced concepts, practices, and tools of total quality management may be unevenly deployed within the work force.	At the initiative of then CEO Robert Galvin, Motorola opened a training and education center in 1980 with a contemplated five-year budget of $35 million. That drive has evolved into a full fledged "university" with 12,000 people involved in training and education, including 110 full-time and 300 part-time staff, and an annual budget of $60 million (plus another $60 million in lost work time.) The quality education program has grown from 3 days to 28 days. Motorola also requires that every employee receive 40 hours of training each year. The top-rated pharmaceutical firm in serving pharmacists and doctors, Merck recognized the need to train salespeople in the technical aspects of their jobs. Its extensive 11-month program provides training in basic medical subjects, Merck's products, presentation skills, and current topics in medicine. A 13-week program includes classroom work, on-the-job training in the field, and medical classes at universities. By the end of this year, all 14,000 of the American Airline's managers and supervisors will have completed the week-long "Quality of Work Life," program. American will spend a total of $15 million on the program. The result: the rate of complaints dropped from 1.2/100,000 in June 1989 to .46/100,000 in June 1990.	

Empowerment and flexible assignments	Authority of employees is derived through title and function.	A Federal Express courier once responded to a Labor Day call from the Memphis trace department regarding a supply of matched blood needed by a child scheduled for surgery. The boy needed the blood by the next morning and the Boston station's beeper was not functioning. When the courier arrived at the station in person, he had to scale a barbed-wire fence (because his key would not open a new lock on the gate), explain the unusual circumstances to the security guard, and find and deliver the package. The hospital received the blood in time and was able to proceed with the surgery on time.
	Decision rights are well-defined and often written down.	
	Empowerment is not viewed as a major employee involvement strategy. Work assignments are flexible when necessary.	
	Middle management is given autonomy to make its own decisions with respect to department or operational unit.	
		A favorite legend at UPS is the regional manager who took it upon himself to untangle a misdirected shipment of Christmas presents by hiring an entire train and diverting two UPS-owned 727's from their flight plans. When top management learned of his actions, they praised and rewarded him.
		USAA has the "Power Down" concept, which empowers employees with decision rights. Key criteria are: (1) Is it good for the customer? (2) Is it good for the company? (3) If yes to both, then do it.

(Continued)

Key Excellence Indicators (Continued)

Excellence indicator	Good company	Excellent company	Your organization
Team and individual recognition	Recognition is well-established within the organization but is usually focused on individual performance. Types of recognition may be limited and often focus primarily on external customers. Exemplary performance with suppliers and internal customers may be overlooked.	Domino's Pizza uses a system called TIPO (Team/Individual/Performance Objectives) to relate monthly bonuses to individual and team performance. The system ties bonuses directly to key satisfaction indicators for each unit and each specific job. If customer-focused quality levels miss targets at Federal Express, all managers lose their bonuses, which can account for up to 40% of a corporate executive's pay. Milliken has quarterly "sharing rallies" where team and individual efforts are recognized. The president and CEO are almost always in attendance. Met Life instituted a recognition program in which employees are eligible to win quality awards of $1000 each. The awards are designed to recognize employees who have performed uniquely to provide excellent service. The awards recognize efforts resulting in a high level of customer satisfaction and enhancing Met Life's reputation for service quality. CEO John Creedon personally selects the winners after reviewing all the entries.	

Contact with the customer	Customer contact is focused primarily on front-line employees. Senior executives typically meet with key customers only when there are problems. Many employees have little or no direct customer contact.	Brand managers at Procter & Gamble spend several hours each week answering the 1-800 customer lines. They hear and respond to customer complaints, problems, and suggestions. At Nordstrom's Department stores, sales clerks keep elaborate repeat customer records that include address, clothing size, style, color preference, birthdays, and anniversaries. Clerks call their customers to announce the arrival of special items or to suggest an appropriate birthday gift. Following a sale the clerk writes a thank-you note to make certain that everything fits well and performs as promised.
Low turnover, accidents, and absenteeism	Turnover rates are par with industry average or perhaps slightly better than average. Yet these organizations have not established themselves as "employer of choice" in the industry or market. Consequently they have no competitive advantage through their work forces.	The insurance industry averages for turnover and absenteeism are approximately 20% and 5% respectively. However, USAA Insurance's Property and Casualty Division has seen decreasing trends in both areas with employee turnover at 9.4% and employee absenteeism at 2.1% in 1988.

(Continued)

Key Excellence Indicators *(Continued)*

Excellence indicator	Good company	Excellent company	Your organization
Category 5: Quality assurance *Quality in design*	Quality in design is a key organizational goal, but design processes may be lengthy due to lack of cross-functional involvement. Contributions of customers and suppliers to product design are often neglected. Design process is not truly prevention-focused.	Computer screens in Federal Express delivery trucks are specially designed to go blank when the truck is in gear. This prevents drivers from causing accidents by reading the computer while they are driving. At Disney's Epcot Center, quality in design extends all the way to the parking lots. Because visitors often forget where they park, Epcot maintains computerized data that tells which parking lots are filled at what time of the day. By asking when the visitors arrived, parking attendants can usually find a "lost" car in 20 minutes or less.	
Focus on response time	Focus is on product and service excellence as defined by defect rates. Response time is important for key service dimensions. Response time for many internal components is often overlooked. This is not viewed as a source of competitive advantage.	Wallace established a Total Response Network that must respond to all inquiries and complaints within 60 minutes. Milliken's suggestion system has a 24-72 rule: All suggestions must receive a "go" or "no go" answer from a supervisor within 24 hours. If it is beyond the supervisor's authority, then it must be forwarded to the quality council and responded to in 72 hours. This fast turnaround built credibility into the system. At Globe Metallurgical, replies to customer inquiries from anywhere in the world must be made within 24 hours. Response time used to range from several days to over a week.	

Focus on continuous improvement of products, services, and business processes	Organizations focus on product and service excellence and some business processes. The focus is on managing results and not processes. Process goals and measurements may be scant. Managers occasionally have process responsibilities in their job descriptions.	Tom Malone of Milliken describes how he noticed that approximately 25% of Japanese managers had job responsibilities for "processes." Milliken managers were subsequently deployed into process-focused positions, as opposed to functional responsibilities only. Xerox has begun design on a new "business architecture" that focuses on cross-functional processes that create products, services, and results. USAA ensures quality of service by "migrating" veteran employees to open new sites. When a new office is opened, part of the trained work force is moved to the site to imbue USAA culture and know-how. USAA feels the expense of relocating employees is worthwhile.
Integration of prevention and correction with daily operations	The presiding mentality is often "If you see a snake shoot it." Employees are good at fire fighting and correcting short-term problems. Employees don't systematically move from correcting problems to root-cause analysis to preventing the problems from ever occurring again.	The SQI system at Federal Express is used for preventive purposes. The scores identify problems for management before customer complaints are typically received. The SQI information helps the company discover and solve individual customer problems without customers having to tell the company that the problems exist. Senior managers lead quality teams for each SQI component. When systemic problems are identified, the quality action team addresses it and eliminates the root cause.

(Continued)

Key Excellence Indicators (Continued)

Excellence indicator	Good company	Excellent company	Your organization
Linkage to suppliers	Expectations are communicated to suppliers and requirements are stipulated by contract. Inspections and audits are fundamental tools to ensure the quality of suppliers' goods and services. Close communications are maintained with a few major suppliers, but suppliers are seldom viewed as partners. Training and recognition of suppliers is limited. Limited or no supplier involvement occurs in activities such as goal setting and planning or in the activities of quality improvement teams.	Motorola has issued a mandate requiring all of its more than 6000 suppliers to apply for the Malcolm Baldrige National Quality Award. Motorola intends to drop any supplier that does not at least make good faith efforts to assess themselves according to the award criteria. As a Baldrige winner, Motorola has offered to advise any of its suppliers in their application process. "Motorola University" has also been opened to all the company's suppliers. USAA has fourteen measures it utilizes to ensure the quality of potential suppliers and to improve the quality of existing ones. Activities include inspection tours, end-user surveys, and supplier-education programs. Whenever a company submits a bid to become a Milliken supplier, the company's representatives are invited to Milliken's headquarters to be given a full day of orientation on Milliken's quality practices. Often, Milliken will not consider a potential supplier until they have gone through the quality presentations.	

Category 6: Quality results		
Meaningful trend data	The organization tracks data but often focuses just on short-term trends (i.e., month-to-month or quarter-to-quarter results) and pays little attention to long-term trends (three-to-five year time horizons). Trend lines may show peaks and valleys or extended plateau effects, suggesting that continuous improvement efforts have lost momentum.	The fuel reliability of Westinghouse Commercial Nuclear Fuels has improved by a factor of 10, reaching today's near-perfect 99.9995% defect-free production of fuel rods. The unit recently set a record of 42 consecutive months of 100% on-time delivery of finished assemblies. Westinghouse has cut its total quality costs by 30% in four years and has seen a 50% reduction in warranty costs. Milliken has reduced total costs by 58% since it began its quality-improvement process. American Airlines quality-improvement efforts have been rewarded with a 62% reduction in customer complaints. American now has the best complaint record in the industry.
Demonstrate close connection between program and outcome	Operating results are attributed to ongoing initiatives without rigorously demonstrating the causal connection of programs and outcomes. Evaluation and improvement cycles are often absent from programs that have been deployed.	After making a $2 billion acquisition of Tiger International, Federal Express's quality indicators dropped as the company worked to align systems and integrate the two companies. Within eight months of completing the acquisition, the company had recovered from the dip in its service quality indicators and returned to meeting goals for its SQI scores set prior to the acquisition. Also, the first year that the SQI system was created, it helped the company reduce failures by 11%, despite a volume growth of 21%.

(Continued)

Key Excellence Indicators (Continued)

Excellence indicator	Good company	Excellent company	Your organization
Improvement in supplier quality	Supplier quality is monitored to meet requirements. Suppliers are not viewed as partners whose quality-improvement efforts are directly linked with the organization's own continuous improvement efforts. Supplier quality trends are a primary focus when they become problematic. Supplier improvement may at times go unrecognized and unrewarded.	Xerox has seen a reduced defect rate on incoming parts from 80,000 defects per million to 300 defects per million. In an effort to improve supplier quality, Motorola has required all suppliers to commit to applying for the Baldrige Award. Says Charles Gonsior of St. Paul Metalcraft, "If we can supply Motorola, we can supply God." Since 1988, IBM Rochester's supplier lead times have been reduced by 80%, and defect rates on incoming parts have improved by 58%.	
Broad base of improvement trends	Key dimensions of product and service quality are steadily improved. The focus is often on defect reduction of products and services for external customers and on operation results. The scope of improvement may be narrow, often with little attention paid to internal and process improvement trends. There is partial or little focus on cycle-time improvement, customer and employee retention rates, process measures, and other quality indicators.	Xerox has reduced unit manufacturing costs by 40%, reduced indirect costs, cut its new product design-and-production cycle by 50%, and increased return on assets by 4.9%. In 4 years, Cadillac has reduced warranty costs by 29%, cut cycle time in die-changing from 12 hours to 3.5 minutes, and reduced durability and reliability problems by 27% to 71% on all car models. Since 1984, IBM Rochester has reduced total cycle time by 60%, cut assembly-line time in half, achieved 42% space savings per system, reduced CFC emissions by nearly 60%, and reduced scrap by 55%.	

Category 7: Customer Satisfaction *Frontline empowerment*	Frontline employees are trained to assist customers; procedures are established to determine ways that employees can and should help customers with routine service requests. Nonroutine requests or problems often need to be referred to a supervisor or to another department.	Motorola allows employees at service centers to give credit up to a \$1000 to make a customer happy, with no prior approval necessary. Any Milliken associate can halt a production process if that person detects a quality or safety problem.
Strategic infrastructure support for frontline employees	Employees are supported with hardware and software that are standard for the industry. Often the range, depth and update speed of information are limited; seldom does the organization "pioneer" new equipment or new applications of technology for its frontline employees.	At L.L. Bean, outstanding customer service is due in part to a computer system which supplies moment-to-moment information on stock. This system allows 99.8% of all orders to be filled with the right merchandise. Florida Power and Light has developed a sophisticated, computer-based lightning tracking system to anticipate where weather-related service interruptions might occur and strategically position crews at these locations to quicken recovery response time. Federal Express drivers carry handheld computer/scanners to package pickup sites in order to record important routing information. On Federal Express delivery trucks, on-board computers provide drivers with up-to-the-minute information.

(Continued)

Key Excellence Indicators (Continued)

Excellence indicator	Good company	Excellent company	Your organization
Service standards derived from customer requirements	Customer satisfaction is the number one objective. Attempts to ascertain the customers' service expectations and requirements are made through surveys or focus groups. However, extensive research on customer requirements is not a focus of the organization, and service standards may still be derived from managerial best judgement rather than from research-based customer requirements.	Federal Express determines customer satisfaction in a variety of ways, including regular customer/sales in-person meetings, customer round tables, customer response calls, a 1–800 telephone number, and market surveys. Federal Express has a Strategic Integrated Systems (SIS) Department to identify customer needs. The department is driven by customer and market research. Some of the services generated as the result of customer awareness are the PowerShip customer automation device, the computerized tracking system called COSMOS, and Ground Operations Digitally Assisted Dispatching System (DADS), all of which help to provide the customer with "real time" package delivery information. A Dow Chemical customer came up with his own specifications for carpet foam backing even though Dow assured him top quality. After the customer returned the shipment for the third time, management finally inquired. The customer said that the foam backing did not pass his "roll-stool test," which entailed 30,000 revolutions of an office chair (if the sample piece didn't delaminate from the foam, it passed). Dow then went back to the labs and developed a foam that could withstand 80,000 office-chair revolutions.	

| Attention to hiring, training, attitude, morale, of frontline employees | Frontline employees are critical hires; thorough initial job training is provided to all new employees, and apprentice programs are part of initial training.

Hiring requirements may be loosely defined and candidates are not screened to determine their conformance with requirements.

Continuing education of existing employees is often overlooked, and employee morale is not monitored as a leading indicator of external customer satisfaction. | Immediately after handling billing problems, American Express mails to customers a questionnaire requesting feedback on the service representative's courteousness, competence, and so on.

Guaranteed Fair Treatment Policy (GFTP) is Federal Express's grievance policy. It has prevented any third-party intervention between management and employees in the history of the company. The GFTP affirms the employees' right to appeal any issue through a systematic review by progressively higher management levels. Issues such as promotions, application of compensation and benefit policies, and discipline are eligible.

The standard orientation training program at USAA Property and Casualty Division consists of more than 40 hours of training. Often company representatives will make house calls to assess the progress of new employees and help those that are having trouble. |

(Continued)

Key Excellence Indicators *(Continued)*

Excellence indicator	Good company	Excellent company	Your organization
High levels of satisfaction	Customer satisfaction levels match or exceed industry averages. Little or no evidence that customers are "fanatical" in their loyalty to the organization.	Globe Metallurgical customer satisfaction and quality ratings became so high that they are now the industry standard. Many customers now specify "Globe Quality" when placing orders for metal alloys. In the most recent syndicated study conducted by the Gallup Organization of the air express industry, 53% rated Federal Express a 10 on a 10-point scale. The nearest competitor was rated a 10 by only 39%. Additionally, 95% of both domestic and export customers expressed satisfaction in the last year.	
Proactive customer systems	The focus is on meeting customer requirements; little or no emphasis is placed on anticipating customers' needs, expectations, or complaints before the customer has recognized and expressed them.	Both Westinghouse and Globe Metallurgical give customers access to company computers, voice mail, and the like to facilitate direct communications and improve customer responsiveness. Procter & Gamble was the first consumer goods company to put a toll-free 1–800 number on all of its packaging. Calls were summarized monthly for board meetings. Toll-free 1–800 numbers remain a major source of product-improvement ideas. American Hospital Supply Co. provides customers with computer terminals from which they can place all orders conveniently. Customer satisfaction has since increased significantly.	

Use of all listening posts	Customer communication strategies utilize one or more listening posts; communication with customers may be infrequent. The organization makes little effort to develop new strategies for communicating with customers.	Sam Walton, founder of Wal-Mart, had his plane drop him next to a wheat field where he met a Wal-Mart truck driver. Giving his pilot instructions to meet him 200 miles down the road, he made the trip with the Wal-Mart driver, listening to what he had to say about the company. IBM created a customer council comprised of representatives from IBM's top 50 clients. It meets regularly to give IBM input in the development and design of computers. Federal Express determines customer satisfaction in a variety of ways, including regular customer/sales in-person meetings, customer round tables, customer response calls, a 1–800 telephone number, and market surveys.
Quality requirement of market segments	Markets are segmented primarily for sales and promotional purposes; quality requirements are not significantly differentiated for each customer market.	When servicemen from Hewlett-Packard visit customers, they gather information about competitors' products (what the customer likes, dislikes, etc.). This information is used by headquarters to develop new and "improved" products. Fidelity Investments surveys customers who also use other financial services (i.e., Fidelity's competitors). Fidelity uses this customer feedback to improve its products and services and to target new markets.

251

16
Baldrige Resources

Available from the Malcolm Baldrige National Quality Award Office

Individual copies of these materials are available free of charge from the Malcolm Baldrige National Quality Award Office, National Institute of Standards and Technology, Administration Building, Room A537, Gaithersburg, Maryland 20899. For further information call 301–975–2036 or telefax 301–948–3715.

- *Application Criteria*
- *Application Forms and Instructions*
- *Malcolm Baldrige National Quality Award Fact Sheets*
- *Winner Profiles*
  2-page information sheet about each winner (1988–present)
- *Winner Contact Sheet*
  Names, addresses, telephone and fax numbers for each winner's public affairs and quality contacts
- *Articles by Curt Reimann*

  "Winning Strategies for the Malcolm Baldrige Award." *The Journal of Quality Management* 1, no. 2 (July, 1990): 9–25.

  "The Malcolm Baldrige National Quality Award." *Proceedings of the Association for Manufacturing Excellence*, October 11–12, 1989.

  "The Baldrige Award: Leading the Way in Quality Initiatives." *Quality Progress* (July, 1989): 35–39.

- *Case Studies*

    Globe Metallurgical, Inc.
    Leach, Kenneth E. *The Development of the Globe Metallurgical Quality System.* Cleveland: Globe Metallurgical Incorporated, 1989.

    Motorola, Inc.
    Smith, Bill. *The Motorola Story.* Schaumburg, IL: Motorola, Inc., 1989.

    Westinghouse Commercial Nuclear Fuel Division
    Performance Leadership through Total Quality: A Case Study in Quality Improvement. Pittsburgh: Westinghouse Electric Corporation, 1989.

    Liberty Bank
    A hypothetical case study based on the 1990 Baldrige criteria, with senior examiner's consensus report and feedback report.

- *Visuals*

    Slide: 35 mm color slide of the Baldrige Award
    Picture: Black-and-white, 8-by-10 photograph of the Baldrige Award

- *Public Law 100–107, August 20, 1987*
    A copy of the Act that established the Malcolm Baldrige National Quality Award

- *Foundation for the Malcolm Baldrige National Quality Award—Sheet*
    Lists members and officers of the Foundation for the Malcolm Baldrige National Quality Award

Available from the American Society for Quality Control

For information call 800–952–6587, fax 414–272–1734, or write Customer Service Department, 611 E. Wisconsin Avenue, Milwaukee, Wisconsin 53201-3005. There is a charge for the following items.

- *1992 Award Criteria* in packets of 10

    Item Number T995: $24.95 plus shipping and handling

- *Award Winners Videos* The videos of award winners are a valuable resource for gaining a better understanding of excellence in quality management and quality achievement. The videos provide background information on the award program, highlights from the annual award ceremony, and interviews with representatives from the winning companies.

1988 - Item Number T993:	$10 each
1989 - Item Number T502:	$10 each
1990 - Item Number T992:	$15 each
1991 - Item Number TA996:	$15 each

- *Case Studies*   The case studies are used to prepare Baldrige examiners for the interpretation of the award criteria and the scoring system. The case studies, when used with the award criteria, illustrate the award application and review process. The case studies are sample applications written about fictitious companies applying for the Baldrige Award. They demonstrate the form and content of an application, providing information requested in the seven categories of the award criteria. Responses are presented for each of the individual items and areas to address. The case studies can provide valuable insights into the award criteria and scoring system for companies interested in application, as well as in self-assessment, planning, training, and other uses.

1991 - Item Number T508: $25 plus shipping and handling (Based on 1991 award criteria)

Alpha Telco, with Senior Examiner's consensus report.

Herton Technology, with Senior Examiner's consensus report.

1992 - Available mid-year, 1992

Available from the National Technological University

For information call 303–484–6050, fax 303–498–0501, or write Advanced Technology and Management Programs, Attn: Ellen Stafford, 700 Centre Avenue, Fort Collins, Colorado 80526. There is a charge for the following items.

- *Quest for Excellence IV Videotape*   Videotape recording of key presentations of 1991 Baldrige Winners from the Quest for Excellence IV Conference held February 3–5, 1992, in Washington, D.C. Extensive visuals and presentation outlines included. Cost: $950.

- *Quest for Excellence III Videotape*   Videotape recording of key presentations of 1990 Baldrige Winners from the Quest for Excellence III Conference held February 13 and 14, 1991, in Washington, D.C. Some visuals and presentation outlines included. Cost: $950.

■ *Quest for Excellence II Videotape*   Videotape recording of key presentations of 1989 Baldrige winners from The Quest for Excellence II Conference held February 22 and 23, 1990, in Washington D.C. Cost: $1900.

Note: Videotapes of the Quest for Excellence I Conference are not available.

Note: Baldrige Award related seminars are offered by NTU, both in live-broadcast form and on videotape.

Available from Audio Archives International, Inc.

For information call 800–747–8069, fax 818–957–0876, or write 3043 Foothill Boulevard, Suite #2, La Crescenta, California 91214. There is a charge for the following items.

■ *Quest for Excellence Conference Audio Tapes*

1992: $152.00 per set of 19 or $10 each cassette

1991: $144.00 per set of 17 or $10 each cassette

Previous years' sets are also available. Contact Audo Archives International, Inc. for additional information.

17

Community, State, Industry-Specific, and National Quality Awards

Limited to a maximum of six winners per year, the Baldrige competition recognizes only the best of the best. Countless other excellent companies would go unrecognized were it not for the many community and state quality awards. Indeed, these awards, many of which are modeled on the Baldrige, also stimulate interest in TQM, in self-assessment, and ultimately, in applying for the national award itself.

Following are some selected community and state quality awards. The list is by no means comprehensive. Initiatives are springing up across the country as the power and appeal of existing award programs become recognized.

At the end of this chapter, we have provided a selection of industry-specific awards, along with a short list of other countries' quality awards. It should be noted that, although the Baldrige criteria have emerged as the definitive quality standard, the Deming Overseas Prize is the only true international competition.

Community Quality Awards

The Erie Quality Award

The first community quality award in the United States, the Erie (PA) Quality Award was established by the Erie Chamber of Commerce, with cosponsorship by the Erie Section of the ASQC, for the purpose of recognizing the quality-improvement efforts of companies and organizations in the area.

Although it is local in character, the Erie Award nonetheless has national implications. "Quality improvement at the community level," according to the Erie Community Quality Coalition, "is a logical 'accelerator' for the transformation of America."

The Erie award program is patterned after the Baldrige, but differs from the national award in several important respects. First, the Erie Quality Award comprises three distinct types of awards: "highest achievement," "significant progress," and "serious commitment."

This hierarchy of awards was created to recognize incremental improvement and to serve as an organization's first steps toward applying for the Baldrige itself.[1] A Pennsylvania state quality award that is pending will add another step to the ladder to be climbed in applying for the national award.

Another difference between the Baldrige and the community award is that the latter, though based on the national model, has been reworded and shortened to encourage smaller organizations to apply.

The Erie Quality Award also differs from the Baldrige in that any publicly or privately held organization of any size is eligible, including service and manufacturing organizations, academic institutions, hospitals and health-care organizations, government (on the local, state, and national levels), trade associations and professional societies, and religious organizations.

Like the Baldrige, no awards are given if an organization does not meet the first award-level criteria ("serious commitment"). However, any number of organizations can win, creating the incentive for companies to cooperate rather than withhold information.[2] Written feedback is provided to encourage companies to reapply.

The Erie Excellence Council also offers a course, twice a year, on how to develop community quality award programs. The course, entitled "Community Quality Award Workshop," led to the creation of programs in Austin, Texas and Mohawk Valley, New York.

For more information contact James H. Brown, Vice President, Erie Excellence Council, c/o Lord Corporation, 2000 West Grandview Blvd., P.O. Box 10038, Erie, Pennsylvania 16514–0038 (814–868–0924).

State Quality Awards

Connecticut Quality Improvement Award

Created in 1988, the Connecticut Quality Improvement Award uses the same-year Baldrige guidelines (i.e., the 1992 Quality Improvement Award guidelines are the same as those for the 1992 Baldrige Award) and is open to small (1 to 100 employees), medium (101 to 500), and large (over 500) companies in both the service and manufacturing sectors. Only one award can be given in each category.

Unlike the Baldrige, applicants for the Connecticut Award must have a minimum of three years of trend data in order to qualify. Because of this rule, program administrator Sheila Carmine turns away more applicants than she accepts. Only two applications, in fact, were accepted in 1991. (There were no winners that year.) Those that do qualify and have their applications reviewed, however, invariably score in the very respectable 400-point range.

The "3-year rule" exists primarily to retain good examiners who put in long hours without pay. "Our examiners are incredibly concerned and conscientious," says Carmine. "To keep them, the examination process has to be a learning experience." The 3-year rule was enacted so that examiners work on only the strongest applications.

The Connecticut Award is funded by various business sponsors and through workshops featuring teams from winning Baldrige companies. Aetna Life & Casualty, in particular, has been a strong supporter of the award.

For more information contact Sheila Carmine, President, Connecticut Quality Improvement Award, P.O. Box 1396, Stamford, Connecticut 06904 (203-322-9534).

The Margaret Chase Smith Maine State Quality Award

Named after a former U.S. Senator from Maine, this state quality award is open to any for-profit or nonprofit business. (Local, state, and national government agencies are excluded.) Large and small (fewer than 100 employees) businesses in both the manufacturing and service sectors are eligible to apply. All applicants receive feedback reports summarizing their strengths, areas for improvement, and overall quality management efforts.

The award criteria are identical to previous-year Baldrige criteria. In 1991, the first year in the award's history, 72 applications were requested and seven companies submitted. Twenty volunteers acted as judges and examiners. In order to qualify, volunteers had to have a minimum of eight years of experience in a quality-related technical, managerial, or professional capacity.

Three companies made it to the second level of evaluation. Of those three, only two merited site visits, which were performed by teams of four quality professionals and an independent observer who was a member of the award committee. National Semiconductor/Digital Logic Division, in the large business/manufacturing category, emerged as the only winner.

Application review expenses are paid primarily through application fees, with partial support provided by various service organizations throughout the state.

For further information contact Jennifer Vachon, Vice President of Member Services, Maine Chamber of Commerce and Industry, 126 Sewall Street, Augusta, Maine 04330 (207–623–4568).

The United States Senate Productivity Awards for Maryland and the Maryland Center Excellence Awards

These awards are given annually to recognize Maryland organizations for achievement in the areas of productivity and quality. The Senate Productivity Award, created by the United States Senate in 1982, can be conferred by any senator from any state, pursuant to the guidelines established by the Committee on Commerce, Science, and Transportation. In 1991, Maryland combined this award with the Maryland Center Award into a single selection process. The two organizations judged the most outstanding in their respective categories (manufacturing, service, and small business) receive U.S. Senate Productivity Awards. Up to 5 additional Excellence Awards are given by the Maryland Center, which provides training, technical assistance, and applied-research support in quality and productivity to public- and private-sector organizations in the region.

The criteria consist of five categories: productivity and quality leadership; human resource excellence; productivity/quality results; customer orientation and results; and impact on the state and local communities.

For more information contact the Maryland Center for Quality and Productivity, College of Business and Management, University of Maryland, 4321 Hartwick Road, Suite 308, College Park, Maryland 20742 (301–403–4535).

Armand V. Feigenbaum
Massachusetts Quality Award

Named after the man who first articulated the concept of total quality control, the Feigenbaum Quality Award is managed by the Massachusetts Council for Quality. The criteria are identical to those of the Baldrige, but without the "areas-to-address." Award categories include service, manufacturing, small business, and nonprofit organizations, including government. Up to two awards can be conferred in each category.

For further information contact Dirk Messelaar, Massachusetts Council for Quality, Inc., University of Massachusetts at Lowell, One University Avenue, Lowell, Massachusetts 01845 (508–934–2490).

The Minnesota State Quality Award

Patterned after the Baldrige Award, the Minnesota Quality Award is sponsored and administered by the Minnesota Council for Quality. Any for-profit business or subsidiary located in the state is eligible to apply.

Like the Baldrige, the Minnesota Quality Award has three categories: manufacturing, service, and small business. (Plans are being made to create additional award categories for government, education, and other nonprofit organizations.) Award types are "Highest Achievement" and "Finalist." Up to two Highest Achievement Awards may be given each year in each of the three award categories. No awards are given if quality standards are not met.

The Minnesota application is patterned after the previous year's Baldrige criteria. However, the questions are less detailed. For example, the Minnesota criteria are grouped by "categories" and "items" and do not include Baldrige-type "areas-to-address."

The first year for the award was 1991. Zytec Corporation, the only winner, also went on to win a Baldrige.

For more information contact Carol Davis, Vice President, Minnesota Council for Quality, 2850 Metro Drive, Suite 633, Bloomington, Minnesota 55425 (612–851–3181).

The Governor's Excelsior Award

New York State's Excelsior Award, created in 1992, recognizes high-quality performance in the public, private, and education sectors of the state's economy. Awards are given to large and small organizations within each of the sectors.

The Excelsior criteria incorporate elements of existing quality awards, especially the Baldrige. Although the applications for each of the three sectors embody the same standard of quality, they vary in their language to conform to the different characteristics of the particular sectors. Another unique feature of the Excelsior Award is that it stresses labor-management cooperation and the management of work-force diversity as fundamental practices underlying quality. For example, the Human Resource category in all three sectors contains an item that addresses how an organization ensures that work-force minority, disability, and gender issues are recognized, dealt with, and assessed. "Partnering" has also been added as an item in the Leadership category in the applications for all three sectors. Organizations are required to "describe the plans and progress of labor and management toward common goals that de-emphasize adversarial relations and build on new forms of mutual cooperation and trust."

The response to the award program has been enthusiastic. For example, the Department of Labor, which coordinates the award activities, anticipated only about 100 applications for the board of examiners. Instead, it received 145. Surprisingly, the majority of requests for applications from the private sector came from small (8 to 210 employees), rather than large, companies.

For further information contact Barbara Ann Harms, Director, Labor-Management Affairs, Harriman State Office Campus, Building 12—Room 540A, Albany, New York 12240 (518–457–6747).

The North Carolina Quality Leadership Award

Open to any publicly or privately owned for-profit business, this award is administered by the North Carolina Quality Leadership Foundation, a cooperative effort by industry, academia, and government to promote quality awareness, recognize quality achievements, and publicize successful quality strategies of North Carolina organizations.

The criteria are the same as those of the previous-year Baldrige Award. Only one award can be given in each of four categories: small and large businesses in both manufacturing and service industries.

North Carolina also has an Honor Roll, recognizing companies that have demonstrated continuous quality improvement, with expectations of greater deployment and/or sustained positive trends for key performance measures. Any number of companies can make the Honor Roll. However, no awards are given if the basic quality criteria are not satisfied.

For further information contact Dr. William A. Smith, President, North Carolina Quality Leadership Foundation, 410 Oberlin Road, Suite 306, Raleigh, North Carolina 27605 (919–733–4856).

The U.S. Senate Productivity Awards for Virginia and the Award for Continuing Excellence

Like Maryland, Virginia offers a U.S. Senate Productivity Award for quality achievement. Only one award can be conferred in each of four categories: private-sector manufacturing, private-sector service, public-sector state and federal agencies, and public-sector local agencies. Plaques are awarded for up to three finalists in each category, and certificates of merit are given, as well.

Virginia also offers an Award for Continuing Excellence (ACE) to recognize past recipients of the Senate Productivity Award who have demonstrated "sustained exemplary effort and performance in quality and productivity management." To win an ACE, an organization is evaluated on the basis of rate and magnitude of improvement and must wait at least three years after receipt of the Productivity Award before applying.

Twenty-three companies have won a Virginia Senate Productivity Award since its inception in 1983. Only two companies have captured the Award for Continuing Excellence, which was inaugurated in 1989.

The twenty-member Virginia Senate Productivity Board, comprising representatives from public and private sector Virginia organizations, reviews applications and determines the winners for both the SPA and the ACE.

For further information contact Elizabeth Ingold, Program Director, U.S. Productivity Award, 567 Whittemore Hall, Blacksburg, Virginia 24061–0118 (703–891–0106).

The Wyoming Governor's Quality Award

The Governor's Quality Award is presented each year to honor Wyoming companies that strive for superiority through their commitment to quality. For the first two years, 1988 and 1989, the award was a carbon-copy of the Baldrige. Unfortunately, the program met with little success. In 1990, the criteria were simplified, garnering the award considerably more "grass-roots appeal." Eighty-nine Wyoming companies, in fact, applied for the award in 1991.

Currently, the "criteria" consist of one open-ended question, to which companies are encouraged to respond in whatever way they feel is appropriate: "Provide applicable quantitative and qualitative information to describe strengths and extraordinary accomplishments specifically related to your company's commitment to quality." Scoring is based on a 5-point system, with 5 points representing the use of quality as a "competitive tool" and "success in a particular field or product category." The Governor's Quality Award is given to only one company each year. Applicants receive a letter of appreciation but no feedback report, and they do not learn their score.

For more information contact Barbara Stafford, Division of Economic and Community Development, Herschler Building 2 West, 122 W. 25th Street, Cheyenne, Wyoming 82002 (307–777–7286).

Industry-Specific Quality Awards

Shingo Prize for Excellence in Manufacturing

Created in 1988, the Shingo Prize is based on the philosophy that world-class status can be achieved through improving manufacturing processes, implementing just-in-time concepts and systems, eliminating waste, and achieving zero defects. Also covered in the criteria are processes related to management leadership; employee involvement; business process, operations, and support-service improvement; and improvements in productivity, quality, and customer satisfaction.

The prize, which is administered by the office of Business Relations at Utah State University's College of Business, is named for Shigeo Shingo who, along with Taiichi Ohno, is recognized as the creator of the revolutionary manufacturing techniques comprising the renowned Toyota Production System.

For further information, contact Ross E. Robson, Executive Director, The Shingo Prize, College of Business, Utah State University, Logan, Utah 84322–3521 (801–750–2279).

The President's Award for Quality and Productivity Improvement

Each year this award is given by the President of the United States to federal organizations that have implemented total quality management in an exemplary manner. A panel of examiners from public- and private-sector organizations evaluates each written application. A maximum of 5 finalists are selected to receive site visits. A panel of judges, also comprised of representatives from the public and private sectors, selects a maximum of 2 winners. All applicants receive feedback reports.

Each award winner is asked to prepare a publication describing its TQM approach and accomplishments; produce a videotape highlighting its TQM efforts; participate in the National Conference on Federal Quality; and make presentations to leaders from across the government.

The award program is administered by the Federal Quality Institute (FQI), whose mission is to promote and facilitate the implementation of total quality management throughout the federal government. In carrying out this role, FQI sponsors a number of major activities, including a "TQM Start-Up Service" to assist federal agencies in laying a sound quality foundation for their long-term efforts; model TQM partnership projects; federal quality conferences; publication of the Federal TQM Handbook series; and a TQM networking and resource center.

The President's Quality Award criteria comprise eight major categories: top management leadership and support; strategic planning; customer focus; employee training and recognition; employee empowerment and teamwork; measurement and analysis; quality assurance; and quality and productivity results. In contrast to the generic Baldrige scoring criteria (approach, deployment, and results), each category in the President's Award criteria has its own set of scoring guidelines. For example, in order to score 80 percent to 100 percent of total point value in the category "Top Management Leadership and Support," managers, among other things, must have routine contact with employees, customers, and suppliers. To score 60 percent to 80 percent of point value, managers must meet "frequently" with employees, and so on. "Contact" with employees warrants 40 percent to 60 percent of point value, and so on down to 0 percent to 20 percent of total point value.

For more information contact either Dick O'Brien or Victoria Elder at the Federal Quality Institute, P.O. Box 99, Washington D.C. 20044–0099 (202–376–3747).

The NASA Excellence Award/
George M. Low Award

Created in 1985, this award is jointly administered by NASA (National Aeronautics and Space Administration) and the American Society for Quality Control. It recognizes contractors, subcontractors, and suppliers to the nation's aerospace program. All NASA contractors, subcontractors, and suppliers are eligible to apply, regardless of their size or the nature of their product/service. Awards can be given to as many applicants as demonstrate the required level of excellence.

Eighteen specific criteria are split among five general categories: customer satisfaction; quality (e.g., quality assurance, vendor quality, etc.); productivity (e.g., software utilization, efficient use of manpower); commitment and communication; and human resource activities.

Each criteria element is scored based on 5 evaluative dimensions: time in place; deployment; performance, ranging from "starts and stays low" to "sustained high performance with constant improvement;" resources, ranging from "poor support" to "commensurate with need and effective;" and planning, ranging from "barely initiated" to "master plan with provisions for feedback and modification."

In order to encourage small businesses to improve their quality and productivity processes, NASA established a separate small business award with the same general criteria but with fewer areas-to-address.

For further information contact Geoffrey B. Templeton, NASA Quality and Productivity Improvement, Programs Division, NASA Headquarters–Code QB, Washington, D.C. 20546 (202–453–8415), or Craig A. Henry, ASQC, 611 East Wisconsin Avenue, P.O. Box 3005, Milwaukee, Wisconsin 53201 (414–272–1734).

Quality Cup

Unlike other quality awards that recognize entire companies, divisions, or departments, the Quality Cup, created by *USA Today* and the Rochester (NY) Institute of Technology, honors small teams and individuals in five organizational categories: service firms, manufacturing firms, not-for-profit organizations and institutions, governmental units and agencies of government, and organizations with fewer than 500 employees.

Awards are made in recognition of exemplary customer service, a valuable improvement in the process for achieving customer satisfaction, or a valuable improvement in the procedure for solving problems. As part of the application process, teams or individuals must describe their accomplishments in a 750-word essay. Quality experts selected by RIT serve as judges and visit with all finalists.[3]

For more information contact Carol Skalski, Quality Cup, USA Today, 1000 Wilson Blvd., 22nd floor, Arlington, Virginia 22229 (703–276–5890).

American Society for Quality Control

The Milwaukee-based ASQC offers 5 awards for outstanding achievements in the area of quality:

1. The Shewhart Medal, awarded to the individual who has made the most outstanding contribution to the science and techniques of quality control or who has demonstrated leadership in the field of modern quality control

2. The Edwards Medal, presented to the individual who has demonstrated the most outstanding leadership in the area of quality administration and fostering professional growth among employees

3. The Eugene L. Grant Award, for outstanding leadership in the development and presentation of a meritorious educational program in quality control

4. The Brumbaugh Award, for the paper which has made the largest single contribution to the development of industrial application of quality control

5. The Lancaster Award, in recognition of dedication and outstanding contributions to the International Fraternity of Quality Professionals

Each award has its own special bylaws. For more information contact Sheila Zelinski, American Society for Quality Control, 310 W. Wisconsin Avenue, Milwaukee, Wisconsin (800–248–1946).

Selected National Quality Awards

Argentina Quality Award

Australian Quality Award—Outstanding Achievement in Total Quality Management

British Quality Award

Canada Awards for Business Excellence

Colombia National Quality Award

Deming Prize (Japan)

European Quality Award (for companies based in Western Europe)

French National Quality Award

India Quality Award

Israel—Quality Prize of the Association of Electronics Industries

Malaysia Quality Award

Malcolm Baldrige National Quality Award (United States)

Mexican National Quality Award

New Zealand Railfreight Awards for Excellence in Manufacturing

Norwegian Quality Prize

Philippines—Outstanding Quality Company of the Year

Polish Committee for Standardization

South African Quality Award

Swedish Quality Award

Turkish Standard Institution

A Quality Glossary

approach: One of the three evaluative dimensions used in Baldrige scoring, "approach" refers to the methods a company uses to achieve the purposes stated in the criteria. Some specific components of the approach concept are the degree to which it is systematic, integrated, consistently applied, and prevention-based.

acceptable quality level (AQL): A concept used with sampling procedures applied to arms-and-ammunition suppliers during World War II, AQL is the poorest quality that a supplier can provide and still be considered "acceptable" or satisfactory. The concept—that some errors or defects are normal—is the antithesis of "zero defects," which holds that the only allowable standard for quality is error-free work.

benchmarking: The practice of setting operating targets for a particular function by selecting the top performance levels, either within or outside a company's own industry. In a broader sense, benchmarking involves searching around the world for new ideas and best practices for the improvement of processes, products, and services.

common cause: The source of random, or natural, variation in a process. Common causes—or "assignable causes," as they are sometimes called—are inherent in the production process itself.

companywide quality control (CWQC): An expression used widely in Japan, CWQC means the application of quality principles to all processes in a company and the involvement of all employees at all levels in the quality-improvement process. The concepts of continuous improvement and customer satisfaction are also embedded in the approach. CWQC is the equivalent of "total quality management (TQM)" in the United States, where the term "management" has roughly the same meaning as the word "control" in Japan.

conjoint analysis: Also called "tradeoff analysis," conjoint analysis is a method for providing a quantitative measure of the relative importance of one product or service attribute over another. In performing this type of analysis, customers are asked to make tradeoff judgments: Is one feature desirable enough to sacrifice another? Conjoint analysis is particularly useful in situations where customer preferences are in conflict and where the problem is to develop a compromise set of attributes.

control: A term applied to the management of processes indicating that quality requirements, standards, or goals are being met and that the output of the process is predictable.

cycle time: The amount of time it takes to complete a particular task. Shortening the cycle times of critical functions within a company is usually a source of competitive advantage and a key quality-improvement objective.

deployment: One of the evaluative dimensions used in Baldrige scoring, "deployment" refers to the extent to which a company's approaches are applied in all relevant areas and activities. For example, reward-and-recognition programs need to be applied to all categories of employees, from hourly workers to top managers.

descriptors: As used in this book, descriptors are relatively specific methods, organizational features, or system/process characteristics that illustrate or help to interpret each area to address in the application.

empowerment: Giving employees relatively broad decision-making authority and responsibility. In order for employees to be empowered, they also need to be "enabled," that is, given the skills and respect needed to do their jobs effectively.

failure mode and effect analysis (FMEA): A technique for systematically reviewing the ways in which a process, product, or service can fail and the impact such failures could have on customers, employees, or other processes. Using this analysis, quality engineers can predict field-failure rates, design recovery systems, and estimate the need for additional parts or personnel.

feedback loop: A system for communicating information about the performance of processes, products, or services. Feedback loops are essential for continuous improvement.

indicators: Measurable characteristics of products, services, and processes that best represent quality and customer satisfaction.

kaizen: A Japanese expression referring to continuous improvement in all phases of a business.

lessons learned: A phrase coined by Joseph Juran to describe a structured approach to analyzing past experience in an endeavor and applying the results of that analysis to improving the quality of future efforts.

pareto analysis: A system of analysis based on the principle that, in any phenomenon, relatively few factors account for the majority of effects. Juran uses the phrase "vital few" to suggest that it is more efficient and less costly to concentrate on the most important sources or types of failures, customers, and so on.

process flow diagramming: A visual, systematic way of examining a process by diagraming all its inputs, outputs, and activities.

process capability: The ability of a process to meet operating goals or internal- or external-customer requirements. "Capability" may differ from actual performance due to "special causes"—conditions or events due purely to chance and not to the production system itself.

quality assurance (QA): A phase in the evolution of the quality discipline, QA differed from statistical quality control, its predecessor, in that all functional groups, not just engineers and workers on the shop floor, were involved in the quality effort. However, QA is more narrowly focused than its successor, total quality management (TQM), which emphasizes senior-executive involvement, the management of quality for competitive advantage, and a strong customer orientation.

recovery: The actions taken by an organization, particularly its front-line employees, in response to unexpected customer problems such as an unusual request or the inconvenience caused by a canceled airplane flight. Less severe than crises, recovery situations can result from an error committed by the company or the customer or from an uncontrollable event like the weather.

reliability engineering: A broad-based discipline for ensuring better product performance by predicting more accurately when and under what conditions a product can fail. Based on the results of such an analysis, engineers can improve designs, set operating limits for equipment, and create backups in case of system failure. Reliability programs also incorporate feedback loops for analyzing product performance in the field and, in particular, product failures.

root cause (cause-and-effect) analysis: A deductive approach to analyzing problems by working backwards from the "effect" to the cause or causes. One of so-called "Seven Quality Tools," root-cause analysis is often facilitated using a "fishbone diagram" in which all the inputs to the process are arrayed in visual format like the bones of a fish.

simultaneous engineering (SE): Also known as concurrent engineering, SE is a general approach to production in which concept development, design, manufacturing, and marketing are carried out in unison. In contrast to a linear, sequential approach in which communication between functions is poor and the production process is marred by rework, scrap, poor quality, and frustration, simultaneous engineering maximizes communication, reduces errors, and shortens cycle times.

six-sigma: A statistical way of measuring quality, six-sigma is equivalent to 3.4 defects per million units of output—a virtually defect-free level of performance. The ambitious, companywide goal of "six-sigma quality" has been adopted, most notably, by Motorola, a 1988 Baldrige Award winner.

special cause: An "abnormal" source of variation that does not arise from the production process itself, but which is extraneous and unpredictable.

statistical process control (SPC): Based on the principle that no two units of output of a process are likely to have the exact same specifications, SPC involves the mathematical determination of acceptable limits of variation. Graphs are used by workers to plot output variables and visually determine when a process is "in" or "out of" control.

statistical quality control (SQC): A relatively early development in the evolution of the quality discipline, SQC relies on statistical concepts and tools (e.g., sampling techniques) to control production quality. SQC techniques are used in total quality management, although the emphasis in TQM is on "building quality in," rather than error detection.

stretch goal: An ambitious, usually long-term quality goal that requires extraordinary effort, innovation, and planning to achieve.

total quality control (TQC): An expression coined by Armand Feigenbaum, TQC involves the application of quality principles in all processes and at all levels of a company.

total quality management (TQM): TQM, as embodied in the Baldrige criteria, represents the latest phase in the evolution of the quality discipline. Distinctive features are a strong and pervasive customer orientation and a view toward managing quality for competitive advantage. The term "TQM" is roughly equivalent to TQC and CWQC in Japan, where the word "control" has the same connotations as "management" in this country.

transfer to operations: An activity or series of activities in which operating personnel are trained in the performance of a new manufacturing or service-delivery process.

zero defects: An approach to quality improvement, based primarily upon increasing worker motivation and attentiveness, in which the only acceptable quality standard is defect-free output or service execution.

Notes

Chapter 1

1. Interview with Curt Reimann (24 September 1991).

2. Constance McLaughlin Green, *Eli Whitney and the Birth of American Technology*, 1st ed. (New York: Little, Brown, 1956), 185–202.

3. Frederick Winslow Taylor, *Principles of Scientific Management* (Easton, PA: Hive Publishing, 1985).

4. Frank Bunker Gilbreth, *Primer of Scientific Management* (Easton, PA: Hive Publishing, 1985).

5. David A. Garvin, *Managing for Quality: The Strategic and Competitive Edge* (New York: The Free Press, 1988), 5.

6. Walter S. Shewhart, *Economic Control of Quality for Manufactured Product* (New York: D. Van Nostrand Company, 1931).

7. Garvin, 6.

8. J. M. Juran, ed., *Quality Control Handbook* (New York: McGraw-Hill, 1951), 37; cited in Garvin, 12–13.

9. Armand V. Feigenbaum, "Total Quality Control," *Harvard Business Review* (November–December 1956): 95, 98; cited in Garvin, 14.

10. Philip Crosby, *Quality Is Free: The Art of Making Quality Certain* (New York: McGraw-Hill, 1980).

11. Robert P. Hanson, ed., *Moody's Industrial Manual, 1987, Vol 1* (New York: Moody's Investors Service, 1987), 1101.

12. David Halberstam, *The Reckoning* (New York: William Morrow, 1986), 39.

13. Milton Moskowitz, Robert Levering, and Michael Katz, *Everybody's Business: A Field Guide to the 400 Leading Companies in America* (New York: Doubleday, 1990), 233.

Chapter 2

1. Neil J. DeCarlo and W. Kent Sterett, "History of the Malcolm Baldrige National Quality Award," *Quality Progress* (March 1990): 21.

2. DeCarlo and Sterett, 21.

3. DeCarlo and Sterett, 21.

4. DeCarlo and Sterett, 22.

5. DeCarlo and Sterett, 22.

6. DeCarlo and Sterett, 21–27.

7. Interview with Curt Reimann (24 September 1991).

8. For a discussion of the impact of ISO 9000, see Gary Spizizen, "The ISO 9000 Standards: Creating a Level Playing Field for International Quality," *National Productivity Review* 11, no. 3 (Summer 1992).

9. Glenn Rifkin, "Pursuing Zero Defects Under the Six Sigma," *New York Times* (13 January 1991): D1, D5.

10. Malcolm Baldrige National Quality Award Office, 1988 Winners Profile.

11. Tom Peters, *Thriving on Chaos* (New York: Alfred A. Knopf, 1987), ii.

12. Milton Moskowitz, Robert Levering, and Michael Katz, *Everybody's Business: A Field Guide to the 400 Leading Companies in America* (New York: Doubleday, 1990), 234.

13. Malcolm Baldrige National Quality Award Office, 1990 Winners Profile.

14. Dave Beal, "The Lessons of Zytec," *St. Paul Pioneer Press* (21 October 1991): C1.

Chapter 3

1. Jeremy Main, "How to Win the Baldrige Award," *Fortune* (23 April 1990): 108.

2. W. Edwards Deming, *Out of the Crisis* (Cambridge, MA: Massachusetts Institute of Technology, Center for Advanced Engineering Study, 1986), 26.

3. Deming, 50.

4. Deming, 315.

5. David A. Garvin, *Managing Quality: The Strategic and Competitive Edge* (New York: The Free Press, 1988), 32.

Chapter 4

1. Christopher W. L. Hart and Gary Spizizen, "Using the Baldrige Criteria for Assessment and Continuous Improvement," *Human Resources Policies and Practices* 40, no. 8 (Englewood Cliffs, NJ: Warren Gorham Lamont, a division of Research Institute of America, 13 April 1992).

2. Hart and Spizizen.

3. Ron Zemke, "Bashing the Baldrige," *Training* (March 1991): 36.

4. Hart and Spizizen.

5. Interview with Debra Owens (13 February 1990).

6. Audio tapes: Quest for Excellence III Conference (13–14 February 1991). Available from Audio Archives International, La Crescenta, CA.
7. "Quality Showcase," a seminar presented at IBM Rochester (23 January 1991).
8. Interview with Tom McElwee (16 March 1990).

Chapter 5

1. Christopher W. L. Hart, James L. Heskett, and W. Earl Sasser, Jr., "The Profitable Art of Recovery," *Harvard Business Review* (July–August 1990): 148–156.
2. Interview with Curt Reimann (5 July 1990).

Chapter 6

1. United States General Accounting Office, *Management Practices: U.S. Companies Improve Performance through Quality Efforts*, GAO/NSIAD-91-190 (Washington, D.C.: GAO, May 1991).
2. Mark Graham Brown, *Baldrige Award Winning Quality: How to Interpret the Malcolm Baldrige Award Criteria*, 2nd Edition (White Plains, NY: Quality Resources; Milwaukee, WI: ASQC Quality Press, 1992), 60–62.
3. J. M. Juran, *Juran on Planning for Quality* (New York: The Free Press, 1989).

Chapter 7

1. W. Edwards Deming, *Out of the Crisis* (Cambridge, MA: Massachusetts Institute of Technology, Center for Advanced Engineering Study, 1986), 315.
2. H. J. Harrington, *The Improvement Process: How America's Leading Companies Improve Quality* (New York: McGraw-Hill, 1987) 136.
3. Harrington, 138.

Chapter 8

1. Mary Walton, *Deming Management Method at Work* (New York: G. P. Putnam's Sons, 1990), 46.
2. Walton, 46.
3. Robert Camp, *Benchmarking: The Search for Industry Best Practices that Lead to Superior Performance* (Milwaukee: Quality Press; White Plains, NY: Quality Resources; 1989), xii.
4. Camp, Benchmarking, xi.

Chapter 9

1. J. M. Juran, *Juran on Leadership for Quality: An Executive Handbook* (New York: The Free Press, 1989), 12.
2. Marion Horton, "The People Side of Quality," *Supply House Times* (October 1990): 150.
3. Alex Taylor, "Why Toyota Keeps Getting Better and Better and Better," *Fortune* (19 November 1990): 79.
4. Andrea Gabor, *The Man Who Discovered Quality: How W. Edwards Deming Brought the Quality Revolution to America* (New York: Random House, 1990), 179.

Chapter 10

1. Mary Walton, *Deming Management at Work* (New York: G.P. Putnam's Sons, 1983), 214.
2. John Simmons and William Mares, *Working Together* (New York: Alfred Knopf, 1983), 17.
3. Frederick Winslow Taylor, *Principles of Scientific Management* (New York: Harper & Row, 1947), as quoted in Simmons and Mares, 24.
4. Frank Caplan, *The Quality System: A Sourcebook for Managers and Engineers*, 2nd ed. (Radnor, PA: Chilton Book Company, 1990), 219.

Chapter 11

1. W. Edwards Deming, *Out of the Crisis* (Cambridge, MA: Massachusetts Institute of Technology, Center for Advanced Engineering Study, 1986), 142.

Chapter 13

1. Theodore Levitt, "After the Sale Is Over," *Harvard Business Review* (September–October 1983): 87.
2. Levitt, 89.
3. David A. Garvin, *Managing for Quality: The Strategic and Competitive Edge* (New York: The Free Press, 1988), 24.
4. Levitt, 91.
5. For more on the subject of recovery, see Christopher W. L. Hart, James L. Heskett, and W. Earl Sasser, Jr., "The Profitable Art of Recovery," *Harvard Business Review* (July–August 1990): 148–156.

Chapter 14

1. Some of the criticisms in this section are derived from our own inquiries. Others are taken from two magazine articles criticizing the Baldrige Award: Ron Zemke, "Bashing the Baldrige," *Training* (March 1991): 29–37; Pat Houston, "Baldie, We Hardly Knew Ye," *Business Month* (July 1990): 41–44.

2. Steven Kreider Yoder, "All That's Lacking Is Bert Parks Singing, 'Cadillac, Cadillac'," *Wall Street Journal* (13 December 1990): A1, A15.

3. Interview with Curt Reimann (24 September 1991).

4. Glibert Fuchsberg, "Non-Profits May Get Own Baldrige Prize," *Wall Street Journal* (14 March 1991): B1.

Chapter 15

1. Tom Peters, *Thriving on Chaos* (New York: Alfred A. Knopf, 1987), 408.

2. Roger van Oech, *Creative Whack Pack* (Stanford, CT: U.S. Games Systems, 1988).

3. "The Human Side of Quality," *Fortune* (24 September 1990): 138.

Chapter 17

1. James H. Brown, "The First Baldrige-Based Community Quality Award," *Journal for Quality and Participation* (September 1991): 86–87.

2. James H. Brown, *The Erie Quality Award—A Celebration of Community Excellence* (Wilton, CT: The Juran Institute, IMPRO, 1990), 9.

3. John Hillkirk, "This Month Will Focus on Quality," *USA Today* (1 October 1991): 1B.

Index

About the Authors

CHRISTOPHER W. L. HART is president of the TQM Group, a Cambridge-based consulting firm specializing in the design and implementation of total quality management programs. A leading voice on the subject of quality and productivity improvement, he has served as an examiner for the Malcolm Baldrige National Quality Award and as a consultant on quality issues for such firms as Federal Express, GTE, Westinghouse, AT&T's Universal Card Services, and many others. He is a former faculty member at Harvard Business School and Cornell, and his writing on quality topics has been widely published in both the academic and business press.

CHRISTOPHER E. BOGAN is a principal and founding member of the TQM Group. An expert on quality in service organizations, he led the TQM Group team that assisted Federal Express in becoming the first American service company to win the Baldrige Award. He has consulted on quality issues for Marriott, MONY, KPMG Peat Marwick, Baldrige site-visit finalist Southeastern Freight Lines, and many others.